THE RIGHT-WING IDEA FACTORY

THE RIGHT-WING IDEA FACTORY

From Traditionalism to Trumpism

Donald F. Kettl

OXFORD
UNIVERSITY PRESS

OXFORD
UNIVERSITY PRESS

Oxford University Press is a department of the University of Oxford.
It furthers the University's objective of excellence in research, scholarship,
and education by publishing worldwide. Oxford is a registered trade mark of
Oxford University Press in the UK and in certain other countries.

Published in the United States of America by Oxford University Press
198 Madison Avenue, New York, NY 10016, United States of America.

Library of Congress Cataloging-in-Publication Data
Names: Kettl, Donald F. author
Title: The right-wing idea factory : from traditionalism to
Trumpism / Donald F. Kettl.
Description: New York, NY : Oxford University Press, [2026] |
Includes bibliographical references and index.
Identifiers: LCCN 2025041527 (print) | LCCN 2025041528 (ebook) |
ISBN 9780197778296 hardback | ISBN 9780197778319 epub | ISBN 9780197778326
Subjects: LCSH: Conservatism—United States—History—21st century |
Right-wing extremists—United States—History—21st century |
Radicalism—United States—History—21st century |
Political culture—United States—History—21st century |
United States—Politics and government—1989-
Classification: LCC JC573.2.U6 K47 2026 (print) | LCC JC573.2.U6 (ebook) |
DDC 320.520973—dc23/eng/20260112
LC record available at https://lccn.loc.gov/2025041527
LC ebook record available at https://lccn.loc.gov/2025041528

DOI: 10.1093/oso/9780197778296.001.0001

Printed by Marquis Book Printing, Canada

The manufacturer's authorized representative in the EU for product safety is
Oxford University Press España S.A. of Parque Empresarial San Fernando de Henares,
Avenida de Castilla, 2 – 28830 Madrid (www.oup.es/en or product.safety@oup.com).
OUP España S.A. also acts as importer into Spain of products made by the manufacturer.

MIX
Paper | Supporting
responsible forestry
FSC
www.fsc.org   FSC® C103567

CONTENTS

PREFACE

Donald Trump was about halfway through his fourteen-year run on *The Apprentice* television reality show when he mused out loud in 2010 about running for president. Rumors about his desire had been circulating for years. "If I did anything, I'd do it, I guess, as a Republican." He'd love not to run, but, he told a reporter, "Somebody has to do something. We are losing this country."[1] It took five more years for his campaign to get into gear.

It seemed a casual start for someone so obviously ambitious but, once bitten by the bug, he couldn't escape the lure of power. Just one-fifth of his way through his second term, two veteran Washington insiders, Jim VandeHei and Mike Allen, wrote, "No president in peacetime has done this much in one year of one term," with "chaos" as his brand.[2]

In focusing on what certainly is an "unprecedented presidency," as VandeHei and Allen put it, it would be easy to ignore the underlying shift from traditionalism to Trumpism. In fact, Trumpism was already emerging in 2010, even before Trump launched his presidential campaign. The US Supreme Court had knocked down restrictions on campaign contributions by special interest groups. The "Tea Party" movement dissolved as the right-wing movement rose, the latter supported by Steve Bannon—then a co-founder of the alt-right website *Breitbart News*—and other voices of the alt-right. By the time the host of *Celebrity Apprentice* decided to become the celebrity candidate, the table had already been set for him, with financial backing emerging, big ideas emerging, and local forces already on the march.

Trump was indeed unprecedented, mostly because of his great instinct in sensing a developing movement and racing to the front of it, proudly holding the flag of leadership he had wrestled away from others. To understand Trumpism, therefore, it is essential to understand the ideas from which it grew and how they broke from the past. That's the foundation of this book.

And this leads to a second question: Just how enduring is Trumpism? The only true thing ever said about predictions came from New York Yankees great Yogi Berra, who explained, "It's tough to make predictions, especially about the future." But, this book argues, just as Trump built his political success on the right-wing ideas others had contributed and big money others had raised, Trumpism will endure for a very, very long time into the future. That's not just because of the long shadow that Trump has cast. It's also because the roots of Trumpism lie at the local level. Those roots grew deeper and stronger during the Trump administrations, often spinning out ideas like removing fluoride from the water supply and banning books from schools and pulling higher education to the right. These ideas energized a new right-wing destined to last long past Trump's time in office. Explaining that process is the second goal of this book.

The book explores how the factory of right-wing ideas produced the movement and why they are destined to last for a very long time. The movement challenges fundamental ideas about American democracy that one-time foes and eventual friends John Adams and Thomas Jefferson spent their last days promoting—and that they would now be profoundly worried to find under assault.

In writing this book, I've been blessed by ideas and encouragement from my longtime friend and colleague, John DiIulio. Two anonymous reviewers provided invaluable reactions, and it's a testimony to them that they might not recognize large parts of the book that are far better for their suggestions.

At Oxford University Press, David McBride encouraged the first steps of this book. Angela Chnapko provided an endless supply of wise and helpful suggestions for sharpening the book's argument, and Alexcee Bechthold skillfully guided the book off the launching pad.

Most of all, I'm grateful to my wife, Sue, who, over fifty years, has been an attentive audience even when far more interesting things beckoned on her iPad. She has been a supporter even during sometimes gusty winds, and she has simply been the best friend I ever could have wished for. I dedicate this book to her and all she's done to help make it happen.

Donald F. Kettl
Austin, Texas
September 2025

Chapter 1

A Factory for Power

For more than two hundred years, traditional conservatives, in their quest to shrink government in defense of individual liberty, dominated the American right-wing. Then, in the 2010s—a momentary blink in the long history of ideas—a new idea factory pushed that version of conservatism to the curb. Instead of a small government, it sought a robust government. Instead of the pursuit of individual liberty, it sought to advance particular social values. And instead of the long-term quest for conservative ideals, it sought to conquer the Left by using ideas as instruments to gain power. This book is the story of how a right-wing idea factory, focused on the pursuit of political power, suddenly became one of the most powerful political and social forces in America and, in many ways, across the rest of the world.

A small group of right-wing ideologues launched a movement that spread across the United States and around the world, redefined conservatism, destroyed the existing Republican Party, knocked the Democrats back on their heels, and then in 2024 created one of the most improbable re-elections in the country's history. At each step of Donald Trump's restoration, the reaction among both the cognoscenti and the public was, "Wow, we didn't see that coming." For those who closely followed the right-wing movement, however, this was no surprise. This movement was the product of an idea

factory whose full dimensions hadn't been understood until the sur-
prises continued to break over the political system, like monster
waves crashing over the bow of an unsuspecting ship.

This singular focus proved remarkably successful, often in ways
that took virtually everyone by surprise, including those on the new
right-wing. It established a moment of political and social change
more significant than anything in the twenty-first century—and
as significant as any but a handful of moments in the twentieth
century as well, like Franklin D. Roosevelt's New Deal and Lyndon
B. Johnson's Great Society. Until 2010, there was a thread of ideas
connecting traditional conservatism from ancient Greece and Rome
through the Enlightenment, then from its robust development to
the country's founders, then to the conservative economic revolution of free-market ideas in the 1950s, and then to Ronald Reagan's
presidency and its pursuit of a smaller government. The 2010s broke
that thread.

Like all stories of modern conservatism, the tale begins with
Reagan. In his 1989 farewell address, he celebrated America as "the
shining city upon a hill," which he drew from a sermon by pilgrim
John Winthrop in 1630. America, he said,

> was a tall, proud city built on rocks stronger than oceans, wind-
> swept, God-blessed, and teeming with people of all kinds living in
> harmony and peace; a city with free ports that hummed with com-
> merce and creativity. And if there had to be city walls, the walls had
> doors and the doors were open to anyone with the will and the heart
> to get here. That's how I saw it, and see it still.

It's a wonderful speech, although it must be said that Reagan's
speechwriter got the quotation and its context wrong. Winthrop did
speak of "a citty upon a hill," but as a tough Puritan he never suggested it was "shining." In fact, Winthrop's sermon wasn't a proud
celebration but a stark warning. "The eies of all people are upon us,"
he said, with a caution that there would be "curses upon us" if the
country did not live up to its vision and promise.[1] With its promise

of freedom and liberty, Winthrop said that the United States had put itself on a pedestal where the entire world would be watching closely to see if the nation could live up to them. It was a note of admonition, not a celebration of success. But the historical details mattered far less than the ringing rhetoric of one of Reagan's best speeches, whose message continues to echo through the halls of the Right.

The bedrock principles of conservatism that Reagan celebrated had changed relatively little since Edmund Burke and his role as the "father of modern conservatism." In his *Reflections on the Revolution in France* in 1790, a book that has constantly been in print since, Burke said he shared many of the values of the French revolutionaries. However, he strongly opposed their efforts to force change through revolution.[2] Burke advocated for changes that proved their worth over time; for evolutionary change instead of revolutionary turmoil; for judgment based on experience instead of broad, abstract principles; and for a steady social order, even if in the hands of the elites. Over the centuries, conservatives added several new principles to Burke's foundation: the importance of individual liberty, especially as expressed through free markets and government deregulation; and a small, limited government, to avoid interfering with that liberty. And that was the foundation for Reagan's speech.

Devotion to these principles, coupled with his infectious "happy warrior" character, made Reagan an enduring hero to Republicans. Thirty-five years after his "shining city" speech, the White House gift shop was still selling Ronald Reagan busts. The president's portrait hung over the president's left shoulder in Donald Trump's Oval Office. In Reagan's first inaugural address, he said, "Government is not the solution to our problem; government is the problem."[3] Republican leaders like George W. Bush, Mitt Romney, Paul Ryan, Ted Cruz, and Donald Trump have repeated this sentence endlessly.

Although the rhetoric has endured, the principles have not. In a very short time, Ronald Reagan's conservatism crumbled. In the early 2010s, big changes in very short succession fed the rise of a new right-wing. This ultimately led to Trump's election in 2016, his re-election in 2024, and the creation of a new right-wing movement with roots deep enough to last long past Trump's political life. The right-wing idea factory that emerged generated a remarkably nimble new movement. Unlike the traditional conservatives' focus on small government as a driving idea, the new right-wing focused far more on gaining power than advancing principles.

Driving the right-wing idea factory were angry grassroots voters who fed their activism with political grievances. After the September 11 terrorist attacks, trust in government was 54 percent. By 2010, it had plummeted to just 22 percent.[4] Upward mobility had declined, with individuals far less likely to earn more than their parents. A 2011 *Time* cover story bluntly asked, "Can You Still Move Up in America?" The answer was blunt: "For most people, it's harder to get ahead than it's ever been in the postwar era." A project by the Pew Charitable Trusts found that people in the bottom fifth of the income scale and who were born in 1970—people aged forty-one at the time—had just a 17 percent chance of making it into the upper two-fifths. "It's hard to imagine a bigger hit to the American dream than that," the magazine reported.[5]

Making it worse was the collapse of the financial and real estate industries in 2008, which doubled the unemployment rate in the next two years. Many workers who kept their jobs had lower wages. Home prices fell 40 percent, eight million Americans suffered foreclosure on their home mortgages, and the stock market lost 40 percent of its value. One-fourth of households lost more than half of their wealth.

The federal government launched major bailouts for the nation's major financial institutions, trying to salvage at least some of the assets from revered Wall Street firms like Bear Stearns, founded in 1923, and Lehman Brothers, which began in 1844 as a small Alabama store operated by a German immigrant. The nation's largest savings and loan, Washington Mutual, went under. Half a trillion government dollars flowed into troubled banks and investment houses. That helped the banks but left most ordinary Americans out in the cold. According to a 2008 Gallup poll, most

Americans—56 percent—favored having the federal government step in to help people struggling to pay their mortgages, but that aid never came. Even more Americans—61 percent—*opposed* having the federal government use public money to bail out Wall Street investment companies.[6] There was a growing sense that the wealthy got the upper hand and kept it, and that the government was using Americans' tax dollars to keep it that way. Meanwhile, immigrants were moving into the country, and the right-wing worried that they took jobs that would otherwise go to current Americans—especially white Americans.

As their anger boiled, CNBC financial analyst Rick Santelli erupted in what the media came to call "the rant heard around the world." Speaking live and unscripted from the floor of the Chicago Stock Exchange, he condemned the government for "promoting bad behavior" by bailing out the big financiers, encouraging them to take big risks and then bailing them out when they got into trouble. He was so mad, he said, that he was going to organize a "Chicago tea party." Protesters around the country loved the reference to the Boston Tea Party of revolutionary days, and they organized similar tea-party protests around the country.[7]

Fox News commentators quickly sensed that the "Tea Party" theme was a ratings winner. Fox News host Glenn Beck began hammering on the big-spending/big-government issue, and Tea Party coverage on Fox took off from nothing. There were 3,124 stories in 2010 and 2,632 more in 2011. As viewer interest in the Tea Party movement died down in 2013, an important element of the right-wing idea factory emerged: There were always new issues rising to replace others that fell.[8] There were stories about transgender issues and abortion. Critical race theory, an abstract academic concept, then moved to center stage before petering out (see Figure 1.1). It was an assembly line that constantly shifted production, generating new products in rapid succession to fuel the movement's energy.

The quick evolution of issues, strategies, and tactics in the right-wing idea factory is very different from traditional conservatism's

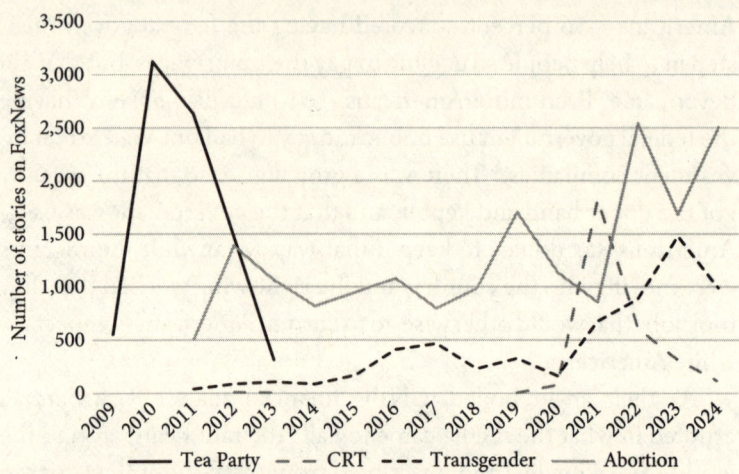

FIGURE 1.1 Cycles of News Stories Rose and Fell on Fox News

Source: TV News Archive, http://archive.org/details/tv. Data as of March 27, 2025.

pursuit of normative constants. with traditional conservatism. Russell Kirk, one of the mid-twentieth century's great conservative thinkers, wrote, "The conservative believes that there exists an enduring moral order. That order is made for man, and man is made for it: human nature is a constant, and moral truths are permanent."[9] One of the bedrock principles of traditional conservatism was the constancy of that moral order, founded in individual liberty, the value of private property, the power of market competition, and the central role of the rule of law. Conservatives sought a smaller government and less federal spending.

In contrast, the right-wing idea factory rejected the idea of a permanent set of principles. Issues were important in terms of their effectiveness in building a movement that, in turn, focused squarely on acquiring, keeping, and using political power. Its proponents sought to impose their values on the country. They talked about a small government but did not hesitate to boost spending to support their goals, and they paid little attention to free-market capitalism. The pursuit of a balanced federal budget, a bedrock principle of traditional conservatism for decades, simply drifted from the scene. In fact, Google searches for "balanced federal budget" in June 2025 were just 3 percent of what they were in June 2006, when the conservative think tanks were pursuing new strategies to "starve the beast" that was, in their view, the federal government.[10] They squeezed "equity" from their lexicon (along with diversity and inclusion), they pushed aside the delicate balance of powers created by the nation's founders in favor of growing executive power, and they showed little reverence for the rule of law. In a very short time, it became a very remarkable new political movement.

The Rise of the Right-Wing Movement

It would be a gross exaggeration, of course, to suggest that traditional conservatism was a constant set of ideas through two millennia, or that the right-wing revolution of the 2010s tossed it all aside. But a remarkable consensus grew over time, as Thomas Jefferson captured in the Declaration of Independence, that the nature of humans provided for fundamental rights. That, in turn, generated support for liberal democracy—not the chase after left-wing causes, but the pursuit of liberty. Jefferson built on John Locke, who explained the importance of individual rights and limits on governmental power. The consent of the governed, Locke contended, should be the foundation of governance. With that came, over time, the division of government into branches to prevent any one branch—especially the executive—from imposing its will on everyone else. There was the pursuit of civil rights and the liberties laid out in the American Bill of Rights. And most of all, there was the fundamental importance of the rule of law, a system that ensured that the law applied equally to everyone and provided free markets and a level playing field. This base laid the foundation for the Republican Party during most of the twentieth century.

That all changed in the early 2010s and, by the end of the decade, the Republican ship had become unmoored from traditional conservatism and liberal democracy. The Grand Old Party—a nickname for the Republicans tracing back to Minnesota in 1874— was old but no longer grand.[11] A new right-wing base had emerged, with Donald Trump as its leader. As Kevin Roberts, president of the right-wing Heritage Foundation, said in 2024, the country is "in the process of the second American Revolution." Then in a chilling threat, he added that the revolution "will remain bloodless if the left allows it to be."[12] Democrats scrambled to make sense of the new reality they faced and to find new ideas to counter the sudden revolution on the right. A movement toward illiberalism, a term popularized by Fareed Zakaria as the opposite of liberal democracy, quickly grew.[13]

Just as it would be a gross exaggeration to suggest that traditional conservatism was a single, unbroken collection of ideas, there was great variation in the ideas surrounding the new right-wing movement that developed during the 2010s. Some of the internal tensions surfaced in the debate leading up to Trump's decision to bomb Iranian nuclear weapons production sites in 2025. Underlying all the new right-wing elements, there was this common premise: Unlike traditional conservatism, which enormously valued the history of the ideas at its core, the new right-wing movement did not grow in the tilled ground of shared basic principles. Rather, it was tactical, with strong grassroots zealots eager to put their ideas—and often their anger—to work to upend existing political power. They seized on whatever fueled their energy, like the reaction to the government's constraints imposed during the Covid pandemic and what they believed was the indoctrination of their children by left-wing woke propaganda. They sought to channel that anger into growing their political power base, both in squeezing out the traditional Republican core and in putting Democrats back on their heels.

Before the 2010s, there was Pat Buchanan, one-time Nixon staff member, political pundit, and presidential candidate in 1992, 1996, and 2000, who helped launch the "paleoconservative" movement (which gave birth to the alt-right), devoted to Christian nationalism and an America-First focus.[14] ("Paleo" here referred to the effort to restore what the movement claimed was a more genuine version of conservatism reaching back deeply into the past.) The debates here gave rise to new conservatives like Richard Spencer, who in 2016 gave a speech that contended, "America was, until this last generation, a white country, designed for ourselves and our posterity. It is our creation and our inheritance, and it belongs to us."[15]

Then there was Steve Bannon, the driving engine of Trump's startling 2016 campaign, who brought genuine message discipline to the battle, the focused attack on Hillary Clinton, and the highlight on immigration. The BBC called Bannon "the Trump-whisperer," a "master provocateur," and "an agent of chaos," before that trail of chaos pushed him outside the Trump orbit.[16] Bannon had managed to do what no one thought possible: remanufacture Trump, a Democratic television star who had supported abortion rights, into a right-leaning, pro-life presidential candidate—who won.

Although Bannon's razor-sharp political skills and rough interpersonal edges led many observers to see him as only a political strategist, he contributed an important intellectual foundation to the new right-wing. He was a disciple of philosopher René Guénon, a metaphysical French writer who died in 1951 after a career developing critiques of modern civilization. Like Bannon, he was a Catholic, but he eventually separated from mainstream Catholicism to embrace Islamism. From there, he continued to push on philosophical boundaries to seek higher states of being. Guénon believed that society was in the process of decay, with the pursuit of materialism and individualism undermining fundamental truths and insight. Moreover, he concluded that time was cyclical, in a reflection of Hindu cosmology. The key to dealing with a decaying society, he believed, was to reach back to fundamental truths, found in "sacred sciences," which provided the guiding philosophy for what society ought to be and where it ought to go, because it could build on what had been. What society needed most, he contended, was a spiritual reawakening.[17]

That in turn proved a heavy influence on Bannon, who believed that the key to creating a stronger society was reaching back in time to older principles, including the Catholicism of generations before, and using these older principles to avoid internationalism and bar the door to migrants. For Bannon, his anti-immigration policy was not just opportunism. It grew out of a deep-seated belief that the culture and language of migrants were disrupting the core values of the country, and that these values could only be reclaimed by returning America to Americans, a proposition with an unmistakably racist tinge to it.

The tech bros, especially Elon Musk, brought a different approach, rooted in a deep distrust of democracy and a firm belief in the inefficiency of modern American government. They brought in the thinking of Curtis Yarvin, a software developer and blogger who created ideas called the "dark enlightenment." Yarvin believed that America's institutions had been taken over by the radical left. The solution, he said, was to smash those institutions and build a new system, driven by technology and led by a single strong official, an "American Caesar" who would have the power to push the radical left aside. Yarvin contended, "It's not that democracy is bad; it just that it's very weak." The answer, he believed, was making government both strong and properly led. He didn't believe in voting. Instead, he believed in a strongman or a monarchy, modern style. "It doesn't have to be Elon Musk," he told a *New York Times* reporter, but Musk certainly did not object to suggestions that he might fit the role well.[18] Governing, in their view, was too important to be left to anyone but the smartest experts, insulated from political pressure by the Left.[19]

There were different ideas driving the new right-wing forward, but ideas alone were not enough. It needed fuel, and that came from an enormous amount of anonymous cash unleashed by the US Supreme Court's 2010 decision in *Citizens United v. the Federal Communications Commission*. In a sharp break with the past, *Citizens United* allowed unlimited spending by wealthy donors and organizations, without disclosure of the source or amount.[20] Liberals and conservatives quickly embraced this new tool, but the conservatives proved far better at it. In six of the eight election cycles between 2010 and 2024, conservative-leaning groups outspent liberal-leaning ones—often by a lot (see Figure 1.2). That money, in turn, made it possible for conservatives to capitalize on new ideas, build political support around them, recruit and champion political candidates, and, in the end, put Donald Trump into the White House. Twice.

The right-wing idea factory grew at the intersection of two powerful forces that united into a single movement. There were *power ideologues* who produced ideas fundamentally different from traditional conservatism. They pushed aside the motivating ideas of the Republican Party and focused instead on the single-minded pursuit of political power. They assembled a loose coalition of activists at the federal, state, and local levels of government who were driven by an agenda of destroying the "deep state," stopping

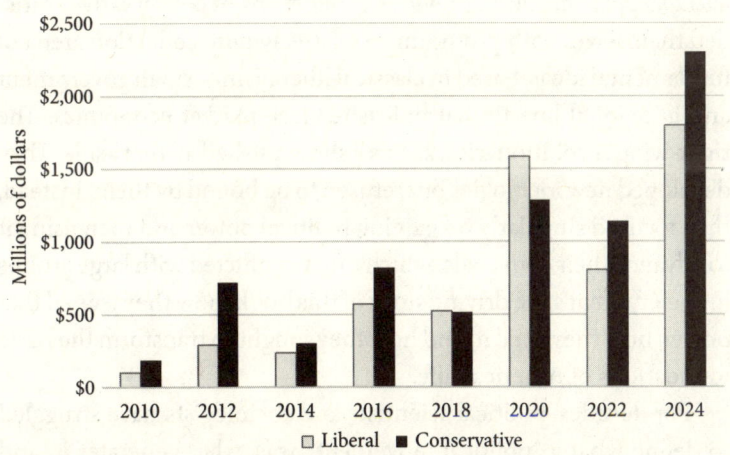

FIGURE 1.2 The Right Outspent the Left with Dark Money

Source: OpenSecrets, "Outside Money, Excluding Party Committees" (various years), https://www.opensecrets.org/outside-spending/by_cycle.

illegal immigration, promoting Christian nationalism, gearing up energy production, abolishing the Federal Reserve, imposing work requirements on welfare recipients, ending "woke propaganda" in local schools, blowing up programs for diversity/equity/inclusion, expanding presidential power, and dismantling significant parts of the civil service system.

Then there were *grassroots zealots*, who came after the right-wing revolution had moved into production. Covid energized them, first in relatively uncoordinated fashion as they pushed back against the government constraints of lockdowns and mask mandates and home schooling. But then they began connecting through social media, and new groups, like Moms for Liberty, rallied like-minded activists on the right. Issues rose and fell in attention. Passionate individuals faded in and out of the movement, but there was a constant genesis of new ideas and fresh advocates to stoke the zealotry. If some ideas didn't work, they quickly moved on to new ones, with state and local governments being the principal sources of action.

It was a political movement that *focused singularly on gaining and wielding political power*. Previous generations of conservatives satisfied themselves with promoting a relatively pure collection arena of fundamental ideas, based in classical liberalism—small government and individual liberty that unleashed free-market economics. The right-wing revolutionaries, as I will show, pushed all that aside. They developed new ideologies but refused to be bound by them. Instead, they focused singularly on gaining political power and then using it to advance their own goals, which often conflicted with large groups in society. That's the driving story of this book: how they gained that power, how they used it, and how they fought to transform the basic foundations of American life.

For decades, political scientists and sociologists have struggled to define what a "political movement" was, what generates it, and what sustains it. They've identified three different patterns. One pattern grew on *grievances*. Neil J. Smelser and Ted Robert Gurr held that a social movement grows out of shared complaints among members of a community. Identifying these intense grievances—and organizing around them—generates and then drives the movement forward. Understanding the grievances, therefore, is the first step in understanding everything else.[21] The right-wing idea factory is full of grievances, but these grievances do not begin to explain its breadth of power.

A second pattern grew with *organizers*. John D. McCarthy and Mayer N. Zald argued that political movements are based on the skill of the organizers and on their ability to attract money. Grievances always exist everywhere all the time, they pointed out. If movements were the product of grievances, they contended, then grievances like deprivation ought to generate many more movements, but this was not the case. They held instead that leadership mattered much more: the ability of individuals to define issues, gather people around them, and raise money to support the work.[22] This approach, however, presumed a fundamentally strategic approach to movements, and the right-wing idea factory has been a far more varied mélange, often not very strategic, and much more dynamic than the leadership pattern would suggest.

Third, there was the *opportunistic* approach. Sidney Tarrow contended that social and political forces combine, sometimes by chance, and create the critical mass to drive big change. "Contentious politics occurs when ordinary people—often in alliance with more influential citizens and with changes in public mood—join forces in confrontation with elites, authorities and opponents," Tarrow wrote. This process made it possible for ordinary people to act when they don't have enough political leverage on their own.[23] This confrontation created political pressure that, in turn, spread like a virus through the political system.

Instead of these three models—grievances, organizers, and opportunities—the right-wing idea factory grew through a fourth approach: *issues selected to drive the single-minded pursuit of power*. The right-wing idea factory was *transactional*: It used its ideas and issues to build power, without necessarily creating sustained relationships among any of the players and engaging each group of players only as long as the relationship was beneficial for everyone involved. The idea of transactional leadership began with the work of sociologist James Downton in 1973, but James McGregor Burns developed the idea in more detail and popularized it in his classic 1978 book, *Leadership*. In this kind of transactional policy, individuals make "an exchange of valued things." However, Burns said, "Beyond this the relationship does not go. The bargainers have no enduring purpose that holds them together."[24] This was the core of each step in the right-wing idea factory and, especially, of Trumpism. There was no broad principle at play. Rather, there were continuing efforts to identify policies that parts of the political base wanted and then to advance those policies to build support in that base. Leaders then identified what might resonate with the base and used accumulated power to generate those policies.

These approaches made the right-wing idea factory very different from traditional conservatism and ensured that the right-wing idea factory was especially effective, both in disrupting existing ideologies and in gaining political traction. Its players staked out the boundaries of the new movement, but they certainly did not ensure—or need—consensus. More important, they began to converge on what the overall movement meant, how the rule of law ought to work, and how that rule of law ought to define the very conscience of the nation.

The idea of "conscience" had long been an important theme for American conservatives. In 1960, Barry Goldwater published a book, *The Conscience of a Conservative*, as he prepared to become a presidential candidate. The book made a powerful argument, rooted in natural law, about the core values of conservatism. Those roots, Goldwater claimed, made conservatism ageless:

> Conservatism, we are told, is out-of-date. The charge is preposterous and we ought boldly to say so. The laws of God, and of nature, have no dateline. The principles on which the Conservative

political position is based have been established by a process that has nothing to do with the social, economic and political landscape that changes from decade to decade and from century to century. These principles are derived from the nature of man, and from the truths that God has revealed about His creation. Circumstances do change. So do the problems that are shaped by circumstances. But the principles that govern the solution of the problems do not. To suggest that the Conservative philosophy is out of date is akin to saying that the Golden Rule, or the Ten Commandments or Aristotle's Politics are out of date. The Conservative approach is nothing more or less than an attempt to apply the wisdom and experience and the revealed truths of the past to the problems of today. The challenge is not to find new or different truths, but to learn how to apply established truths to the problems of the contemporary world.[25]

Traditional conservatives are classical liberals, part of the movement established in the Enlightenment. The right-wing idea factory leaders are neither traditional conservatives nor classical liberals. They talk about liberty but seek to impose their values on everyone else. They talk about a small government but haven't hesitated to boost spending to support their goals or harness government to advance their values, and they pay little attention to free-market capitalism. They have squeezed equality from their lexicon and they have pushed aside the delicate balance of powers created by the nation's founders in favor of growing executive power. Russell Kirk wrote that "the conservative believes that there exists an enduring moral order. That order is made for man, and man is made for it: human nature is a constant, and moral truths are permanent."[26] The right-wing idea factory has rejected this principle, along with the traditional conservatism and the rule of law it generated. It has, instead, pushed the bedrock rule of law aside in a raw and blatant grasp for power. The factory operates out of zeal for its cause, without worrying about constraints in pressing it on everyone else, in the quest for ever greater power.

Who Are We?

In a 2025 speech, retired Admiral William McRaven made the link between the nation's conscience, its values, and the rule of law. McRaven had a long career with enormous impact, from overseeing the capture of Iraqi dictator Saddam Hussein to the mission that took out Osama bin Laden, the director of the September 11, 2001, terrorist attacks. During his thirty-seven years of experience in the US Navy, McRaven had developed a basic question for the nation's leaders—and for anyone who cares about how the nation is led:

> "Who Are We?" Who are we as a nation? Because, if we don't know who we are as a nation, if we don't understand our principles, our values, our strengths, our limitations and our aspirations, then all the decisions that follow—will be flawed.

And his answer was simple:

> We are the guys who provide aid and comfort to the weak and downtrodden. We are the guys that free the oppressed and stand up for the little guy. We are the good guys. We are Americans. That's what we do.... Our values, our principles have been our north star, our guiding light in dealing with our own citizens and the rest of the world.

McRaven, however, feared that the nation was losing sight of this north star and was, instead, increasingly becoming "transactional," willing to do things only if the country got something in return.[27] It was a remarkable echo of Burns's notion of leadership.

Despite the criticisms of traditional conservatism, it did have a superior virtue: It had a set of strong anchoring principles. Even one of conservatism's strongest detractors, left-leaning economist John Kenneth Galbraith, said in 1963, with tongue firmly in cheek, that conservatives were engaged "in one of man's oldest, best financed, most applauded and, on the whole, least successful exercises in moral philosophy. That is the search for a truly superior moral justi-fication for selfishness."[28] But traditional conservatives did have an answer to the "Who are we?" question.

With the 2010s, however, there not only was a strong break on the right from traditional conservatism. There was also a big step away from any effort to answer the "Who are we?" question. A se-ries of factories in the states began cranking out a new collection of big ideas. Their creators made little effort to attach their new work to the old principles. Instead, their work was purely transactional, in the ways about which McRaven warned, and their currency of trans-action was the pursuit of political power. If traditional conservatives had high-minded ideals as their goals, the new right-wing ideologues sought power to advance their social policies.

This work preceded Trump's ascent to power, but it then pro-duced Trumpism. It was destined to long outlast it. This transition, and why the change from traditionalism to Trumpism matters, is the puzzle I will explore in the book. The next chapter, however, be-gins with an even more fundamental story: how the Covid outbreak in 2020 created a wedge between traditional conservatives and the new right, between the traditional approach of a small government to enhance individual freedom and harnessing the government to promote social values, which not only came to define society but which also marked a sharp break from the path.

What matters most is why these values matter and how we use government to produce them. As Pulitzer Prize–winning historian Jon Meacham put it, "History tells us that we can chart our national progress in terms of how close we come to, or how far we fall from, realizing the implications of the Declaration [of Independence] and accordingly interpreting or amending our Constitution—and ourselves."[29] Both the Declaration and the Constitution are living documents. There is an enormous controversy about whether to take either one literally, given the centuries that have passed since they were written. On one thing, however, there can be no con-troversy. The way we live the values captured in these documents defines our national character and the meaning that the documents have in our daily lives today.

And on this, there is great controversy: Just what do we want those values to be? That's the question of this book. The answers have fundamentally changed since 2010.

Chapter 2

The Grassroots Uprising

The outbreak of the Covid virus at the end of 2019 switched the right-wing idea factory into high gear. It was an enormous public health crisis. At the beginning of the pandemic, the respected Institute for Health Metrics and Evaluation at the University of Washington projected that the death toll would reach 93,765 persons, a number that at the time seemed horrific and beyond comprehension.[1] In the end, more than 1.2 million Americans died. A team of University of Southern California researchers put the economic toll at $14 trillion in the three years after the virus's outbreak, with conventions, bars and restaurants, and air travel suffering the most.[2] During Covid's worst months, 22 million Americans were unemployed, more than in any downturn since the Great Depression. It took more than two years for the labor market to bounce back to where it was before the outbreak.[3]

For many years, public health experts had been planning for what they predicted would be a truly global pandemic, and they warned that such a pandemic could devastate countries on health, social, economic, and political fronts.[4] Covid seemed "the big one" for which they had been preparing.

Companies shut down their offices and employees learned to work from home. To stay afloat, restaurants and bars scrambled to develop delivery and pickup services. "Margaritas to go" became exceptionally popular in Texas, with the state legislature afterward making that a permanent innovation. On the advice of experts, local schools shut down. Teachers scrambled to learn how to teach online; frustrated parents struggled with the technology and worried that their kids were lagging farther and farther behind in their schooling.

Many Americans got increasingly angry at public health experts, whose advice shifted as the virus progressed. The director of the federal Centers for Disease Control and Prevention, Robert R. Redfield, said that it was not necessary for healthy people to wear masks. Anthony Fauci, who directed the National Institute of Allergy and Infectious Diseases at the National Institutes of Health, suggested saving supplies of protective equipment for doctors and nurses. Then, a few weeks later, the advice changed. The Centers for Disease Control recommended that individuals wear face coverings when they couldn't socially distance and suggested that simple masks, made from t-shirts and rubber bands, would be enough. Sewing circles sprang up around the country to produce these masks for first responders and healthcare workers amid a major mask shortage, only to be told later that the masks did little to block the virus.

Should people work hard to track down more expensive masks? Did social distancing really matter? Was the "wonder drug" ivermectin, typically used to treat people with intestinal worms, effective against Covid? When would a vaccine be available? Should people get vaccinated and, if so, what about boosters? Were the vaccines safe? When it came to the schools: Should they be closed and, if so, for how long—or was the closing of schools a vast overreaction? What about treatments that Trump promoted in 2020, including hydroxychloroquine and chloroquine, typically used to treat malaria? Trump took to the White House podium to suggest health experts examine injecting people with bleach to fight off Covid. State poison control hotlines were flooded with calls to check on the remedy.[5] A population increasingly distrustful of experts went shopping for unproven antimalarial drugs.[6]

Americans wondered whether they could trust the news. In 1998, trust in the mass media was about the same among Republicans and Democrats. By 2024, however, trust among Democrats had declined slightly, from 59 to 54 percent.[7] Republicans, on the other hand, came to trust social media more, with trust rising from 19 percent in 2021 to 45 percent in 2025.[8] With the advice of experts shifting, as they learned more about this new outbreak, and with so many people shuttered at home, relying more on friends, smartphones increasingly became the guide for Republicans.

Many Americans concluded they did not know which expert to believe—or whether to believe any expert at all. White House officials, including President Trump and Vice President Pence, publicly went back and forth on whether they believed in masks and whether they would wear one themselves. Trust in physicians and hospitals dropped from 71.5 percent in April 2020, just weeks into the pandemic, to 40.1 percent in January 2024.[9] Faced with such serious social and economic pain, Americans wondered whether they could trust any institution. According to Edelman, 54 percent of Americans lost trust in government in 2024 because of Covid.[10] They turned instead to the friends they knew and the social media that connected them. That spilled over, in particular, to worries that "public K-12 education in the US is generally going in the wrong direction," with Republicans worrying more than Democrats by a margin of 65 to 40 percent.[11] That, in turn, fed a grassroots movement of parents trying to gain stronger control over local schools.

The Birth of Moms for Liberty

In 2020, two Florida school board members, outraged over their schools' Covid policies, created a new group, "Moms for Liberty." The name said it all: parents concerned about their kids and who distrusted experts. They wanted the freedom to make their own choices. It quickly became a national phenomenon in Republican circles. "Moms for Liberty didn't exist 3 years ago. Now it's a GOP kingmaker," the *Washington Post* wrote in 2023. Donald Trump and Ron DeSantis (who at that point was Trump's strongest challenger in the 2024 race) came to the Moms annual summit in Philadelphia that weekend and sought support from the group. Trump told the summit, "In school board races, PTA meetings and town halls across the nation, you have taught the radical left Marxists and communists a lesson they will never forget: Don't mess with America's moms." He concluded, "You're the best thing that's ever happened to America."[12]

The roster of speakers at the summit was a who's who of the conservative Right. There was the president of the Heritage Foundation, Kevin Roberts; critical race theory opponent James Lindsay; and Tim Barton, the president of WallBuilders, a group dedicated to exposing what it called the "lies" about America's past. By 2024, the group counted 310 chapters in forty-eight states with 130,000 members.[13] In a very short time, the group had grown into the most powerful right-wing force in K-12 education.

Moms for Liberty had modest beginnings. One founder was Tiffany Justice from Indian County, which included Vero Beach. Joining her was Tina Descovich from Brevard County, just to the north, near the Kennedy Space Center. They had become increasingly concerned—and annoyed—by the conflicting signals about Covid they got from the experts: mask or not mask; distance or not distance; close schools or keep them open; and, ultimately, vaccinate or not. They worried about how the shutdowns affected the educational performance of the kids—and how Covid was driving the unfettered power of big government. So in 2021, they launched Moms for Liberty, a group dedicated to reopening the schools and throwing away the masks. Justice explained, "Parents often feel they are up against a machine and are left feeling unheard and frustrated." Descovich added, "The balance of power in education has dramatically shifted away from parents and communities to unions and bureaucrats." She concluded, "Moms for Liberty is fighting to restore parents to the role of primary decision maker for their children by helping them organize and amplify their voices."[14]

The chapters aggressively spoke out at school board meetings, and many local school administrators complained that the groups were bringing chaos to the sessions. In Brevard County, Gary Shiffrin, the head of the local association of school administrators, said that Moms for Liberty had been responsible for more upset than at any since the desegregation battles two generations earlier. "They have decided they are going to be the spokespeople for conservatism, and this won't end when COVID ends," he said. He couldn't have had a better crystal ball. As Descovich put it, "Now is the time to capture these parents for the long term."[15]

Descovich came up with the name, "Moms for Liberty." Justice developed the group's catchy brand, "We do not co-parent with the government," which they printed on merch for sale at the group's website. Descovich said she had been motivated to create the group when her seventh-grade son came home with a 100-plus grade on an assignment. How had he gotten such a great score? He explained he had created "a 'wanted' poster for Christopher Columbus, for 'crimes against humanity.'" How, she wondered, had school changed so much since her time in school? She concluded that education had been hijacked by left-wing activists, and she added that complaint to the same worries about the Left's response to Covid.[16]

The group's leaders believed that Covid had led bureaucrats, especially in Washington, to grab too much power over individuals' lives, and they pledged to win that power back. "Once a parent loses the right to direct the upbringing of their child, we've lost everything," Descovich argued. "You've lost your family. You've lost your community. You have lost the basic unit of society." That showed up in the basics like reading, Justice contended. "The reading proficiency rates we have in America right now pose the greatest national-security threat of anything for the future of this country. If you have a nation of children and adults who cannot read, where does that leave America?"[17] These issues had been simmering for some time, but it was Covid that provided the spark to light the kindling of such educational policy issues.

The cornerstone of their strategy was recruiting candidates for school board races around the country. In 2022, Moms for Liberty fielded about 500 candidates, and 55 percent of them won. In 2023, it was less successful, with just 43 percent of 202 endorsed candidates winning their races. Descovich chalked that up to "happenstance." Critics weren't so sure. "Sowing chaos is a lot easier than governing," said Jack Schneider, an education professor at the University of Massachusetts, Amherst. "It's one thing to smear teachers or to level outrageous claims about the curriculum. It's another thing entirely to convince local voters—people who have a stake in the schools actually functioning—that you have the good sense and the practical skills to oversee school district operations."

The Moms movement also hit a major speed bump with a sex scandal that undermined the group's claims on morality. Bridget Ziegler, of one of the group's other founders, and her husband Christian Ziegler, the Florida Republican chair, found themselves accused by a third woman of planning a sexual threesome. According to their accuser, Bridget had not been able to make it. But Christian was there, and the woman accused him of raping her and filming the encounter. Police later concluded that the incident was "likely consensual," but the publicity led to his ouster from the GOP chairmanship, a political black eye for her, and an embarrassment for Moms. Descovich then lost an election for her Brevard County School Board seat.

Despite these problems, Moms for Liberty continued its roll. Trump appeared with Justice at a Moms for Liberty summit in July 2024. Soon after his 2025 inauguration, she amplified the new administration's policy by working with the US Department of Education to create an "End DEI" web portal, where users could make "reports of discrimination based on race or sex in public schools." She dismissed criticisms of the portal as a "snitch line" and said it was a way to expose "the breadth of indoctrination" that was happening in public schools.[18]

Moms created M4MU (Moms for Liberty University), "an academic approach to educating, equipping, and empowering parents to fight for their children."[19] Among those involved was former Sheriff Mark Lamb, who had become famous for his many appearances on Fox News claiming that sheriffs have no obligation to enforce policies they believe are unconstitutional, like Covid's stay-at-home order. M4MU also featured programs on how parents could combat the threat of violence in local schools and ensure that their children received "an appropriate education." The Moms website included videos of its members speaking forcefully at public meetings, to encourage more members to do the same. And they were, indeed, all moms.[20]

Their power stretched into the second Trump administration. When the president signed the 2025 executive order directing his education secretary to shut down the US Department of Education, Moms for Liberty had a special place at the ceremony—and on the White House website supporting the decision. Moms celebrated Women's History Month with a "Liberty Sword" award to recognize "an individual that unabatedly stands for the principles of Liberty."[21] They had a "Moms for Liberty Day at the White House."[22] The group rolled every media event into an occasion for growing its base—and for raising money.

Which Books to Ban?

That fight for parental control soon morphed into a campaign to ban books. With school closures, many parents found themselves acting as their children's teachers and, as they worked with the materials school districts distributed, confronting—and sometimes objecting to—what their kids were taught. The fiercest early book-banning battle occurred in a small southern Pennsylvania school district, with about 5,500 students and 375 teachers. It was in York, a reliably red county that went almost two-to-one for Trump in 2016, 2020, and 2024, and which the Democrats had not won since Lyndon B. Johnson's trouncing of Barry Goldwater in 1964. By 2022, the district had banned more books than any other in the country—a total of 441 different titles.[23] The campaign also fueled a furious battle between students, parents, and the school district.

Soon after George Floyd's tragic murder in May 2020, a diversity committee in Central York School District compiled readings for teachers and students over the summer. After they reviewed the guide, however, two school board members charged that the committee was advancing issues like "white privilege," which, they said, could push students toward socialistic and anti-religious points of view. A few months later, the school board decided to ban all the resources that the diversity committee had prepared.

One of the banned items was a policy from the Pennsylvania Association of School Boards that called for a campaign against racism. "If racism is ever to be eradicated, our public schools will need to play a significant role in leading the effort," its public statement said. Another was *I Am Not Your Negro*, a 2016 film documentary based on James Baldwin's work that had been nominated for an Academy Award. There were children's books including *Peeny Butter Fudge* by Nobel laureate Toni Morrison; *I Am Rosa Parks* by Brad Meltzer; Laurie Wallmark's biography of Grace Hopper, a black scientist who helped invent one of the first computer languages; and Margot Lee Shetterly's award-winning book about the women whose mathematical work had helped launch the American space program and had inspired a movie nominated for the Best Picture Oscar in 2017.[24]

Long school board debates about how to manage Covid temporarily pushed the issue to the back burner, but when the 2021–2022 school year began, students began demonstrating every day outside the school to demand the books be put back on the shelves. Parents began collecting copies of the banned books, and thousands of copies poured in from around the country.[25] School board officials tried to sidestep the growing controversy by claiming their decision really wasn't a "ban" but a "freeze" until the board could review the materials in more detail, but that did not quiet the students. Edha Gupta, a high school senior, said that the board's decision "was a slap in the face." Another senior pointed to a video jointly produced by CNN and Sesame Street, *Coming Together: Standing Up to Racism,* which featured Elmo and Big Bird.[26] She asked, "Why is a Sesame Street episode threatening the education of children? If anything this school board is threatening education."[27]

The controversy made teachers increasingly nervous about assigning materials that might get them into political trouble. One teacher, Ben Hodge, said he needed to "think twice about whether or not I should or could use a James Baldwin quote as an opening for my class." Patricia Jackson, a twenty-year veteran in the district, explained, "There are teachers looking over their shoulders wondering if someone's going to be at their door." She continued, "I am not an enemy of the state. I am here to take care of your babies when they walk into my classroom."[28] One teacher added, "You have Black children who want to learn about themselves, and now teachers who live in fear of presenting that information to them." The teacher continued, "This targets Black people, and now my concern is you have teachers afraid to teach."[29]

Parents were split. One mom, Brandi Miller, said, "I don't think that a board that lacks diversity is the appropriate authority to determine what qualifies as appropriate material to address race in this community." However, another mother countered that "the community is 100 percent against a critical race theory indoctrination agenda." She added, "Schools are not the place for politics or identity to be shaped." (Critical race theory wasn't being taught in York and none of its materials promoted the theory, whose complexity lay far beyond the capacity of high-school students. I will turn to this issue in the next chapter.) For one parent, Matt Weyant, it was a simple issue: "I don't want my daughter growing up feeling guilty because she's white." The ongoing conflicts led the high school principal, Ryan Caufman, to ban the use of *any* of the materials in the classroom. As for charges that the school board was engaging in racism, Jane Johnson, the school board's president, said that it was just a coincidence that all the materials were about people of color or prepared by them.[30]

The students' ongoing pressure on the school board eventually led its members to vote unanimously to reinstate all the materials on the list. One teacher praised the students, saying, "They are heroes and should be celebrated as bastions of American freedom and democracy. I want to be clear, these kids did this."[31] Their victory did not last long, however. The school board soon took two of the books back off the shelves. One was *Push* by Sapphire, the basis for the film *Precious,* which won two Academy Awards and was nominated for Best Motion Picture. The other was Sarah J. Maas's *A Court of Mist and Fury,* a *New York Times* best-seller. The pressure campaign started up again on the school board and the board relented yet again, but the board instructed the district's librarians to spend the summer break examining more than two thousand books for adult content, which was sure to set up the next battle.

At the center of the York controversy was Rhonda Graman, head of the York chapter of Moms for Liberty, who called her group a collection of "joyful warriors," "united and conquering" as part of the Moms campaign in York public schools.[32] Pushing hard on the issue, too, was Faith Casale, who had narrowly lost election for a seat on the school board in 2021. She had taken the lead in attacking Maas's book for what she called its "detailed sexual content." *Push,* she said, contained objectionable "racial slurs, foul language, [and] sexual content," and hoped to use her complaints to catapult her onto a school board seat.[33] The criticisms generated attention on the school board but not enough for her ongoing school board campaigns, which she lost in 2021 and 2023. A local newspaper found that she had been responsible for anonymously challenging most of the books, all in a lost cause—except for rousing right-wing activists in York.[34]

Under the banner of parental choice, the book-banning movement spread across the country, with a focus on books about

LGBTQ issues and a small group of individuals leading the charge in each community. A *Washington Post* investigation revealed that there were 1,065 complaints about books across the country during the 2021–2022 school year. Almost half—43 percent—dealt with LGBTQ issues. Thirty-six percent were about issues of race. The most-challenged book, the *Post* found, was *All Boys Aren't Blue* by George M. Johnson, which dealt with both race and LGBTQ themes. Second was *Gender Queen* by Maia Kobabe because of its focus on LGBTQ issues. Strikingly, the *Post* found that only eleven people were responsible for 60 percent of the challenges—the *Post* called them "serial book challengers." The biggest reason for seeking to ban the books, they said, was to protect children from sexual content (in 61 percent of the challenges). Where did their lists come from? The *Post* reported that 51 percent of them learned about the books from news reports. Another 30 percent found out about them from other parents and from lists prepared by a handful of national groups.[35]

Parents used social media, especially Facebook, to share lists of books that ought to be banned. There were groups like Patriot Mobile, which called itself a Christian cell phone company; the Florida Citizens Alliance, which partnered with Gov. Ron DeSantis and Moms for Liberty; and Utah Parents United.[36] In addition, other groups largely unknown outside the right-wing echo chamber were very influential inside it: US Parents Involved in Education, No Left Turn in Education, MassResistance, Parents' Rights in Education, Mary in the Library, County Citizens Defending Freedom USA, and Power2Parent. Of the book-banning groups active in 2022, 73 percent had formed since 2021.

The different groups had similar tactics: similar complaints and a focus on a relatively small collection of books.[37] Social media allowed the movement to spread quickly and operate cheaply. PEN America estimated that these groups heavily influenced at least half of the book bans created across the country, with at least 20 percent directly linked and much more connected indirectly.[38]

Right-wing grassroots groups were quick to claim credit for their influence. MassResistance, for example, said its parents forced a "middle school Principal to pull graphic pornographic books from library," including books that "included descriptions of anal rape of a child, bloody suicide, and other horrible scenes." Parents had been working for months to get the schools to withdraw the book, but then "MassResistance gets involved—things start happening!" its website bragged.[39] The Florida Citizens Alliance held a "Protecting Our Children Summit," which promised a PowerPoint presentation that was "extremely graphic in nature," demonstrating that "porn and obscenity" were being forced on children as young as five years old. "No minors will be allowed in the room during the presentation," the group titillated.[40] The campaign led to bans of materials in several school districts throughout the state. In Missouri, a Facebook group of parents filed complaints to take sixteen books off the shelves. They were successful.[41]

The lists propagated across the groups. In Florida, the Citizens Alliance produced a "Porn in Schools" report, with books cited on the website for Christian Patriot Daily. That list, in turn, had come from a graduate student who had developed the short catalog for a completely opposite purpose: an LGBTQ+ guide for caregivers. The list spread to Georgia, where forty-one challenges came from the Florida Citizens Alliance report. The movement then jumped to Michigan, with a group called Forest Hills Parents United. In many states, the lists seemed the product of cutting-and-pasting, with book titles appearing in the same order, with the same typos.[42]

Moms for Liberty produced a 111-page book list, complete with ratings that ran from zero, suitable "for everyone," to five, with "aberrant content." The ratings also had QR codes, one of which took parents to books that, the rating said, were "pornographic," something that made them a "public health crisis." (Just what "pornography" meant, however, was very much in the eye of the reader, as US Supreme Court Justice Potter Stewart put it in 1964: when it came to pornography, he said, "I know it when I see it.")[43] A different QR code allowed parents to concentrate on own their school's library catalog and compare books' ratings with the books on the shelves.[44] Another right-wing group, No Left Turn in Education, compiled its own list. Most of the books focused on what the groups identified as "critical race theory," "anti-police" themes, and "comprehensive sexuality education."[45] It shared the same zero-to-five rating tool that Moms for Liberty displayed and then allowed users of its site to map the presence of troublesome books anywhere in the country.[46] Both of the groups, in turn, linked to RatedBooks.org, which provided a search engine to check any book.[47]

As the Covid crisis of 2020 and 2021 sent more kids to their parents for homeschooling, more of the parents became engaged with what their kids were reading, and many were surprised by what they saw. Parents started talking with each other—in person, in texts, and through Facebook groups—about what their kids were learning and about what they should be reading. At one Laramie, Wyoming, school board meeting, a large crowd gathered to oppose mask mandates in schools. But then one mom interrupted the debate about the masks and began reading from books available in the district's school libraries. One was *Monday's Not Coming*, which had won its author, Tiffany D. Jackson, the Coretta Scott King–John Steptoe Award for New Talent. But the mom objected to the book's frank language about sex, even though that played a relatively minor part of the book. The mom then turned to another book, Ellen Hopkins's *Traffick*, about five teens who found themselves victims of sex trafficking. She said, "Parents like myself had no idea this stuff was here." A dad at the meeting, who had come to talk about the district's response to Covid, said, "I would never have known these extreme leftists that are controlling our school district had I not gone to voice my opposition to the masking."[48]

The Covid battles and book bans easily flowed back and forth into each other. Some parents objected to books simply based on their titles, without having read them. Other parents fed on social media complaints, which led to bans of notable books like Toni

Morrison's *Beloved*; Khaled Hosseini's award-winning book *The Kite Runner*; as well as classics like John Steinbeck's *Of Mice and Men* and Harper Lee's *To Kill a Mockingbird*, which had won the Pulitzer Prize. A Texas state legislator compiled a list of more than 850 books that, he said, could cause students "discomfort, guilt, anguish or any other form of psychological stress." Of the first one hundred books on the list, ninety-seven came from the pens of women, LGBTQ authors, or minorities. That was enough for a school district in San Antonio, which took 400 books on the legislator's list off the library shelves.[49] There had been no complaints from parents, and there was no review of their contents. The legislator was Matt Krause, who was hoping to fuel his run for attorney general. He lost.

Covid became a major driver for the movement, explained Tiffany Justice from Moms for Liberty. Parents, she explained, had been invigorated by working with their kids at home during Covid. "We had never really been able to get parents as invigorated as they have been seeing the curriculum up close and personal while they were sitting with their child doing the work," she said. And that helped fuel her movement. "We saw it as an opportunity to really engage parents even more and to get them involved in their children's education."[50]

At one school board meeting in a town near Austin, a parent pulled selective quotes from Ashley Hope Pérez's novel *Out of Darkness* and complained about anal sex, which wasn't even in the book. *Jimmy Kimmel Live!* and TMZ both used video of the complaint for laughs, but the speaker won support in right-wing circles for battling "filth." Pérez said she soon began receiving phone messages calling her a "degenerate piece of s—," was called SATAN on social media, and received a letter saying she was "no better than a slut or a hooker." The book had received a positive and mostly quiet reception when it was published in 2015. The *New York Times* praised it, with its review saying "Her layered tale of color lines, love and struggle in an East Texas oil town is a pit-in-the-stomach family drama that goes down like it should, with pain and fascination, like a mix of sugary medicine and artisanal moonshine."[51] The book, however, doesn't contain anything about anal sex.[52]

Research by PEN America showed that a relatively small handful of organizations, especially Moms for Liberty and No Left Turn in Education, fifty organizations and local chapters in all, mostly launched since 2021—were responsible for many of the book bans. PEN America traced 20 percent of the book bans directly to these groups. Another 30 percent of the bans showed evidence of the groups' influence, including common lists of books, language, and tactics.[53]

Book banning isn't new, of course. As long as writers have been writing and readers have been reading, there have been campaigns to ban books. In 213 BCE, Chinese Emperor Shih Huang Ti burned all the kingdom's books—and 460 Confucian scholars along with the books, because he wanted to claim that he was the beginning of recorded history, a claim difficult to disprove when the previous records and experts were gone.[54] In ancient Rome, the emperor Augustus exiled the poet Ovid in 8 CE because he thought the poet's book, *Ars amatoria* (*The Art of Love*) was a bit too explicit—but also because, some historians believe, Ovid had accused the emperor of committing incest with his own daughter Julia—or maybe that Ovid had himself slept with the emperor's daughter—or maybe that Ovid had discovered someone else doing so—or maybe because of all of the above.[55] The book was so racy that the US Customs Service banned the book's import until at least 1928. It has since reappeared on Amazon as a "modern library classic."

During the Renaissance, the Catholic Church developed its own banned-book list, the *Index Librorum Prohibitorum* (or the Index of Forbidden Books, published in 1559), which among other things banned any version of the Bible in a native tongue. Over time, it included everything written by Jean-Paul Sartre, David Hume, and Thomas Hobbes. *Paradise Lost*, by John Milton, made the list. So did work by Erasmus, Voltaire, Montesquieu, Francis Bacon, Nicolaus Copernicus, and Edward Gibbon. Daniel Defoe's *Robinson Crusoe* was on the list as well, along with Victor Hugo's *Les Misérables*. In the early days, anyone possessing any of the books on the Index could be excommunicated. The church eventually ceased publication of the index in 1966, as part of the general reforms that came with the Second Vatican Council and the overload of new books to review.

English theatergoers couldn't watch *King Lear* from 1810 to 1820, during the reign of King George III and until his death in 1820, because the king banned the play. The connection between one mad king and another was too much for George to bear. The Soviet Union banned *The Adventures of Sherlock Holmes* in 1929 because of "occultism." In 1931, Hunan Province in China banned *Alice in Wonderland* because animals couldn't talk. The government of East Berlin viewed Mickey Mouse as an "anti-Red rebel" in 1954, while Penguin Books won a 1960 trial that sought to hold D. H. Lawrence's *Lady Chatterley's Lover* as obscene. The US Post Office had banned the book from the mail, but a federal judge concluded that the Post Office had no power to decide whether anything was obscene. The whole debate, of course, did nothing but boost sales of the book. Throughout Germany in 1933 the Nazis burned books by Albert Einstein, Sigmund Freud, Ernest Hemingway, and Helen Keller, among others.

There's never been a time since the invention of books when some book didn't strike someone as offensive. L. Frank Baum's 1900 classic, *The Wizard of Oz*, with its tornadoes, witches, flying monkeys, a yellow brick road, and ruby slippers, captivated children and their parents for generations. It even surprisingly spun off a Broadway prequel in 2003, which played on stage for decades, and a hit movie that debuted in 2024. But Detroit's libraries banned the book in 1957. The director of the Detroit Public Library at the time said, "There is nothing uplifting or elevating" about the book, and he argued it had "no value." The "negativism" of the book was a problem. "Instead of setting a high goal," the Associated Press reported the director as saying, "they drag your minds [down] to a cowardly level," a conclusion that apparently missed its unintended pun on the book's Cowardly Lion, who wanted courage.[56] Boston banned Ernest Hemingway's *The Sun Also Rises* in 1930. So did two California communities in 1960, because the book's profanity and promiscuity were too much for residents of Riverside and San Jose to bear.[57] Strongsville, Ohio, banned Joseph Heller's classic, *Catch-22*, because of what officials saw as indecent language. And, of course, there's J.D. Salinger's *The Catcher in the Rye*, which has been the focus of controversy since its 1951 publication. George Orwell's *1984* ranks as one of the most-banned books ever. (Both of these books ranked in the top two hundred books on Amazon during the 2020s.)

But book banning increased massively in the 2020s. In part, this was because of growing sensitivity to issues of gender diversity and increasing sales of books devoted to these issues. For example, NPD, a leading market analysis company, documented a rapid increase in sales of LGBTQ fiction as part of what one of its analysts explained was "a generational shift toward a more open and inclusive attitude toward gender diversity and sexual orientation," in which niche titles became mainstream.[58] Shifting cultural values brought issues of sexual identity to the surface, which both encouraged publishers to publish more books on the topic and made it possible for more readers to explore them.

The number of book bans grew from 2,532 in 2021–2022, to 3,362 in 2022–2023, and then tripled in the next year, to 10,046. The number of banned titles tripled as well in just one year, from 1,557 in 2022–2023 to 4,231 in 2023–2024. The book bans were most numerous in Florida and Iowa, which accounted for 8,232 book bans in 2023–2024, followed by Texas and Wisconsin, all states with majority-Republican legislatures and all but Wisconsin having a "trifecta," with Republicans controlling the governorship and both houses of the state legislature. Florida required that any book for which someone made a charge of "sexual content" be removed from libraries until it was thoroughly reviewed. Iowa mandated that all books be "age-appropriate," without defining what that meant. Discussions of LGBTQ+ issues—and therefore any materials exploring them—were banned from the classroom. In many states, just a few school districts accounted for the banned books; in Kentucky and Missouri, one district was responsible for all the bans. Banned books likewise tended to focus on a small number of subjects. Fifty-seven percent were about sex or sex-related topics; 44 percent on people of color; and 39 percent on LGBTQ+ characters.[59] And, as the *Washington Post* found, a small number of actors were responsible for most of the action.

The book-banning movement energized school board members across the country. In Granbury, Texas, a school board member who had run on a campaign platform to root out "sexually explicit" books from the school system wormed her way into a school library after closing and, armed with a flashlight, set out to discover dangerous books. Her school board colleagues later censured her—not for her zealotry, but for being in the library after hours without permission.[60]

Then, when at the start of his second term, Trump signed his executive order terminating all diversity, equity, and inclusion (DEI) programs in the federal government, administrators of Department of Defense schools on military bases scrambled to scrub books with DEI overtones from any curriculum and from school libraries. DOD's school system is enormous and provides education for the children of military families who are, in many cases, based far away from the United States, in lands where English and American culture are typically not part of the curriculum. The system reaches 67,000 students in 160 schools, a system larger than those in Seattle or Boston, and in standardized tests outranks the scores of every state, in both math and reading in both the fourth and eighth grades.[61] Following the Trump executive order, school officials sent a memo to parents saying it was taking a close look at library books "potentially related to gender ideology or discriminatory equity ideology targets." One item was a picture book designed for fourth to eighth graders, *No Truth without Ruth*, about the late Supreme Court justice

Ruth Bader Ginsberg. Another was *Freckleface Strawberry*, a picture book for four- to eight-year-olds about dealing with freckles. It was written by Julianne Moore, a five-time Oscar nominee and 2015 winner for her performance in the movie *Still Alice*. Moore was striking for her bright red hair—and freckles.[62]

The Trump executive order rippled out to the nation's service academies. At the US Naval Academy, for example, officials identified several books that threatened to incur the ire of Defense Secretary Pete Hegseth. Library items included *The Autobiography of Martin Luther King, Jr.*; a biography of Jackie Robinson, who broke the color barrier in major league baseball; and *Einstein on Race and Racism*, by Fred Jerome and Rodger Taylor.[63] After a public uproar, all but twenty of the books were returned to the shelves. The Pentagon, however, did not disclose which titles were still being withheld. Not long afterwards, Defense Secretary Pete Hegseth removed the academy's commandant, long before the scheduled completion of her appointment.

Covid, along with the political changes it brought, transformed education. It increased parents' determination to decide how education worked. Especially in towns dominated by the right-wing idea factory, they pushed aside the control of experts for their own judgment. Covid also inflamed the even bigger DEI debate over who ought to control what children read in schools. That, in turn, turned old flashpoints about race and DEI into new battlegrounds.

Most of all, it radically transformed the right-wing, from a broad movement committed to shrinking government and promoting liberty to a movement eager to expand governmental power, in unprecedented ways, to promote social goals. Traditional conservatism had an extraordinarily well-developed collection of ideas. This new brand of right-wing activism had outrage, channeled not toward promoting liberty but toward removing ideas that ordinary individuals—dads and especially moms—found offensive. It sought not the protection of freedom but the accumulation and exercise of political power, not the protection of individual choice but the imposition of the values of a few on everyone. It was tactical, not strategic. At its core, it was not ideological but pragmatic.

Most of all, it pushed aside traditional conservatism, with its focus on individual liberty and market-based choice, for a new right-wing strategy that wasn't shy about marshaling government power and using it promote a very particular set of social goals. It's not likely that Burke, Friedman, Goldwater, Reagan, or Buckley would have approved. But it did set the stage for a brand-new, grassroots-driven right-wing approach.

And, as we will see in the next chapter, it fed off Covid in generating a broad and powerful new movement.

Chapter 3

The New Populists

During his remarkable rise to political power, the global media focused on Donald Trump's transition from real estate developer and reality television star to the presidency—twice—an arc that at first seemed improbable even to Trump. (He had done very little to prepare for winning the 2016 race, and that led to a slow start that plagued him during much of his first term.) The underlying story, however, is both more important and more interesting. Trumpism—and the new populism on which he ran—was in full gear before Trump's golden escalator ride in 2015 when he kicked off his run.

Political impresario Steve Bannon, who was the chief executive officer of the campaign before becoming Trump's short-lived chief strategist in the White House, had already built the superstructure of ideas on which Trump ran. Trump and Bannon were populist-nationalists, a budding movement focused on putting people first (as opposed to resting control in an elite) and America first (as opposed to an internationalist view). They were Republicans by convenience and certainly were not conservative, in the movement's traditional terms. Bannon, in fact, said, "I think conservatives are [expletive.]" In fact, Bannon claimed the movement he promoted was about much more than putting Trump in the White House, because Trumpism is "always going to fade."

What the debate should be about, he said, was "the core," the populism that supplied Trump's support and which would sustain the movement when Trump was no longer politically active.[1] There was little agreement among scholars and other experts about just what this "populism" meant, but it did focus on a broad appeal to the people, a reaction against social elites, and an impatience on shifting governmental power toward the executive.[2]

Bannon's influence on Trump in 2016 was even more remarkable because he did not join the campaign until August of that year. After the inauguration, he quickly flamed out as a member of the White House staff, in part because members of Trump's inner circle tagged him as one of the key sources for an embarrassing tell-all book, Michael Wolff's *Fire and Fury*.[3] He also burned all his bridges with Trump's family, especially in revealing a meeting that Don Jr. held with Russians during the campaign in Trump Tower, an episode that Bannon called "treasonous."[4] Just as important, his hard-charging style rubbed most of the White House staff the wrong way.

Bannon's path to Trump's strategist was as unpredictable as was Trump's rise in politics. *New York Times* columnist Ross Douthat laid out the improbable biography in a rapid-fire story: "Working-class Kennedy Democrat, a blue-collar Catholic family whose father was essentially a foreman at the phone company and got to lower management. He spent 50 years there, as his father did, and helped organize the Communication Workers of America back in the '30s before it went off the rails. Stay-at-home mom, five kids. Land-grant university, naval officer. Educated at Harvard Business School—that's the West Point of capitalism, particularly, at the time, globalization. Studied under Michael Porter, the great theoretician of competitive advantage and globalization." Bannon worked with Andrew Breitbart to develop and fund Breitbart News, which became one of the most important voices of the right-wing cause, and then took over the news site when the founder died just days before its launch.[5]

During the early years of his career, Bannon was a Hollywood producer, with twenty-one film credits. None were big moneymakers; almost all were documentaries that promoted his increasingly right-wing leanings, like the 2010 film, *Generation Zero*, which told the tale of how social changes helped stimulate the 2008 financial crisis. (Viewers of the film gave it a 29 percent approval on *Rotten Tomatoes.*)[6] Filmmaking whetted his appetite for a more direct role in politics. He abandoned Hollywood, investment banking, Democrats, unions, universities, Harvard Business School, and especially globalization. Bannon became increasingly convinced that globalization was responsible for enormous economic and social problems in America, especially for lower- and middle-income Americans. He renounced permissive immigration, convinced it had undermined the economic prospects of working-class Americans. That built the foundation for his populist nationalism, and he found a ready audience in Trump for his views.

Although Bannon developed a reputation as the rough-talking muscle of the new right-wing, there was a deceptively complex ideology behind his work. Bannon opposed the free-market capitalism of the traditional conservatism, which he viewed as a system that rewarded only the rich, and he embraced social conservatism, from his Catholic upbringing. He helped generate the "America First" approach of the right-wing. Bannon's opposition to globalization led him to advocate high tariffs and energy self-sufficiency. He argued that the United States should back away from international alliances and temptations for nation-building, so the country could focus squarely on defending its own national interests, instead of broad international alliances. He opposed immigration and favored banning travelers from Muslim-majority nations, to emphasize and reinforce American cultural identity. This message appealed, in turn, to white Protestants, who worried that rapid-fire cultural changes were eroding their identity—and their political dominance. In 2016, Trump called him "the best talent in politics."[7]

Bannon built his strategy around these ideas. He believed that it was essential to return to the proper social order, especially by blocking the influx of migrants, and to curb individual rights in favor of promoting the social good in sync with lasting traditions. For the

West to return to its roots, he believed, the Catholic Church's grand traditions provided the guide (and not the more modern one focused on social justice and championed by Pope Francis and Pope Leo XIV).[8] His strategy had an apocalyptic side as well. In 2013, Bannon said, "Lenin wanted to destroy the state, and that's my goal too." He explained, "I want to bring everything crashing down, and destroy all of today's establishment."[9] Bannon became convinced that a "deep state" of bureaucrats had been captured by the dominant left-wing ideology, much as the Catholic Church had been captured by a left-leaning "synodality" (with a focus on dialogue and collaboration, not a focus on core truths, as he saw it). This deep state had made government increasingly unaccountable, and the only solution was to vilify them before pushing them out. If Trump sometimes seemed intent on taking out the framework of government, it came from Bannon.

Bannon was certainly abrasive, but he had been effective. He was a superb tactician, but his loud and abrasive tone and disheveled hair disguised the deceptively deep philosophical model he had developed. He pushed aside the debris of the Republicans' self-reflection to lay out a game plan that proved enormously successful for raising money and personally successful for Trump, even if Bannon himself soon swung into a different orbit—and into a four-month sentence in a federal prison for two counts of contempt of Congress for refusing to testify about the January 6, 2021, attack on the Capitol.

Leo and the World of Dark Money

Parallel with Bannon's work, but only partially in sync with it, was the remarkable fundraising prowess of Leonard Leo. He became the unquestioned master of exploiting the opportunities that opened with the Supreme Court's *Citizens United* decision. Few Americans knew about him, but nearly everyone knew what he accomplished. His primary tool was the expert use of dark money and in negotiating the corridors of even darker money that lay behind it.

Leo was "the man who rebuilt the Supreme Court," as Bari Weiss, editor at *The Free Press*, put it, before becoming editor-in-chief of CBS News. Leo became "one of the most powerful people in the United States," although "most people don't know who he is because, well, he doesn't want them to know." He convinced George W. Bush to nominate Justices John Roberts and Samuel Alito to the Supreme Court and, during the Trump administration, he worked behind the scenes to secure the nominations of Neil Gorsuch, Brett Kavanaugh, and Amy Coney Barrett. He "has cultivated talent across every level of the judicial system," including in the lower federal courts and state supreme courts. And he was "the architect" of the Supreme Court majority in *Dobbs* that overturned the 1973 *Roe v. Wade* Supreme Court precedent establishing a woman's right to an abortion.[10] Even when Trump turned on Leo through a series of Truth Social posts in 2025, it quickly became clear that Leo, not Trump, would prevail in the long run.

Leo's climb began in the wake of *Roe v. Wade*, when a conservative activist named Phyllis Schlafly launched a fight to overturn it. She had worked as an analyst for the American Enterprise Institute, then the foremost think tank on the right, and had enthusiastically promoted her self-published book, *A Choice Not an Echo*, in which she attacked the "Eastern Republican Establishment" as being insufficiently conservative.[11] (It remained available on Amazon into the mid-2020s, in its third edition, a remarkable feat for any self-published book.) In any big movement, it's always too easy to make too much of any one person, but Schlafly was certainly the driving force behind the anti-abortion movement in the years after *Roe*. With her movement to stop the campaign for the Equal Rights Amendment to the US Constitution, she helped Republicans build support among the religious right, which set the stage for their expansion in the 2010s and, ultimately, for the reversal of the *Roe* decision.

The support of the religious right helped elect Ronald Reagan and then George H. W. Bush, but conservatives were disappointed that they had not made more progress in reversing *Roe*.

Right-wing leaders concluded that what they most needed was a cohort of conservative judges who could help them shift the ideological balance of power on the federal bench.

The central figure in this quiet campaign was Leonard Leo, a Cornell graduate who had founded one of the first chapters of the Federalist Society, an organization founded in 1982 to encourage intellectual debate on the principles of limited government. When he graduated, he took a job with the fledgling group and, in the years that followed, he fashioned it into an increasingly important pipeline for recruiting conservative talent for the federal courts. Along the way, he got to know an upcoming federal jurist, Clarence Thomas, and eventually assembled the six jurists who overturned *Roe*.

In just a few years, Leo wove together a remarkably complex, interconnected network of organizations. There were right-wing groups like Liberty Council, which hired Thomas's wife Ginni Thomas as its president, as well as several Catholic groups opposed to abortion and same-sex marriage, including the Catholic Association and the Catholic Association Foundation. He connected with a wealthy conservative donor, Rebekah Mercer, as well as Steve Bannon, then chairman of Breitbart News. Mercer became a major contributor to the Trump campaign, and Bannon took on the job of Trump's campaign manager.

Leo headed three different nonprofits—BH Fund, the Freedom and Opportunity Fund, and America Engaged, which served as fundraising fronts. In turn, they became interlocking parts of an even larger conglomerate of dark-money organizations, many of which had neither employees nor websites. Because of the limited federal requirements for overseeing such groups, they reported only the most rudimentary financial information to the IRS. Loosely allied with Leo's groups was the vast nonprofit network established by billionaires Charles and David Koch, including the Charles Koch Institute, Americans for Prosperity, Americans for Prosperity Foundation, and Freedom Partners. The sheer scale of their activities was enormous.

The 2010 *Citizens United* decision spawned an even larger network of organizations whose mission was inscrutable behind their patriotic names: Majority Forward, America Votes, Duty & Honor, and Defending Democracy Together (supporting the Left). There was the American Action Network and America First Policies (supporting the Right). Then there was the National Association of Realtors, which took no chances by supporting both.[12] It was even harder to identify the networks behind the networks—the connections between Leo's empire, the Koch organizations, and the organizations they supported.[13] It was simply impossible to chart who was doing what. But one thing was clear: The Right was considerably more effective than the Left in taking advantage of the new rules that came after *Citizens United* in 2010.

Without the dark-money boom, it would have been impossible to bring big new ideas to market. It would have been like trying to launch a new car by designing the assembly line but not turning on the energy to run the lights or power the line. Leo knew that the most important part of the assembly line was finding the right place to stage an issue, that this was often likely to be the federal courts, and that putting favorable judges onto the right benches was the key to moving policy.

He was right.

Thanks to *Citizens United*, it was possible to construct new, nearly invisible networks. That's just what the left-wing attempted to do, of course, and it achieved substantial success with money contributed by George Soros. However, the right-wing had a broader collection of donors, was far better financed, was often cleverer, and, in the end, was far more successful. Leo's strategy yielded a large number of lifetime appointments, which paid off far more than investing regularly in expensive congressional races, where it was never clear how long a new member might last and where even successful members had to run for re-election. When sworn in, Chief Justice John Roberts was fifty. His fellow justices likewise had long careers ahead of them: Clarence Thomas was forty-three when sworn in; Samuel Alito, fifty-six; Neil Gorsuch, fifty; Brett Kavanaugh, fifty-three; and Amy Coney Barrett, forty-eight. The Supreme Court's 2022 *Dobbs* decision, which overturned Roe, would have been impossible without this fundamental shift in the Court's makeup.

But Leo's campaign to remake the courts didn't stop there. Before the end of Trump's term in 2021, he had appointed 228 federal judges—54 judges to the appeals court and 174 judges to district courts, or about a quarter of the federal judiciary. That's almost as many judges in just one term as Obama managed in two, but not quite as many as Biden pushed through in his single term, as he struggled to reverse Leo's success. Trump's appointments to the federal appeals courts—the level of federal courts between the district courts and the US Supreme Court—were especially significant. With the determined help of Senate Majority Leader Mitch McConnell, he flipped three of the federal appeals courts from Democratic-appointed majorities to Republican.[14] And, of course, he achieved a supermajority of members of the Supreme Court.

The shifting balance of the lower courts was especially important, because most federal cases never reach the US Supreme Court. In 2023, more than 339,000 cases were filed before the federal district courts. The federal courts of appeals had 40,000 new filings. The US Supreme Court hears only about 70 cases per year.[15] Changing the balance in the lower courts therefore had an enormous and far-reaching, if often quieter, impact on the thousands of issues that never made it to the high court. It was so important that, in preparing his second term, Trump put extra attention on starting the confirmation process of like-minded judges all over again.

Leo's strategy was as simple as it was effective. He identified promising right-leaning students while they were still in law school. He then used his vast—and growing—network of contacts to place them in key clerkships and other prime jobs. As their careers developed, he nursed them through personal challenges and put them into an ideological cocoon to protect them from drifting off the policy course. Then he worked closely with the White House, beginning with the George W. Bush administration, to recommend individuals for key administration jobs and for judicial nominations. One Bush White House aide in an email said that Leo was the point person for "all outside coalition activity regarding judicial nominations." He worked closely with Bush aides to promote the nomination of John Roberts and then Samuel Alito. As one major donor said, "Nothing has been more consequential in transforming the courts and building a more impactful conservative movement than the network of talented individuals and groups fostered by Leonard Leo."[16]

Part of Leo's success also came from supporting justices even after they reached the bench. The last thing he—and his right-wing allies—wanted was to have their investments walk off the Court to a cushy law practice. As George Conway, a one-time Trump supporter turned harsh critic, put it, "Part of what Leonard does is he tries to keep them happy so they stay on the job." Leo regularly hosted dinners where one or two justices could dine with supporters and donors. "It made the justices happy to meet people who revered them," Conway explained. "It made the donors happy to meet the justices and no doubt more inclined to give to Leonard's causes." There were small fishing trips bringing together justices and donors as well as private donor retreats. Robin Arkley II, a California mortgage company executive, told *ProPublica*, "Nothing has been more consequential in transforming the courts and building a more impactful conservative movement than the network of talented individuals and groups fostered by Leonard Leo."[17]

The Federalist Society's connections to right-wing policymakers and donors remained murky, but its influence had become clear. During the first Trump administration, roughly half of the president's nominees to the federal bench were Federalist Society members.[18] Trump blew the group's cover by saying, during the 2016 presidential campaign, "We're going to have great judges, conservative, all picked by the Federalist Society," which meant through Leo's influence.[19] With his nominations of Gorsuch, Kavanaugh, and Barrett, all of whom shared Federalist Society connections, that's just what Trump did. Leo said that his long-held goal was "a federal court system dominated by conservative judges who believe the Constitution must be interpreted literally," a right-wing code word for an originalist philosophy that, in turn, was a stark rejection of progressive jurisprudence. With Trump, that's just what he accomplished. The Federalist Society, as Steven M. Teles explored in detail, helped drive what he called the *conservative legal movement.*[20]

There were big bumps in that road. In 2024, for example, *Pro-Publica* received the Pulitzer Prize for its investigation of billionaire Harlan Crow's funding of luxury travel, a real estate deal, and a child's private school tuition for Justice Clarence Thomas. *ProPublica* also probed Paul Singer, a billionaire hedge fund manager who was alleged to have had business before the Supreme Court and who funded a luxury fishing trip for Alito to Alaska. Alito did not recuse himself from Singer's court proceeding. Crow and Singer were both Republican mega-donors.[21]

Despite these investigative reports, decades-long work of the Federalist Society—and of Leonard Leo in particular—came together in June 2022 with the *Dobbs* decision. The *Roe* precedent crumbled with the decision, written by Alito, that "the Constitution makes no reference to abortion, and no such right is implicitly protected by any constitutional provision."[22] The right-wing won its anti-abortion victory after decades of work, but the win came more than anything else from Leo's dogged work to ensure that the right judges were sitting in the right places at the right time.

But his work was scarcely done. In 2023, Leo secured a $1.6 billion donation from Barre Seid, a ninety-one-year-old former head of an electrical products manufacturer. Seid donated the company (not a cash contribution, but the entire company) to Leo's nonprofit, Marble Freedom Trust, which helped Seid sidestep a huge tax obligation and provided Leo with what was believed to be the single largest political donation in the nation's history. (Compare that with about half a billion dollars that George Soros, the largest financial contributor on the left, donated to political campaigns and related nonprofit organizations in 2021 and 2022.)[23] The financial trail, virtually impossible to disentangle, allowed Leo to increase his spending to right-wing causes through dark-money 501(c)(4) contributions. Previous donations to the trust flowed into the Rule of Law Trust and the Concord Fund, which further muddied the money trail—and further increased Leo's leverage.[24] Then, armed with Seid's contribution, Leo planned a foray into bankrolling Hollywood movies, in a bid to move American culture to the right.[25]

Trump's enthusiasm for Leo's work waned in his second term, especially after the US Court of International Trade, constituted especially to deal with foreign trade issues, blocked the president's tariffs. The reason, Trump believed, was that "his" judges—the ones he appointed in his first term—had not proven loyal to him in the second. "I am so disappointed in The Federalist Society because of the bad advice they gave me on numerous Judicial Nominations. This is something that cannot be forgotten!" He was especially unhappy with Leo. Trump said he had "openly and freely" accepted his recommendations through the Federalist Society, "but then realized that they were under the thumb of a real 'sleazebag' named Leonard Leo, a bad person who, in his own way, probably hates America, and obviously has his own separate ambitions."[26] The attack made many members of the right-wing nervous about what Trump might do to fill future nominations and what his ongoing connections with the right-wing base might be.

But Leo had already established himself as a quiet but enormously powerful figure on the right-wing. And that, in turn, had helped him move abortion policy to the right in many states.

Before the Court handed down *Dobbs*, many states anticipated that the Supreme Court would toss out the *Roe* precedent and leave abortion policy to the states. Thirteen states passed laws that automatically triggered much tighter state restrictions on abortion if the

Court ruled against a federal right to an abortion. Another thirteen states passed new anti-abortion legislation soon after the decision.[27] When the court handed down *Dobbs*, therefore, the impact was nearly instantaneous in more than half of states. Before *Dobbs*, 15 percent of women were at an hour's drive away from where they could obtain an abortion. After *Dobbs*, that percentage doubled.[28]

There was no evidence of overt coordination among the anti-abortion states. In the decade before *Dobbs*, however, state legislative activity on abortion significantly increased, to an average of fifty-four laws passed per year (or an average of at least one law per state over that period).[29] If there wasn't formal coordination, there certainly was an indirect network among the states.

Two right-wing organizations, Americans United for Life and the National Right to Life Committee, promoted the trigger laws. They distributed model laws, lobbied to get the bills passed, provided legal assistance to state activists, and ensured that right-leaning states moved quickly as soon as *Dobbs* made that possible. In the Americans United for Life 2020 annual report, for example, the association pointed to legislation in Idaho and Utah that came directly from its work.[30] Over the years, sixteen states adopted the National Right to Life Committee's model legislation banning abortions after twenty weeks of pregnancy. Thirteen states passed the committee's legislation using the committee's definition of "dismemberment" of a fetus.[31] Legislation restricting abortion after the detection of a heartbeat passed in seven states by 2019, just before *Dobbs*. Bit by bit, these two groups chipped away at *Roe's* foundation under *Roe* until it crumbled with *Dobbs*.

Americans United for Life put together a playbook for state legislators, which produced more than four hundred similar anti-abortion bills introduced in forty-one states. It was, one analysis suggested, a matter of "cut, paste, legislate." Such "copycat bills amount to the nation's largest, unreported special-interest campaign, supplanting in some states the traditional approach of writing legislation from scratch," the authors concluded. The groups provided a "full-service" approach, with a team of attorneys re-searching the background of the issue and adapting proposed leg-islation to the needs of each state. The groups provided experts for consultation and testimony and support for state attorneys general when the inevitable court challenges arose.[32] Then, when pressures increased to create exceptions to strict anti-abortion laws, the right-wing groups rallied their troops to hold the line.[33]

Support for these right-wing groups led back to Leo. His CRC Advisors has worked with Americans United for Life, the March for Life, and the Human Capital Project, which launched an aggressive campaign against Planned Parenthood. All this work circled back through the Judicial Crisis Network, set up to advance the nomina-tions of Leo's picks for the Supreme Court.[34] The sprawling network of right-wing organizations that operated in the pro-life space was impossible to map because of its vast size, enormous funding, and shape-shifting collection of organizations. But there's no doubt that the road from *Roe* to *Dobbs* and then to state restrictions ran through them—and that Leo had paved the road.

Religious Fuel for the Right-Wing Base

Leo's campaign carried a heavily religious connection. After Barrett's confirmation in 2020, there were six Catholics on the Court, includ-ing five of the six justices who voted to overturn *Roe*. (The count was a bit complicated: Gorsuch grew up a Catholic but worshiped as an Episcopalian. The sixth Catholic justice was Sotomayor, on the progressive wing of the Court.) The link between the candidates that Leo promoted and the Catholic Church was not hard to ferret out. A devout Catholic, Leo received several awards from associa-tions affiliated with the church. He joined the Knights of Malta, a group dating to the twelfth century. The Vatican named him and his wife Sally as Stewards of St. Peter, an honor bestowed on those donating at least $1 million to the church. He received the John

Paul II New Evangelization Award from Opus Dei, a conservative Catholic organization that named the award in honor of the "barbarians, secularists, and bigots" who promoted "the woke idols of our age." In fact, he said, "The secularists are fine with Catholics in the public square so long as we don't, you know, practice our faith." Mary Jo McConahay, the author of a book on the links between Catholic bishops and the far right, concluded, "Leo wanted to see his own moral principles become the law of the land. And now he wants his moral principles to be the culture of the land."[35]

Rippling out from Leo's hub, CRC Advisors was a complex network of Catholic organizations. The website for CRC Advisors had just a single page, which described the incubation of "public policy projects, coalitions, and groups: mission-driven, focused, results-oriented."[36] Beyond that, it was impossible to tell what CRC was, who was behind it, how much money it had, who its clients were, and what ideas it promoted. Its predecessor was The Polling Company, a firm then owned by Kellyanne Conway, herself a Catholic, who sold it to CRC when she joined the Trump administration. But that only reinforced the connection between Leo and Trump's team. Staffing CRC were many conservative Catholics. The firm made contributions to Catholic organizations connected to Leo, and many of those organizations in turn were clients of CRC. A writer for the *National Catholic Reporter* called CRC "the marketing arm for the Catholic right." Clients have included the US Conference of Catholic Bishops, the Eternal Word Television Network (a cable network devoted to religious issues), and many pro-life groups.[37]

The reason for the connections was simple, as author John Gehring pointed out. "Conservative Catholics have been talking about ending *Roe* for decades. Leonard Leo went out and did it." For activist Catholic organizations that are seeking support, "You certainly want his money because he has a lot of it."[38] That became clear during Brett Kavanaugh's bruising confirmation fight in 2018. The effort to seat Kavanaugh got big support from the Judicial Crisis Network, funded by dark money. In the run-up to the confirmation campaign, JCN received $17 million from a single donor, who remained anonymous because of the Supreme Court's 2010 ruling in *Citizens United*. Much of JCN's money came from yet another organization, the Wellspring Committee, all of which shared links to Leo.[39]

From this tangled tale, two things become clear. One is that the interlocking right-wing networks acquired enormous power because of the huge resources behind them and the secrecy within which they operated. The other is that, after campaigning for many years to unwind abortion policy, the right-wing in general— and the Catholic Church in particular—saw Leo as the strategist to make it happen. After *Roe*, the church's position was clear and consistent, but it had relatively little impact until the rise of Leonard Leo. It took his considerable skill, his penchant for recruiting allies and their money, the relationships he cultivated, and his increasingly large but relatively invisible network to transform *Roe* into *Dobbs*.

The religious alliances spilled over into a large part of Trump's team. There was J. D. Vance, who converted to Catholicism; CIA Director John Ratcliffe; Sean Duffy, Secretary of Transportation; Lori Chavez-DeRemer, Secretary of Labor; Robert F. Kennedy Jr., Secretary of Health and Human Services; Kelly Loeffler, administrator of the Small Business Administration; Linda McMahon, Secretary of Education; Mario Rubio, Secretary of State; and Elise Stefanik, US ambassador to the United Nations.[40] Other Catholics include Press Secretary Karoline Leavitt; border czar Tom Homan; chair of the Federal Communications Commission Brendan Carr; and National Security Adviser Michael Waltz. On Fox News, Sean Hannity was a Catholic but left the church, while Laura Ingraham converted to Catholicism. Brett Baier is a Catholic, as is Martha MacCallum. Steve Bannon is a Catholic. And although not known to be a Catholic, OMB Director Russell Vought is a strong Christian nationalist, a person whom *The Economist* called "Trump's holy warrior."[41]

The role of Catholics in the right-wing idea factory—not the Catholic Church, but Catholics—is unmistakable. Bannon's brand of firebrand conservatism—anti-immigrant, pro-America-first, believing in an America in decline—laid the foundation for much of the movement. Bannon was allied with the conservative wing of the church opposed to Pope Francis. In 2014, during ceremonies in Rome to canonize two of the pope's predecessors, he visited with Cardinal Raymond Burke, one of the strongest opponents to Francis who, in the minds of some of Francis's allies, verged on being a heretic. Those allies, in a journal known to be reviewed closely by the Vatican, criticized Bannon as a "supporter of an apocalyptic geopolitics," with a foundation "no different from the one that inspires Islamic fundamentalism."[42] In a 2017 interview on *60 Minutes*, Bannon charged that the church's real interest in supporting migrants was economic, because "they need illegal aliens, they need illegal aliens to fill the churches."[43]

The religious overtone went deeper than borrowing the apocalypse and ecclesiastical economics. There was a sense that Trump's first victory was a response to the prayers of religious Americans, even more so following the survival of the attempt on his life during the 2024 campaign. Trump had been spared for a larger purpose, his supporters believed. Trump himself was not a religious man. During the 2016 campaign, he struggled to name his favorite Bible verse, famously talked about "Two Corinthians" instead of "Second Corinthians," then (correctly) talking about the verse's mention of liberty, and eventually straying into a mention of Liberty University.[44] Shortly after his 2025 inauguration, however, he said, "God was watching me." He continued, "It changed something in me. . . . I feel even stronger. I believed in God, but I feel much more strongly about it. Something happened."[45]

Some suggested it was a cynical ploy to appeal to his base, but Trump unquestionably came into his second term with greater abandon, fueled with more religious zeal among his closest advisers, with fewer guardrails constraining their work, and a stronger sense of mission. Bannon was largely squeezed out of the inner circle, but the apocalyptic, anti-immigrant, America-first vision, driven by extraordinary self-assurance among his aides and cabinet officials, drew heavily from the zealotry that Bannon first staked out early in the 2010s and then into Trump's 2016 presidential campaign.

Pope Francis had wanted "to break the organic link between culture, politics, institution and Church," a Vatican-connected journal said.[46] After Trump promised "mass deportation," Francis called it a "major crisis" and continued, "The act of deporting people who in many cases have left their own land for reasons of extreme poverty, insecurity, exploitation, persecution or serious deterioration of the environment, damages the dignity of many men and women, and of entire families, and places them in a state of particular vulnerability and defenselessness."[47] Vice President Vance said he was "surprised" by the pope's criticism and criticized the nation's bishops' conference, saying it "has, frankly, not been a good partner in common sense immigration enforcement that the American people voted for." He added, "I hope, again, as a devout Catholic, that they'll do better."[48] But Vance worked hard to nurture the Vatican alliance, meeting with Pope Francis the day before he died and then with Pope Leo XIV soon after he assumed the papacy.

This was more than an internecine feud between different brands of Catholicism. It was a schism between moderate and progressive Catholics, on the one hand, and the Catholicism that characterized most Catholics in the Trump administration. It was a bridge to the religious right whose members had long been part of the right-wing idea factory's base and, at the same time, energized this broader base in support of restrictions on abortion—and used abortion to reinforce the base. Since the late 1970s, Republicans had cultivated the religious right. It was Bannon's embrace of classical libertarian thought and his brand of zealous anti-immigrant Catholicism that connected Trump to more Catholic voters. Even as Bannon faded into the background, his strategy boosted Trump's share of the Catholic vote from 50 percent in 2020 to 54 percent in 2024.[49]

Traditional populism built off the economic grievances of the people, amplified by a sense that their basic values were under assault. Populist leaders often worked from the outside, to take advantage of popular anxieties to transform the political system.[50] The new populism of the right-wing worked more from the inside, especially through skilled operatives like Leonard Leo and the religious zealots around Trump. It sought to re-establish basic values that had been thought lost, and it pivoted to a political movement focused squarely on building political power to restore those values. That, in turn, made the right-wing's political populism an impressive force on transforming American politics.

And that made the use of abortion as a political turnaround tool even more important, as I will show in the next chapter.

Chapter 4

Abortion and the Populist Turnaround

For many in the right-wing, the generations-long battle to overturn the US Supreme Court's decision in *Roe v. Wade* was the genesis of the factory. The decision brought together a broader coalition of groups than had ever been assembled before in conservative circles. It attracted the interest of politicians like Richard Nixon, who believed he could use it as a wedge issue to pry apart the Democratic coalition. The anti-*Roe* battle generated support from religious leaders and, perhaps most important for its long-term success, it attracted a substantial flow of money that made its longer-term success possible. Sex—the debate over what women would be permitted to do with their bodies, and who would decide—was the catalyst at the core of the right-wing idea factory. It was the critical element that converted the Right from a collection of ideas to an agenda for action.

No twentieth-century issue but civil rights had the explosive power of abortion. Some commentators, in fact, contended that the legalization of abortion threatened to undermine the American political system. Twenty-two years after the 1973 US Supreme Court decision that women had a right to an abortion, *New York Times* columnist David Brooks wrote,

> Justice Harry Blackmun did more inadvertent damage to our
> democracy than any other 20th-century American. When he and

his Supreme Court colleagues issued the *Roe v. Wade* decision, they
set off a cycle of political viciousness and counter-viciousness that
has poisoned public life ever since.

Brooks contended, "When Blackmun wrote the Roe decision, it
took the abortion issue out of the legislatures and put it into the
courts."[1]

Nearly two decades after Brooks's column—and nearly
fifty years after *Roe*—the Supreme Court overturned its precedent.
In *Dobbs v. Jackson*, the Court held that there was no federal constitutional right to abortion. Instead, it was up to the states to decide
whether to allow the procedure. That set in motion a quick chain
of events. Anticipating the ruling, thirteen states had already passed
"trigger laws" that would ban abortion if the Court shifted the
decision to them. Conservatives in other states got to work creating
their own abortion bans.[2] In blue states, policymakers worked
feverishly to shore up the rights previously provided under *Roe*.

Brooks vastly underestimated the conflict that state-based policymaking would create. He had suggested it would produce "a series
of state-by-state compromises reflecting the views of the centrist
majority that's always existed on this issue."[3] Precisely the opposite
occurred. With what Robert Post and Reva Siegel called "*Roe* rage,"
the result was fierce warfare and division among the states not seen
since the battles over states' rights that culminated in the civil rights
conflicts of the 1960s.[4]

Abortion opponents spent fifty years building the foundation
to overturn *Roe*. Abortion opponents in Mississippi had passed a
state law in 2018 banning abortions after fifteen weeks of pregnancy,
except for severe fetal abnormalities or medical emergencies. The
state's only abortion provider challenged the law, claiming that it was
unconstitutional under *Roe*, and the federal district court agreed.
Mississippi appealed, with Thomas Dobbs, an official in the state's
health department, as plaintiff. The Supreme Court ruled that the
Constitution did not create a right to privacy covering abortion, as
the previous Court had ruled in *Roe*. Since there was no federal right,

decisions had to be made by state governments. The red-state trigger laws kicked in.

The argument for sending abortion decisions back to the states did not satisfy anti-abortion advocates, however, who wanted to ban abortions in blue states as well. The reverence for the principles of federalism, it turned out, depended on who was winning and losing. Many conservatives turned into advocates of big government, to use government to ban abortions everywhere.

Control over abortions, as well as a collection of other policies dealing with sex practices, including the regulation of birth control and the treatment of LGBTQ individuals (indeed, whether the LGBTQ label ought even be recognized), moved to the front lines of the culture wars. Protests arose about whether to allow trans athletes, characterized by some on the right-wing as "as nefarious gender interlopers," to compete in sporting events.[5] During the 2024 presidential campaign, experts estimated that Republicans spent at least $215 million on ads suggesting that trans people were harming society. Campaign strategists placed many of these ads on NFL and college football broadcasts, as part of the party's efforts to appeal to men, with ads claiming that Democrats wanted to put "biological men in girls' locker rooms."[6] During the 2024 presidential campaign, another ad said, "Kamala's for They/Them. President Trump is for you." Indeed, half of all voters—and 80 percent of Trump voters—believed that support for transgender rights had gone "too far."[7] Only 1 percent of Americans identified as trans; the number of trans athletes therefore was minuscule. But the ads—and the issue—proved one of the most powerful, divisive, and effective messages driving turnout of the right-wing base in the 2024 election.[8]

The left-wing had long depended on top-down campaigns to drive its policies. The 1954 *Brown v. Board of Education* Supreme Court case defined basic rights, and the Civil Rights Act expanded on that a decade later. Then came the expansion of federal urban renewal programs, the War on Poverty, Medicare, and Medicaid, which pumped out enormous amounts of federal money transforming state, local, and private policy, all of which were transformative policies driven from Washington. In contrast, the right-wing idea factory built its work on the power of grassroots zealots in a quest to upend the progressive left.

The modern story of the Left's work on women's issues dates from 1963 and journalist Gloria Steinem's undercover job as a Bunny at Hugh Hefner's Playboy Club. Her two-part story of sexism and sexual harassment was explosive, doing for the women's movement in the 1960s what the "#MeToo Movement" did in the 2010s.[9]

Steinem built on the fame she acquired from those stories to co-found *Ms. Magazine*, which became the leading voice of the women's liberation movement. Joining her in the campaign were two members of Congress from New York, Shirley Chisholm and Bella Abzug, along with feminist Betty Friedan. Together they established the National Women's Political Caucus, which prepared the political ground for the abortion rights movement. In 1972, *Ms. Magazine* ran a two-page spread featuring fifty-three well-known women, including athletes, actors, and writers, who had undergone abortions, most of which were illegal.

To make abortion legal, they needed a defendant with the legal standing for filing the case and a federal court jurisdiction most likely to produce the most favorable result. Two attorneys working on the case, Sarah Weddington and Linda Coffee, set their sights on Texas, which had especially restrictive abortion laws but which also had one of the federal district courts most likely to rule in her favor. They then identified a plaintiff, known simply as "Jane Roe," who had been denied an abortion, and they filed suit. Their strategy worked, with the US Supreme Court ultimately ruling 7–2 in favor of Roe, later identified as Norma McCorvey, against the Texas attorney general, Henry Wade. It was, Ronald Dworkin wrote later, "undoubtedly the best-known case the United States Supreme Court has ever decided."[10]

The abortion story is typically told as a judicial procedural: Cases come before courts, the cases frame the big issues, courts decide based on precedents, and sometimes they reverse those precedents in setting new policy. As Linda Greenhouse and Reva B. Siegel point out, however, this form of judicial storytelling misses the deep social divisions and careful political strategies underlying the issue. On one side, they wrote, it was a "a time when more Republicans than Democrats supported abortion's decriminalization, when Catholics mobilized against abortion rights but evangelical Protestants did not, when feminists were only beginning to claim access to abortion as a right."[11] It had become the signature issue for the women's rights movement, but it was also a wedge issue for the Republican Party, which, under Richard Nixon, sought to bring Catholics and social conservatives into the fold.

These tensions have defined the politics of abortion ever since. Abortion therefore needs to be understood not just as a debate over women's rights but also as an issue creating political conflict in the quest for party realignment.

The Road from *Roe*

The political battles underlying abortion became even more important after *Dobbs*, when the states became the primary policymakers on abortion policy. Forty-one states created abortion bans of some kind in the next two years, including fourteen states with a total ban on abortions; seven states with an abortion ban at or before gestation of eighteen weeks; twenty states with some abortion ban after that period; and nine states plus the District of Columbia with no restriction on abortion.

These numbers, however, fail to capture the variations among the states. In the seven states that had imposed bans in the first eighteen weeks there were limits ranging from six weeks (Florida and Georgia) to fifteen weeks (Arizona). For the twenty states with a ban after eighteen weeks, standards varied. Some went by the viability of the fetus (California, Connecticut, Delaware, Hawaii, Illinois, Maine, Montana, Rhode Island, and Wyoming); others imposed time limits, from twenty-two weeks (Iowa, Kansas,

New Hampshire, Ohio, and Wisconsin) to twenty-four weeks (Massachusetts, New York, and Pennsylvania) to the third trimester (Virginia). Some states had exceptions to the bans, based on the threat to the life of the woman, the general health of the woman, pregnancy resulting from rape or incest, or a diagnosis of a lethal fetal condition, and then with varying restrictions based on the gestational period.[12] The center of abortion policy had become the states; following *Dobbs*, any semblance of policy coherence and clarity evaporated.

Physicians struggled with the syntax of many of the state laws. Some states had exceptions that allowed an abortion in case of an imminent risk of death to the mother but, as Lisa H. Harris wrote in the *New England Journal of Medicine*, "What does the risk of death have to be, and how imminent must it be? Might abortion be permissible in a patient with pulmonary hypertension, for whom we cite a 30-to-50% chance of dying with ongoing pregnancy? Or must it be 100%?" For women with some cancers, the health risk of not having an abortion might only surface years later. In reviewing the range of issues that they treated, physicians found "countless similar questions."[13]

In Texas, legislation in 2021 banned all abortions once a fetal heartbeat was detected. Supporters of the bill praised it for saving lives. "Texas is the first state to successfully protect the most vulnerable among us, preborn children, by outlawing abortion once their heartbeats are detected," said Chelsey Youman, legislative director of Human Coalition Action Texas.[14] However, as a study published in *JAMA Pediatrics* in 2024 found, the law also resulted in hundreds of additional infant and neonatal deaths in Texas.[15] Texas law banned virtually all abortions unless "in the exercise of a reasonable medical judgment," a doctor determines that the patient is experiencing "a life-threatening physical condition aggravated by, caused by, or arising from a pregnancy that places the female at risk of death or poses a serious risk of substantial impairment of a major bodily function." Most physicians were nervous about trying to interpret these standards, especially since they could lose their license if the Texas Medical Board later determined that they had violated them.[16] The enforcement of the law also depended in part on citizens' reporting. A citizen who reported a doctor for aiding an abortion could be rewarded with a $10,000 bounty.

Not long after the Texas abortion ban went into effect, Josseli Barnica found that her near-term baby would not survive. Doctors delayed treatment until there was no heartbeat. By that point, however, Barnica developed a severe infection and died three days later because physicians were afraid to provide the standard of care that would have allowed the professionals to intervene to protect Barnica from the infection. In Georgia, two women died because they didn't receive care in time.[17] One, Amber Nicole Thurman, had taken abortion medications but the fetus was not expelled completely from her body. The standard treatment in such cases is a dilation and curettage, but the state had made the procedure a felony except in rare circumstances. Doctors intervened twenty hours later but, by that point, it was too late.[18]

In Texas, Kate Cox's doctor told her that her unborn baby girl had a serious birth defect and "there's no outcomes at the end of this, where I take home a healthy baby girl," she said.[19] The state's anti-abortion law made it impossible for her to get an abortion and, she said, "That's when I came across the Center for Reproductive Rights."[20] The center was unsuccessful in battling Texas, so it helped her travel to another state, which remained unnamed, to get the abortion. The nonprofit, founded in 1992 to contest efforts to overturn the Supreme Court's 1972 *Roe v. Wade* decision, had been one of the leaders in contesting the policies of Texas and other states that have sought to end or restrict abortion. A network of other organizations sprang up to help Texas women travel out of state to get reproductive care. Fund Texas Choice,[21] for example, coordinated and paid for travel and lodging for women seeking an abortion. Another nonprofit, Power to Decide,[22] created the AbortionFinder[23] website, which locates providers of abortion, while

NeedAbortion.org[24] built a network of nonprofits that provided, co-ordinated, and paid for care, including at the Women's Reproductive Clinic of New Mexico,[25] just five minutes from El Paso.[26]

This counterpunching led to direct legal warfare among the states. A Texas state judge ordered an ob-gyn in New York to stop mailing abortion pills to Texas patients and, in addition, levied a $100,000 civil penalty. New York officials countered that the physician was protected under the state's "shield law," which safeguarded healthcare providers from consequences that came from another state's abortion restrictions. Arkansas issued an arrest warrant for the same doctor, Margaret Carpenter, for violating its law against prescribing abortion pills. The local district attorney said, "We expect Dr. Carpenter to come to Louisiana and answer to these charges." New York Governor Kathy Hochul fired back, "I will never, under any circumstances, turn this doctor over to the state of Louisiana under any extradition requests."[27]

A volunteer group, Elevated Access, recruited private pilots to fly women to states where abortion remained legal.[28] The pilots didn't ask why individuals were flying; the passengers didn't need to tell them. The organization, in turn, connected with other nonprofits to help women find the air service, in a network of organizations that rivaled those on the right for complexity.[29] These efforts infuriated red-state policymakers, since it did little good to ban abortions if nongovernmental organizations created a workaround. The Guttmacher Institute, an abortion support group, found in 2023 that about one in five women receiving abortion care were traveling out of state, with Illinois and Colorado as big travel destinations.[30]

The abortion bans also vastly complicated the education of physicians. Medical residents wanting to be certified in ob-gyn had to receive training in abortions, according to the national accrediting body. That meant they either had to leave the state for this part of their medical training or enroll in residencies outside Texas to begin with.[31] Physicians already practicing in Texas, along with Florida,

Ohio, and North Carolina, reported they had decided to move their practices elsewhere because of the abortion bans.[32] Idaho lost 22 percent of its practicing obstetricians in the first two years after *Dobbs*.[33]

With *Dobbs*, therefore, the relatively uniform approach that had been in place since *Roe* evaporated. The only truly uniform remaining piece was its un-uniformity, because each state had the power—and responsibility—to set its own course. The result was a tangled web of rules that made physicians uncertain about what procedures they could perform in many places, led some physicians to leave some states, and left women with even greater uncertainty about their options.

In 2022, voters in California, Michigan, and Vermont approved constitutional amendments establishing a right in the state to abortion. Ohio voters made a similar decision in 2023. That encouraged Democrats, in preparing their 2024 presidential game plan, to believe they could turn a large bloc of female voters to the party. That just didn't happen. In 2024, advocates for abortion rights won in seven of the ten states where the issue was on the ballot (Arizona, Colorado, Maryland, Missouri, Montana, Nebraska, Nevada, New York); it failed in three states (Florida, Nebraska, and South Dakota), although in Florida, abortion proponents won a majority of the vote but fell short of the two-thirds of the vote required to expand reproductive rights. During the 2024 election, abortion rights often polled above Kamala Harris's share of the votes. Biden won 57 percent of the female vote in 2020, but in 2024, Harris lost ground, taking 52 percent. In the 2024 election, abortion was the most important issue for 11 percent of voters, compared with the economy (39 percent) and immigration (20 percent).[34] Pro-abortion forces mobilized support for their referenda; Democrats could not translate the pro-abortion victories into wins for their candidates.

By the time the Left rose up to protect abortion procedures, the right-wing had already opened a new front in the anti-abortion campaign, this time on medication abortion. In 2008, the use of medicines to induce abortions accounted for just 17 percent of all abortions. Fifteen years later, in 2023, it was 63 percent.[35] The right-wing calculated that this could create a route to a national challenge on abortion.

In 2000, the FDA had approved the drug mifepristone to induce abortions. As of 2016, it could be used until the seventieth day of gestation. Researchers also found that a two-drug approach—mifepristone along with misoprostol (a drug long on the market to treat stomach ulcers)—could make the process up to 98 percent effective until the eleventh week of pregnancy. For pregnant women, the medication procedure had many advantages. Women could take the drug at home. If they did not live near an abortion clinic, they could get the pills from their local pharmacy or by mail. Telemedicine, a major development during Covid, also made it easy to prescribe the medications and ship them across state lines, and women pursued this option in states that prohibited abortion after *Dobbs*.

Doctors could prescribe the pills after an online conversation, and pharmacies could ship them in unmarked envelopes, which made tracking and stopping them virtually impossible. But Leo led a counterattack. With his support, the Alliance for Hippocratic Medicine, a play on the Hippocratic oath and its pledge to "do no harm," created an umbrella under which several anti-abortion groups, including the Catholic Medical Association, the American Association of Pro-Life Obstetricians and Gynecologists, the American College of Pediatricians, and the Christian Medical and Dental Associations, could challenge medication abortions. They filed suit to upend the Food and Drug Administration's approval of mifepristone, the key ingredient in the two-drug regimen. They contended that the fast-track process the FDA used in approving the drug had not adequately considered its possible risks. The FDA's approval process had gone on for more than four years, so it was not rushed, but opponents thought they had a winning argument. The litigants also challenged the FDA's approval of distribution of the drug by mail and for allowing its use for pregnancies of longer gestation.

The plaintiffs chose western Texas to file their challenge, with a suit led by the Alliance Defending Freedom, a right-wing legal group based in Arizona. Reporters found that the Marble Freedom Trust provided funding to support the case and that the trust's money came from the $1.6 billion that Leonard Leo had raised from the Chicago industrialist Barre Seid. The Alliance Defending Freedom filed suit on behalf of the Alliance for Hippocratic Medicine, based in Amarillo, Texas. The complex interweaving of these organizations made their genesis hard to track. The group had carefully picked this location because the case would be heard by Judge Matthew Kacsmaryk, a Trump appointee who had been a counsel to the First Liberty Institute—which previously paid CRC Advisors and was connected to Leo. Kacsmaryk had been a member of the Federalist Society since his days at the University of Texas at Austin Law School.

When the case reached him, Kacsmaryk ruled in favor of the Alliance for Hippocratic Medicine, a decision that sent shock waves through the pro-abortion community. It was only afterward that investigators found that he had submitted a law review article six years earlier disparaging women who sought abortions and the Obama administration's protections for transgender individuals. In the draft article, the *Washington Post* reported, Kacsmaryk criticized the Obama administration for not supporting religious physicians who "cannot use their scalpels to make female what God created male" and "cannot use their pens to prescribe or dispense abortifacient drugs designed to kill unborn children." When it appeared likely that he would be nominated by Trump to the federal bench, he removed his name from the article, on which he had been the sole author, and replaced it with the names of two colleagues who worked at his legal group, First Liberty Institute, which had the financial connections with Leo. When the time came to fill out the questionnaire for the Senate Judiciary Committee, he did not disclose that he had written the article, which the *Texas Review of Law and Politics* later published.[36] The left-wing appealed Kacsmaryk's decision, but the Fifth Circuit Court of Appeals upheld it. All three of the judges who heard the case themselves had Federalist Society ties.[37]

The US Supreme Court tossed out the case, ruling that the groups contesting the use of mifepristone didn't have standing to bring the case because they had not been directly affected by the drug and its use. But the battle soon shifted to the states. Louisiana passed a law identifying both mifepristone and misoprostol as controlled substances, which made possession without a prescription subject to a jail sentence. That made it harder for doctors to prescribe mifepristone, even though it was a standard treatment for miscarriages. North Carolina imposed a requirement that prescribing the pills required an ultrasound and then a three-day waiting period. Restrictions on abortions of all kinds in the South created a wall of prohibition, and women had to travel a great distance to obtain an abortion.

In Guam, an ongoing battle over the territory's laws, the limited number of doctors, and restrictions on obtaining medication by telemedicine led some women to contemplate an eight-hour plane flight to Hawaii, the closest place with abortion clinics and legal medication abortions. Idaho legislators made it illegal to supply a minor with abortion pills or help them leave the state to obtain the pills without a parent's consent. The left-wing battled back, with the Northwest Abortion Access Fund[38] and the Indigenous Idaho Alliance[39] successfully suing to stop implementation of the law. Meanwhile, Idaho Abortion Rights[40] promised support for women to get free abortion pills online. The *New York Times* found that 171,000 women crossed state lines in 2023 for an abortion.[41] Meanwhile, to create a federal roadblock to shipping the pills across state lines, right-wing groups explored whether they could use the Comstock Act, a law passed in 1873, which forbade the mailing of pornography—and contraceptives.

The question of how to enforce that prohibition surfaced yet again, but the right-wing found a strong ally in Justice Thomas, who took an increasingly broad view of the procedural options. His concurring opinion in *Dobbs* contended that the Court "should reconsider all of this Court's substantive due process precedents" in the *Griswold, Lawrence,* and *Obergefell* decisions, which defined constitutional rights to privacy, due process, and equal protection. Reconsidering those decisions, in turn, would challenge the rights for birth control and same-sex marriage.[42] Thomas thus not only laid out the future path for the right-wing idea factory in sexual matters. He also unmistakably signaled that he would be happy to hear— and overturn—them. Between 2014 and 2022, in fact, the number of same-sex marriages more than doubled.[43]

Meanwhile, in the decision unanimously overturning Kacsmaryk's decision, Brett Kavanaugh laid out a strategy that the groups wanting to challenge medication abortions could use in the future. For the left-wing, no policy leaning its way could be counted on to stick for long.

Leonard Leo and his right-wing allies nimbly morphed their production methods to stay a step ahead of the left-wing. They cemented their anti-abortion policy in many states and then worked hard for it to ripple out to others.

Organizing the Right-Wing Idea Factory

Nothing demonstrates the strategies, tactics, and impact of the right-wing idea factory better than the decades invested in unwinding the *Roe* decision—and the long collection of related issues that have grown up in their wake. There was right-wing dark money, which generated the fuel to drive its machinery. There were the enclaves of the judiciary, not only on the US Supreme Court but also in the lower federal courts and the state courts as well. There was the right-wing's mastery of American federalism, which allowed the movement to advance deeply into policy issues in the states most friendly and outflank the left-wing with even more sophisticated tactics and polished strategies when it tried to counterattack. Then there was a grassroots movement that sprang up across the country, often in apparently free-standing form, but, in fact, synchronized with the broader movement. The vast realm of social media reinforced the agenda of the right-wing factory without all its participants necessarily knowing where it came from—and certainly without most of those outside the right-wing empire realizing the deep and hyper-sophisticated process at work.

Conventional news reporting tended to tell the story like a police procedural, but the process was inherently political, with remarkable twists and turns along the way.[44] The stories increasingly revolved around a shadowy world of dark money, behind-the-scenes actors, and a transformation of politics in which the right-wing has become increasingly practiced and in which the Left has often been relatively hobbled.

The issues have also been shape-shifting. The right-wing idea factory never took its victories for granted; it always looked for the next opportunity to advance its cause and, if necessary, to shift its means of production to adjust to new political forces. From its *Dobbs* victory, the right-wing rolled into a new crusade against gender-affirming care. From 2022 to 2024, for example, the number of states that have banned such care increased from four to twenty-six. The Williams Institute at the UCLA School of Law found that in 2023 alone, state legislators introduced more than five hundred bills designed to restrict the rights of LGBT+ individuals. In addition to restrictions on gender-affirming care, legislation would also limit participation in sports, access to bathrooms, and the use of certain pronouns for certain youth. The institute's study also found that 90 percent of transgender youth in the United States between the ages of thirteen and seventeen live in states where policymakers have either imposed or proposed such limits.[45]

Traditional conservatism staked out basic principles, like free-market economics and deregulation, and then returned to them over and over again. The right-wing idea factory, in contrast, was far more agile in shifting to new issues and new political opportunities with new sources of funding. The right-wing, however, tended to concentrate its operations in states most likely to be receptive to its work—and, of course, the same was true of the Left. Activists on the left, however, found themselves losing ground because of the remarkable energy and prodigious funding on the right. As Hillary Clinton wistfully said in 2004, "One thing I give the right credit for is they never give up." She added, "They are relentless. You know, they take a loss, they get back up, they regroup, they raise more money." Their resources are remarkable. "It's tremendously impressive the way that they operate. And we have nothing like it on our side."[46]

This pattern has led to very different policies in different parts of the country, depending on the relative power and effectiveness of the right-wing idea machine. In red states, and especially in right-wing leaders like Florida and Texas, the new movement became exceptionally well organized, which spilled over to policy success on issues like abortion. Moreover, while Trumpism was on the rise in the nation's capital, the right-wing continued with breakneck speed to advance its agenda in its state-centered base. Indeed, as Trumpism sought to consolidate its national power, the right-wing's state base sprinted ahead of the national movement. There were frequent questions about what was to become of Trumpism without Trump, and of the Republican Party without the president. The state-based forces answered that question, often in ways that few national observers noticed. These forces were under steam before Trump launched his presidential campaigns, and, even as Trump proclaimed his national power, the right-wing forces in the states were operating powerfully and independently, in ways that guaranteed their continued impact when Trump was no longer on the scene.

But that does not mean that the impact of the right-wing was uniform across the states. Indeed, as I have argued, the United States of America increasingly has become the divided states of America, where the government that Americans get depends on where they live, even in red states.[47] That played itself out as well through the ongoing role of race in society and in the schools. I turn to that issue in the next chapter.

Chapter 5

Grassroots Power and Racial Politics

In 2019, the *New York Times* published a series of articles about how slavery shaped the country. Called "The 1619 Project," it marked the four hundredth anniversary of the arrival of the first slaves in Virginia. The project's leaders wrote, "Most Americans still don't know the full story of slavery. This is the history you didn't learn in school."[1] The 1619 Project's goal was to retell the story of America through the lens of slavery and race, beginning with the anniversary of the slaves' arrival. Many academics read the series enthusiastically. It found its way into thirty-five hundred classrooms, and its creator, Nikole Hannah-Jones, won the Pulitzer Prize for Commentary.[2] New York University's Arthur L. Carter Journalism Institute called the project one of the ten greatest works of journalism of the decade, and an Emmy-winning 2023 television mini-series evolved from it. The 1619 Project soon became one of the most awarded journalistic works ever produced.

It soon also became one of the most vilified as well. Several historians pointed to factual errors, but that was nothing compared with the ferocious attacks that came from right-wing critics who complained that the 1619 Project undermined the history of the country's greatness. In *Reason* magazine, Phillip W. Magness charged that the 1619 Project was "junk history." The Cato Institute published a critique by adjunct scholar Timothy Sandefur, in which he charged that the series "ignored the fact that the racial conflicts that have plagued American history are far from unique to the United States." He continued, "Whatever else America might be, it is a land of idealism," and he complained that the project had wrung out "everything . . . that makes America great."[3]

Conservative activists became convinced that by focusing on slavery and the story that surrounded it, the project was a woke effort aimed at tearing down America, its values, its system of government, and its contributions to freedom. To them, the 1619 Project represented the worst parts of the woke movement, a focus on values extraordinarily out of sync with those of most Americans and an effort to push those values on everyone else. Legislatures in Arkansas and Mississippi called the project "a racially divisive and revisionist account." In Iowa, a proposal to ban teaching the 1619 Project said it attempted "to deny or obfuscate the fundamental principles upon which the United States was founded."[4] The South Dakota legislature debated denying funding to K-12 schools and colleges that used the project in the classroom.[5] During his 2020 re-election campaign, Donald Trump criticized the project as "toxic propaganda, ideological poison that if not removed will dissolve the civic bonds that tie us together," a collection of ideas that "will destroy our country." During his first term, he created a presidential commission aimed at countering a narrative that, he said, portrayed that "America is a wicked and racist nation."[6]

These charges fed off a broader right-wing critique that the Left was bringing "critical race theory" (or CRT) into schools, and that this initiative was dangerous. CRT was an approach to racial studies, created in the 1970s, which had previously been relatively unknown outside a small circle of advanced academic researchers. One of its foremost scholars, Columbia Law School professor Kimberlé Williams Crenshaw, described CRT as "a prism for understanding why decades after the end of segregation, over a century and a half after the end of slavery, after genocide has occurred, why racial inequalities are so enduring."[7] It was, in short, a study of how American institutions reinforced and then benefited from slavery and racism.

CRT scholars approached the issue with advanced statistical techniques, complex methodology, and concepts like "intersectionality" (how the identity of both groups and individuals lead to both privilege and discrimination). Teaching and research about CRT concentrated in law schools and advanced university graduate programs in the arts and sciences. It relied on a very complex methodology and technical language which were both very tough going even for advanced college undergraduates. It was virtually impenetrable for high school students, their teachers, and their parents, let alone grade school students. That, in turn virtually guaranteed that CRT would stay out of K-12 education, because the subject was too complex for anyone in the K-12 world to comprehend, debate, or proselytize about it.

That didn't matter, because it became an effective rallying cry for those campaigning against the Left, viewed as the source of CRT and the woke education they believed surrounded it. Those seeking to ban K-12 knew what they knew of CRT not from reading it but from reading about it, especially in social media posts designed to incite opposition. That led, in particular, to a consensus that CRT criticized America and undermined its greatness. That sparked the right-wing movement against a shadow problem: teaching CRT in places where it never had been taught, espousing ideas that were never part of it.

The national campaign boiled over into individual school districts. One district near Dallas was dealing with the hiring of the first black principal of Colleyville Heritage High School. The high school is in a small town—the population was just twenty-five thousand in 2020—and a high-income one—the average income was more than $210,000.[8] Blacks made up only 4 percent of the population, so James Whitfield's hiring before the 2020–2021 school year was a big decision for this suburb in the Dallas Metroplex and a big move for Whitfield, who previously had been a geography teacher, basketball coach, and then an assistant principal for a middle school in Colleyville.

Whitfield didn't have the chance to celebrate his appointment for very long, however. Soon after he took the job, he got a call from his boss, who told him to check his computer. What Whitfield found was a picture on Facebook of him (a black man) embracing a woman (who was white) on a beach. Accompanying the picture was a message asking, "Is this the Dr. Whitfield we want leading our schools?" Another critic suggested that the photo was "overly intimate." The school district asked him to take down the photo and then issued a public statement:

> When a social media concern is brought to the attention of the district, we have a responsibility to review it. Some of the photos the district received contained poses that are questionable for an educator, especially a principal or administrator. It had absolutely nothing to do with race. As a new campus principal, we wanted to provide a smooth transition for Dr. Whitfield to Heritage Middle School, which is why we advised him of the concern and made a request for the photos to be taken down from Facebook.[9]

What the district neglected to point out was that the woman was Whitfield's wife, that the photo had been taken by a professional photographer, that the couple was on a beach trip to celebrate their wedding anniversary, and that the photo was not prurient in any possible way. In fact, *People* magazine published it in a profile on Whitfield.[10]

The controversy continued to hang over Whitfield's first steps as principal. Soon after the deaths of three black Americans at the hands of police in 2020, he sent a message to the school community saying sadly that systemic racism was "alive and well." He called on the entire community to work together toward "conciliation for our nation." Moreover, he wrote, "Education is the key to stomping out ignorance, hate, and systemic racism. It's a necessary conduit to get 'liberty and justice for all.'" The message got nothing but support from members of the Colleyville High School community.[11]

In the late summer of 2021, however, Stetson Clark, who previously had run and lost for a seat on the local school board, used the message to attack Whitfield for "the implementation of critical race theory in our district." (It's worth noting, of course, that the message that Whitfield sent had nothing to do with CRT, and it wasn't clear that anyone making or hearing the charges knew what CRT was. It *was* clear that the school district wasn't teaching CRT.) School board officials reminded Clark multiple times that individual employees couldn't be criticized by name during the meetings, but Clark persisted. One audience member piped in with "How about you fire him?" Clark continued, complaining that Whitfield was "working to destroy our businesses, our school district, our city, even our state," and he called on the district to fire the principal.[12] As Clark finished, the audience cheered. A few weeks later, the school district sent Whitfield a disciplinary letter about the message, put him on administrative leave, and ultimately decided not to renew his contract. The reason officials gave: communication problems and insubordination.

Whitfield later told a reporter, "I am the quintessential boogeyman for these people." He continued, "Anything that has to do with anything related to equity, or inclusion or diversity—they're going to try to attach it to CRT."[13] Whitfield landed on his feet as the new superintendent of Treetops School International, a charter school in Euless, Texas, about eight miles away from Colleyville. The CRT controversy didn't end, however. Governor Greg Abbott signed legislation banning the teaching of "critical race theory" in Texas public schools, an unnecessary step because no one had produced any evidence that it was being taught there. Lieutenant Governor Dan Patrick applauded the battle against the "debunked 1619 founding myth." CRT, he said, was a "ridiculous leftist narrative."[14] One of the bill's sponsors, Republican Representative Steve Toth, told his colleagues, "We don't need to burden our kids with guilt for racial crimes they had nothing to do with."[15]

All of that had exploded from a tame anniversary photo of a principal with his wife, as well as a call for education to advance liberty and justice for all, a phrase from the famous pledge written in 1892 by a Baptist minister, Francis Bellamy.

CRT and DEI as the Factory's Engine

Conservative activist Christopher Rufo made a career campaigning against CRT and other forms of what he saw as excessive left-wing influence on the schools. For example, he charged that "The Arizona Department of Education has created an 'equity' toolkit claiming that babies show the first signs of racism at three months old and that white children 'remain strongly biased in favor of whiteness' by age five."[16] If babies could be "racist" before they could talk, then CRT surely must be crazy, and it was a tale that people could easily connect with. Where did this argument come from? There was a one-pager that the US Department of Education had prepared about research in Philadelphia, which suggested that babies, by the age of three months, tended to look more at faces that matched the race of their caregivers. Babies weren't being indoctrinated. They just made the connections that were most familiar.

Then there was Rufo's condemnation of a Missouri training program, in which "A middle school in Springfield, Missouri, forced teachers to locate themselves on an 'oppression matrix,' claiming that white heterosexual Protestant males are inherently oppressors and must atone for their 'covert white supremacy.'"[17] Rufo told people that this was evidence that CRT attacked whites, heterosexuals, males, and Christians. In fact, two trainers did hold a diversity training program for teachers, but the charges about an "oppression matrix" came from a participant who didn't like the program and who might or might not have been reporting the training session accurately. Rufo tried to support his story with a link to "whistleblower documents," but the "documents" were not from insider whistleblowers but from stories he had written. That made it impossible to tell what had really happened, but it did generate a powerful headline, "'Antiracism' Comes to the Heartland."[18] Rufo's campaign made him, according to *The Times* of London, "America's most effective conservative."[19]

Then, when the governing board considered the candidacy of Santa Ono, the sole finality for the presidency of the University of Florida, Rufo sprang into action again. He pulled stories from the University of Michigan where, Rufo said, Ono had promoted diversity, equity, and inclusion (DEI) initiatives. In fact, Ono had spent months trying to dismantle Michigan's DEI programs, but that didn't matter; his critics found steps Ono had taken fifteen years before to use in attacking him. Rufo's campaign derailed Ono's candidacy, and he then called for "a new process that brings in conservative leaders," "to ensure that this debacle does not happen again." The presidential search committee pondered how best to re-launch its work.[20] Ono ended up at the Ellison Institute of Technology in Oxford, England.

But Tucker Carlson found ratings fodder in CRT. In August 2020, a segment on his Fox News show featuring Rufo charged that top officials at a federally funded nuclear laboratory were made to undergo "white privilege" training that was nothing short of "racism masquerading as anti-racism." The executives, he said, had to "confess their sins to diversity trainers," and, at the end of the session, "they actually had to write letters of apology to women and people of color based on what they learned about their own privilege." Rufo charged, "It's nothing more than a cult indoctrination session that's based on critical race theory, something that is spreading like wildfire through our public institutions."[21]

Rufo was back on Carlson's show a few weeks later. "It's absolutely astonishing how critical race theory has pervaded every institution in the federal government," he said. "What I have discovered is that critical race theory has become, in essence, the default ideology of the federal bureaucracy and is now being weaponized against the American people." It amounted to nothing less than "cult indoctrination," based on "Black Lives Matter and neo-Marxist rhetoric."[22] He later told the *Washington Post*, "I basically took [a] body of criticism, I paired it with breaking news stories that were shocking and horrifying, and made it political." The result, he said proudly, "turned it into a salient political issue with a clear villain."[23] To make the attacks stick, he prepared a "briefing book," directed especially at "winning the language war." Among the suggestions he made was referring to CRT as "race-based Marxism" and "state-sanctioned racism." In one case, he said, "Buffalo Public Schools taught students that 'all white people' perpetuate systemic racism and forced kindergarteners to watch a video of dead black children warning them about 'racist police and state-sanctioned violence who might kill them at any time.'" Then, in Santa Clara, California, the "County Office of Education denounced the United States as a 'parasitic system' based on the 'invasion' of 'white male settlers' and encouraged teachers to 'cash in on kids' inherent empathy' in order to recruit them into political activism."[24]

A group spurred on by Rufo conducted a public opinion poll, which reinforced his arguments. It headlined its news release, "Americans Overwhelmingly Reject 'Woke' Race and Gender Policies in K-12 Education." The poll, the group stated, found that 70 percent of respondents said it was either not important or not at all important for schools to "teach students that their race is the most important thing about them." When asked whether they opposed teaching students that white people are inherently privileged, 74 percent agreed, and 69 percent said they opposed teaching children that America was founded on racism and was, as a result, structurally racist.[25]

Rufo called on Trump to issue an executive order to end the exposure of federal officials to CRT, either by government employees or by government contractors. A few weeks before the 2020 presidential election, Trump did just that. Without mentioning the 1619 Project by name, the executive order condemned the "destructive ideology" that was "grounded in misrepresentations of our country's history." It was, the order said, an attempt to "resurrect the discredited notions of the nineteenth century's apologists for slavery who, like President Lincoln's rival Stephen A. Douglas, maintained that our government was 'made on the white basis by white men, for the benefit of white men.'" The executive order forbade federal employees or federal contractors "to inculcate such views" among government employees.[26]

The right-wing attacks on CRT rippled across the country. In Loudon County, Virginia, one mother criticized CRT as "a tactic used by Hitler and the Ku Klux Klan on slavery very many years ago to dumb down my ancestors so we could not think for ourselves."[27] (To make the obvious point, neither Hitler nor the Klan could ever have used CRT, since the theory hadn't been invented yet, and it would have been repugnant to them in any case.) At another meeting, an angry parent asked, "Why can't we let the public know that you're teaching our children to go out and murder our police officers?"[28] (There was nothing in CRT that even hinted at police assassinations.) In the first six months of 2021, five hundred viral Facebook videos took on CRT, often with inflammatory language like "Watch this parent absolutely obliterate Critical Race Theory at an Illinois school board meeting."[29] In nearly two dozen states, Republican legislators introduced bills that would restrict how teachers could talk about race and racism. Most banned the teaching of CRT.[30] In 2021, the number of mentions of CRT at local government meetings grew fifteen-fold, and nearly two-thirds of these mentions came at forums other than school board meetings.[31]

On Capitol Hill, Republican members of Congress jumped into the fray. Thirty Republican members of the House co-signed a bill to prohibit teaching "anti-American and racist theories," including CRT, at any program run by the US armed forces. (Local schools and colleges and universities were outside the direct reach of Congress, but, because the federal government funded service academies and military training programs, they were targets.) "Critical race theory is a divisive ideology that threatens to poison the American psyche," said one of the bill's supporters, Representative Dan Bishop (R-NC). From April 20, 2021, to September 5, 2023, Republican members of Congress repeatedly hammered on the issue. There were 453 mentions of CRT in their e-newsletters, compared with just three among Democrats.[32] In addition, many individuals interviewed and identified as experts on Fox News about CRT also turned out to be Republican strategists.[33]

Nowhere was the issue more politically important than in Virginia Republican candidate Glenn Youngkin's run for governor. He charged, "We actually have this critical race theory moved into all of our schools in Virginia." Fox News had reported that one county school district had spent $34,000 "on critical race theory coaching for administrators." The money, however, had gone for instruction on equity issues, with just $3,125 allocated for "coaching support" for school leaders about CRT issues. Youngkin's campaign cited a tweet by a vice principal as proof, but the tweet supported the 1619 Project without embracing CRT. Then there was a web page posted by the state Department of Education entitled, "Anti-Racism in Education," featuring a book by Ibram X. Kendi, *How to Be an Anti-Racist.* Kendi was a CRT advocate, but his book developed the theme that all races are equal. The fact check organization PolitiFact concluded that Youngkin's claim was false.[34]

Youngkin nevertheless campaigned vigorously on the message and converted it into a broader message about "parental rights." His Democratic opponent, Terry McAuliffe said, "I don't think parents should be telling schools what they should teach." The right-wing media pounced on McAuliffe's words as a rejection of the rights parents had in shaping the curriculum of local schools. Youngkin charged, "If you had any doubt—any doubt whatsoever—about Terry McAuliffe's principles, he laid them bare last week when he said, he said parents do not have a right to be involved in their kid's education."[35] It would be harder to imagine a stronger setup for Youngkin's closing argument weaving together CRT, banning books, and parental rights. McAuliffe, the Democratic incumbent, had been ahead in the polls, and no Republican had won statewide office since 2009. But with McAuliffe's blunder and Youngkin's CRT attack, he squeaked out a victory. Political analysts called it a "shockwave."[36] Republicans concluded it was a strategy that worked.

Steve Bannon saw the idea as a pivotal strategy for retaking control of Congress in 2022. "Hey, this is how we're going to win," he said. He saw the local school board fights as "the Tea Party to the

10th power," as he referred to the conservative movement created in 2009 to fight Barack Obama's programs. It was powerful, he explained, because "this is mainstream suburban moms—and a lot of these people aren't Trump voters."[37] It worked to give Republicans control of the House.

There was the blizzard of coverage on Fox News, with more than nineteen hundred mentions of CRT on the network from mid-February through June 2021.[38] A senior official at the Heritage Foundation called CRT one of the group's top two issues, along with tightened voter laws. "Heritage Action for America," the 501(c)(4) arm of the conservative think tank, distributed an online pamphlet, "Reject Critical Race Theory." CRT, the pamphlet said, was "destructive" and "rejects the fundamental ideas on which our constitutional republic is based." It contained talking points such as "True equality will be achieved by maximizing the ability of Americans to become self-sufficient, not by dividing Americans on the basis of race and apportioning resources based on skin color." There were ideas about how to post criticisms of CRT on social media, how to stop CRT in local schools, how to contact members of Congress, where to download anti-CRT graphics, and how to submit an open records request to find out just who was teaching what.[39]

The campaign against CRT spilled over to the work of right-wing think tanks between the two Trump administrations. Russ Vought, who had directed Trump's Office of Management and Budget and later came back to the job in the second Trump term, created Citizens for Renewing America, a quieter but powerful analogue to the Heritage Foundation. Vought's group focused on renewing "an American consensus of a nation under God" and on "individuals' enjoyment of freedom." It called CRT a threat to local communities, "rooted in Marxism." Its web page on CRT featured a hammer and sickle, the symbol of the former Soviet Union, against a red background, the color of the former Soviet flag.[40] Vought's center posted a thirty-four-page pamphlet it called "Combatting Critical Race Theory in Your Community: An A to Z Guide on How to

Stop Critical Race Theory and Reclaim Your Local School Board."
The pamphlet began with a quotation from Martin Luther King's
"I Have a Dream Speech" and condemned CRT as a "radical ideology" that "will attempt to take over your cultural institutions,
including all educational institutions."[41] By 2022, it had brought in
more than $44 million in income.[42]

Meanwhile, the 1776 Project PAC pursued "changing education
one school district at a time" by supporting conservatives who believed in parental rights. The organization featured a young black
child on its home page as it opposed CRT and diversity, equity, and
inclusion programs. There was a button on the website for candidates to "apply for endorsement," a store for buying merch including
"Make Education Sane Again" hats and "Education Not Indoctrination" coffee mugs.[43] It was a "super-PAC," which could spend money
to support political candidates but could not coordinate its activities
with them.

The issue was, as Bannon planned, enormously polarizing. By
November 2021, 36 percent of Republicans were "extremely" or
"very" familiar with CRT, compared with 30 percent of Democrats
and just 20 percent of independents. Seventy-three percent of
Democrats favored teaching "how racism continues to impact
American society today," compared with 47 percent of independents and just 24 percent of Republicans. Forty-four percent of
Democrats supported the teaching of CRT in public schools; for
Republicans, it was just 8 percent, even though it was hard to find
any public school where it actually was on the curriculum.[44] CRT
powerfully motivated those on the right because, as political scientist Brandon Rottinhaus explained, "People believe [critical race
theory] to be the threat to the traditional suburban way of life."[45] It
was a remarkable result for a technical research issue that the com-
batants had never read but which, nonetheless, became the center of
an enormous ongoing conflict.

There still was no evidence that anyone in K-12 education was
teaching it.

From CRT to DEI

Public and media attention to CRT began to slide 2022, but the right-wing idea factory pivoted to eliminating the pursuit of diversity, equity, and inclusion (DEI). The DEI movement started with the argument that Black men tended to underachieve in college not because of their own weaknesses but because colleges and universities had failed to give them enough support.

Underlying that argument was the notion of "implicit bias"—subconscious attitudes that had permeated the belief systems of individuals because of their own upbringing and education. Researchers concluded that everyone has implicit biases. The solution, they said, was discovering them; "awareness of bias is one step toward changing one's behavior," wrote Harini S. Shah and Julie Bohlen for the National Library of Medicine.[46] As one of the strongest voices for educating people about diversity, equity, and inclusion issues, Shaun Harper, explained, "When people go into our democracy and do racist, homophobic things, colleges and universities are partially responsible for that." The alternative, he contended, rested on education. "If we don't teach about race and racism and inequality, we leave them terribly underprepared to confront those issues and address them—and, in fact, they are complicit in perpetuating those issues," he said."[47]

Right-wing opinion leaders latched onto DEI. As he was trying to fuel his ultimately failed presidential campaign, Florida Governor Ron DeSantis pledged to "expose the scams that they ["the woke mob"] are trying to push onto students across the country." He said he'd lead the way in Florida, where "students will receive an education, not a political indoctrination." As was so often the case, Texas Governor Greg Abbott jostled with DeSantis for the top rung of the public ladder. He ordered public universities to stop using DEI statements in hiring new employees. Referring to the communist-baiting times of the early 1950s, a *Politico* reporter called DEI "the new Red Scare for red states."[48]

Early in Trump's second term, he issued an executive order "ending radical and wasteful government DEI programs and preferencing," which he called "illegal and immoral," as well as another to end DEI and what it called the "illegal discrimination" that DEI generated.[49] To that, he added an instruction to the Department of Transportation to end DEI hiring policy that he called "illegal and dangerous."[50] He blamed the DEI policy for the tragic collision of a military helicopter and a passenger jet over the Potomac River in Washington, which took sixty-seven lives. In hiring air traffic controllers, he said, the Obama administration "actually came out with a directive, too white." In response to the president's argument, the US Department of Transportation signed a $2.1 million contract to determine whether DEI policies had anything to do with the crash. A controller called it a "waste of money."[51] In fact, the general hiring policy had existed during his own first term, and there was no evidence that FAA hiring policies had anything to do with the collision.[52] But it did provide yet another opportunity for signaling a connection between race and big problems.

This was a powerful illustration of how, as one issue faded on the right, the right-wing idea factory produced another to replace it. Figure 5.1 shows the rise and fall of searches on CRT and DEI, using the Glimpse tool in Google Trends. As the searches for "critical race theory" ebbed, Trump's assault on "diversity, equity, and inclusion" soared. Issues produced by the right-wing idea factory constantly progressed and evolved, with new topics always bubbling up from the grassroots.

For those attacking DEI, colleges and universities became the prime target. Through mid-2025, the *Chronicle of Higher Education* counted 127 bills introduced across thirty states and in Congress, with 29 becoming law. All the bills that became law emerged from red states, with Florida and Texas taking the lead. The focus of the attack on DEI came in trying to shut down DEI offices and fire their staffs, on ending mandatory DEI training, on banning diversity statements, and ending identity-based preferences for hiring

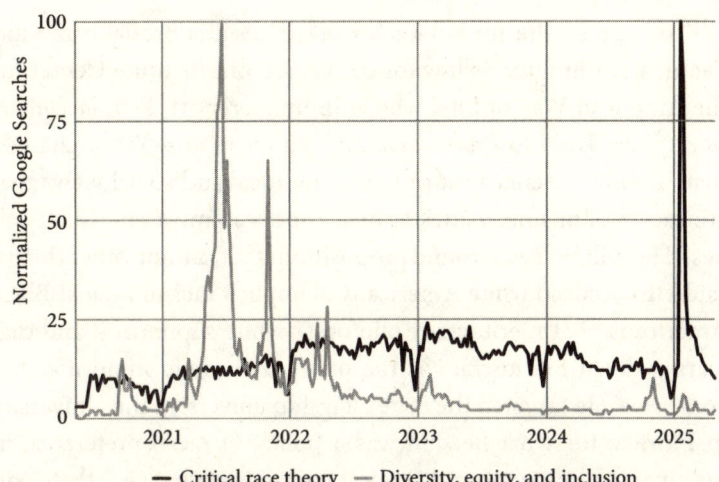

— Critical race theory — Diversity, equity, and inclusion

FIGURE 5.1 DEI Replaces CRT in Google Searches

The figure charts the normalized number of searches. Each data point is divided by the total searches in the United States during the given time range, to compare relative popularity.

Source: Glimpse, from Google Trends, as of April 28, 2025.

and admissions.[53] The race to produce new anti-DEI policy, however, made it hard for colleges and universities to determine what they needed to do, both to ensure compliance with the new state legislation and to collect the information required for federal grant proposals and reaccreditation reviews. The result, the *Chronicle* reported, has been "an inconsistent and confusing landscape."[54]

Florida and Texas led the way with the most aggressive anti-DEI policies in the country. Florida Governor Ron DeSantis took on DEI in March 2023 in a roundtable he titled "Exposing the DEI Scam." He said, "In Florida, we are not going to back down to the woke mob, and we will expose the scams they are trying to push onto students across the country." His office's press release coupled CRT with DEI, and said, "These concepts are in no way inclusive, and instead force exclusion and division withing higher education, and do not in any way contribute to learning or knowledge."[55]

To support the roundtable's work, DeSantis brought in Scott Yenor, a Washington fellow for the Claremont Institute Center for the American Way of Life, who authored a report, *Florida Universities: From Woke to Professionalism.*[56] In his report, Yenor charged that "DEI represents a set of radical political and social views that are turning our universities against America's most cherished values." He built his case around propositions that, among other things, said DEI accused white Americans of implicit racism against Black Americans, that meritocracy reinforces white supremacy, and that tearing down meritocracy is the only way to help minorities become free. He targeted the state's flagship university, the University of Florida, for what he said was a policy of racial preference in hiring and admissions and "radical curriculum changes" that "will tear Florida apart."[57] The report accompanied other work by Claremont, including a column in *Newsweek* titled "Americans Deserve to Know Who Funded BLM Riots," with the clear suggestion that the Black Lives Matter demonstrations across the country must have had external support.[58] Claremont pointed to its mission "to restore the principles of the American Founding to their rightful, preeminent authority in our national life."[59] Funding Claremont's operations, according to an investigation by *Rolling Stone*, was a small group of billionaires, through the Dick and Betsy DeVos Foundation, the Bradley Foundation, and the Sarah Scaife Foundation. Claremont, in turn, supported Trump's claims that the 2020 election was stolen.[60]

This complex network connected a handful of rich individuals promoting right-wing causes, their support of a right-wing think tank generating ideas that support their right-wing leanings, the work of the think tank producing intellectual support and backup for state-level policy, and the use of that research in support of the DeSantis policy agenda (and his ambitions, at the time, for the presidency). This network in turn helped push DEI onto the national policymaking agenda. DEI, in fact, peaked on the Google search engine just as DeSantis pressed his legislative campaign to abolish college DEI activities. It's impossible to know, of course, how much DeSantis's agenda generated broader interest in DEI or whether it was the reverse, but ultimately that did not matter. What mattered most to the right-wing idea machine was the interplay of candidates seeking office and the ideas they used to excite their base. The campaign worked. Two months later, DeSantis signed legislation that banned state colleges from spending federal or state dollars on DEI initiatives. And then it led to the decision not to hire Santa Ono as the University of Florida's president.

Close behind was Texas Governor Greg Abbott, who championed similar legislation banning DEI activities on state colleges and universities and signed a bill in June 2023. One sponsor of the bill, Senator Brandon Creighton, called it "the most significant ban on Diversity, Equity, and Inclusion in the nation."[61] Across the state's sprawling thirty-six four-year campuses, however, both uncertainty about just what the law required and enthusiasm for implementing it created what one national education reporter called "a messy patchwork of campus policies, procedures, and approaches."[62]

Abbott had his allies in the foundation world, especially with the right-leaning Texas Public Policy Foundation, which created a hotline for anyone to report suspected violations of the law. The legislation, reported Jonathan Pidluzny of the Washington-based America First Policy Institute, one of the new right-wing think tanks established following Trump's 2020 loss, was the "best piece of anti-DEI legislation that has been passed at the state level."[63] AFPI got its money from MAGA donors. The Texas Public Policy Foundation was part of the State Policy Network, a collection of right-wing think tanks throughout Canada, the UK, and the United States. It connected to one of the oldest right-wing groups working at the state level, the American Legislative Exchange Council and Americans for Prosperity, which was funded by the Koch family, one of the largest funding sources for conservative causes. The board of directors of the State Policy Network includes officials from the Bradley Foundation, the Heritage Foundation, the Walton Family

Foundation, and other conservative groups. The Texas Public Policy Foundation, meanwhile, had its own financial links to the Charles Koch Foundation.[64]

The Florida and Texas cases lay out a complex collection of connections, some directly overlapping, some not, but all part of a vast, loosely linked network whose members were intent on advancing policy change. Moreover, these are tales of just two states, albeit two of the most aggressive in advancing the right-wing idea factory agenda. (There were, after all, more than two dozen other states in the anti-DEI battle.) The movement rippled across the country into other right-leaning statehouses. It was a combination of aggressive idea marketing and eager program makers who found a happy alliance in advancing a new brand of policy, with the states as the center of action. Colleges across the country, which had established DEI offices in 2020, began shuttering them, either because of pressure from state officials or as a precaution to forestall it. Companies began worrying that DEI was commercial poison. The country's largest retailer, Walmart, decided in 2024 that it would cut back on its DEI initiatives. Target, Amazon, Tractor Supply, Victoria's Secret, Goldman Sachs, Paramount, Bank of America, Coca-Cola, Pepsi, JP Morgan Chase, Deloitte, and Disney all trimmed their DEI programs as the right-wing stirred up opposition to the practice.

At the University of Virginia, the ongoing efforts by the Trump administration to push out its president, Jim Ryan, led to his resignation in June 2025. The Justice Department had been investigating the school's DEI programs and demanded Ryan's resignation as a condition for settling the dispute. Several of the university's board members, appointed by Republican Governor Glenn Youngkin, had negotiated with the Justice Department and were told that one important step in ending the dispute was jettisoning Ryan. The president said, "I am inclined to fight for what I believe in," but "I cannot make a unilateral decision to fight the federal government," which could cost the jobs of hundreds of employees and researchers who would lose federal funding. The DEI battle pushed another top-ranking official to the side.[65]

There was a simple process at work here and in the other cases in the right-wing idea factory. Take a personal grievance or an idea like DEI. Develop outrage. Find like-minded allies. Organize protest through social media. Dig to find conservative thought leaders, like Milton Friedman on school choice, who could provide intellectual energy. Discover well-heeled contributors to support the work, often through dark money. Use that base to create a national conversation as right-wing opinion leaders—Fox News anchors, editors of right-wing newsletters, and bases of right-wing authority in national think tanks—latch onto the work to generate a national movement. And then, as issues and worries change, evolve by shifting to different issues.

It's hard to maintain the vigor of early leaders. But the right-wing idea factory has discovered the power of generating a steady stream of new ideas and reinforcing it with a constant infusion of big cash.

The great success of the factory during the 2010s was the discovery of issues that could generate funding and then shift those issues to maintain momentum and the flow of money. Unlike traditional conservatives where there were bedrock principles, the right-wing idea factory was far more tactical, focused on building and growing a political power base with the ideas and policies that had the most potential—and then moving off those policies quickly as their utility faded away or more promising ones evolved. This tactical movement had a singular focus on acquiring and building political power.

That's the story of the policy oligarchs to whom I turn in the next chapter.

Chapter 6

Policy Oligarchs and Policy Clusters

At the nation's founding, two big concepts shaped the debates about power: federalism, to accommodate big differences between the states without breaking the union; and the chief executive, to get things done. In federalism, there's always been the concern that differences between the states would fracture the nation's unity. In the chief executive, there's always been the worry that making the executive strong enough to implement policies effectively would recreate the very executive-as-king that the colonists had gone to war to end. Just as there's always been tension in how to answer these questions, there have always been differences among the states. Those differences have clustered, eventually producing two very different countries, red and blue, with very different results for their residents.

Even before American independence, the country's thought leaders debated the importance of the national unity and concentrated power. Benjamin Franklin's *Pennsylvania Gazette* in 1754, for example, published an editorial cartoon warning that the colonies faced a stark choice: "Join, or Die."[1] Without bringing the colonies together, Franklin warned, the colonies would be picked apart by European powers eagerly eyeing the continent's wealth. The search for unity continued with the Declaration of Independence. It pointed to a catalog of problems that made it "necessary for one people to dissolve the political bands which have connected them with another," a theme that kept the colonies together as they found toward their unlikely victory over the British army.

The debate over just how much centralizing glue the country needed, however, has never been resolved. The American Constitution–Version 1.0, the Articles of Confederation, failed miserably. For the national government to do anything, it needed support of nine of the thirteen states, and getting that supermajority was often impossible. Some state delegations often didn't bother to show up, let alone contribute to debate and the vote. The national government couldn't collect taxes, and each state conducted its own foreign policy and printed its own money. The Articles aspired to "perpetual union," but it was hard to make good on that dream when rebels like Daniel Shays organized a group of farmers in western Massachusetts to raid a government armory and the federal government proved incapable of stopping it. The whole country was embarrassed to discover that it took the state militia to do something that was the federal government's job.

Just about everyone agreed that had to change, starting with a far more powerful executive. Hamilton argued for a national "governor" who would serve for life and who would appoint state governors. That was too much concentrated national power for the other founders to stomach, so eventually most of them (even Hamilton) coalesced around Madison's plan for national power balanced between three branches of government. But some founders feared that Madison's plan would still lead to too much concentration of power. In debating whether his state of Virginia ought to support the plan drafted by Madison, another Virginian—Patrick Henry, he of "give me liberty or give me death" fame—warned of the dangers in the Constitution:

> This Constitution is said to have beautiful features; but when I come to examine these features, sir, they appear to me horribly frightful. Among other deformities, it has an awful squinting; it

squints toward monarchy, and does not this raise indignation in the breast of every true American? Your president may easily become king.[2]

Madison and Hamilton countered that the Constitution contained numerous safeguards against the concentration of power in the president, especially in the balances provided by the Congress and the courts. Hamilton pointed to federalism as a big safeguard against overreaching power of the national government because "the people of the several States, would control the indulgence of so extravagant an appetite" that might overwhelm the presidency, as he wrote in Federalist 17. The states had power over many of the issues that were closest to the people, and that would restrain the power of the national government, Hamilton contended. He and Madison and other founders won the day.

The ratification of the Constitution, of course, did not resolve the question of who would exercise power, and that pushed the issue into the debate about the very existence of the union. Lincoln was pragmatic about everything, even the future of slavery—except for the preservation of the union itself. In 1862, amid some of the war's darkest days, he wrote Horace Greeley, "I would save the union." He continued, "If I could save the Union without freeing any slave, I would do it, and if I could save it by freeing all the slaves, I would do it, and if I could save it by freeing some and leaving others alone, I would also do that."[3] He believed in "Join, or Die." Any alternative that risked disunion, he feared, would destroy the union and, with it, the grand American experiment in democracy.

The founders sought union without a clear idea about how best to achieve it. After Shays's Rebellion, there was a consensus for stronger national power; to prevent national power from getting too dominant, leaders like Hamilton saw federalism as a brake on national power. That theme has continued since. During the 1930s, for the Progressive New Dealers (with "Progressive" here in the context of the good-government, anti-trust, worker-protection, women's-rights chain of policy), federalism was an opportunity for moving policies forward more quickly than federal policymakers might be able to support.

The states, Justice Louis Brandeis famously suggested in 1932, could serve as laboratories of democracy "and try novel social and economic experiments without risk to the rest of the country."[4] His argument had a twin edge to it. The states could experiment with new ideas without the people always asking the federal government to solve every problem. And with forty-eight states (at the time) each working on their own alternatives, there would be a brake on national policymaking. Of course, Brandeis was certainly not blind to the profound problem of slavery, one of the reasons that slave-owning colonies had insisted on federalism before agreeing to ratify the Constitution. However, critics have charged since that he was blind to the implications of the "separate but equal" doctrine that had dominated legal debates since the Civil War, and that he was guilty, perhaps, of "jurisprudential inconsistency."[5]

State Clusters

In making the case for state-based laboratories of democracy, Brandeis certainly did not anticipate the way in which the right-wing idea factory would later turn his pragmatic approach into a divisive ideology. The factory, during the 2010s, produced a two-track America, where the government people got depended on where they lived.[6] This was because of the clusters in which the factories worked.

First, within each state, ideas do not emerge from completely separate idea factories. They are more like separate facilities in the same chain, generating menu ideas that can vary from store to store, like poutine as a Canadian side dish, the McOz in Australia (a quarter pounder with beetroot) and, of course, mayonnaise for the fries in the Netherlands and "Le Royal Cheese" in France instead of the Quarter Pounder.

The right-wing idea factory thus needs to be understood not as a manufacturer of individual concepts, but as an interrelated, sometimes interlocking campaign to transform policymaking in state governments. Moreover, the machinery in each state does not, nor ever has, run in isolation. State policymakers pay careful attention to ideas in other states and, especially, to proposals emerging from groups like the American Legislative Exchange Council. I once talked with a state capitol reporter in Austin who said, "I pay attention to what's happening in Tallahassee. I know that anything that comes out of Florida will be on the floor of the Texas legislature within forty-eight hours." As a result, the states have settled into different clusters, with some states running their right-wing idea at full speed while others barely turn the machinery on. The red states take cues from each other; blue states do the same, and they closely follow each other in searching for ideas to block conservatives.

The coordinated work of state attorneys general both reinforces these patterns and is the product of them. For years, the National Association of Attorneys General aligned state officers on issues they had in common, including the 1998 national tobacco settlement of the 1990s, worth billions of dollars, as well as the $50 billion opioid settlement in the mid-2020s. The group's discussions sometimes create strange bedfellows, with some of the nation's most conservative legal officers working together with some of the most liberal ones, all in the cause of creating the strongest bargaining position.

As party polarization increased, however, collaboration across party lines eroded. Each party created its own Attorneys General Association, and the two state associations became important players in national politics. During the Biden administration, for example, the Republican Attorneys General Association sued to block the administration's requirement for background checks at gun shows, minimum staffing at nursing homes, and vehicle emissions rules. *Politico* said that the group took a "blowtorch to the Biden agenda."[7] For example, six Republican attorneys general successfully took the Biden administration to the US Supreme Court in 2023 to block its college student loan forgiveness program.[8]

When Trump came back into office in 2025, the Democratic Attorneys General Association used the same strategy. The group repeatedly sued the administration, first to block the administration's plan to end birthright citizenship and then to stop the administration's effort to take away federal grants to the states. They sued to block the proposed shutdown of the Department of Education, public health spending, and a variety of other programs. By day 80 of the second Trump administration, the attorneys general had already filed twenty-five suits to stop administration policy.[9] The campaign by the attorneys general, often organized in daily conference calls, marked one of the party's few bright spots as it sought to right itself after the 2024 election.[10] As Table 6.1 shows, these ongoing battles—and, especially, the aggressive right-wing-idea machine—produced big policy and political differences between the states. The most-aggressive states in running right-wing idea factories were also far more likely to vote for Trump in the 2024 presidential election. In fact, the average Trump vote in these states was nearly 20 percent higher than in the states that swung to Kamala Harris.

Did the factory generate higher Trump support—or did higher Trump support reinforce the right-wing idea factory policies? The right-wing idea factory tended to be much more strongly associated with some policy outcomes. Per capita income, life expectancy, and educational attainment (defined by the percentage of residents with a BA or higher in 2025) were all lower in the factory leaders. The states with the most active right-wing idea factories tended to have higher levels of financial stress, as WalletHub measured it, as well as lower social mobility, as measured by the nonpartisan Archbridge Institute. These numbers suggest cause and effect. People in some states have higher levels of stress than in others. Economists and demographers have demonstrated that social mobility has become more difficult for those at the bottom of the income scale since at least the 1960s. For children born in 1940, more than 90 percent earned more than their parents, but for children born in the mid-1980s, the likelihood they would out-earn their parents fell to just

TABLE 6.1 A Comparison of Social Measures in Factory Leaders, Factory Avoiders, and the States in Between

Right-Wing Factory Index Cluster	Trump vote (2020)	Per capita personal income (2024)	Life expectancy in years (2025)	Educational attainment, BA degree or higher (2025)	Total stress score (2025)	Social mobility (2023)
Factory leaders	58.9%	$64,996	74.5	30.6%	45.9	4.8
Middle	47.7%	$71,922	76.4	35.0%	44.3	5.2
Factory avoiders	39.7%	$75,254	77.7	38.0%	43.9	5.1

See the appendix for the sources for the table.

50 percent, according to Opportunity Insights. Moreover, areas with higher mobility produce lower poverty rates, better schools, more stable families, and stronger social networks.[11]

The policy work tended to cluster in about 40 percent of the states, across a very large number of policy areas. On the other hand, strong opposition to the right-wing agenda arose in one-fourth of the states, where elected officials and public interest groups fought hard to create barriers against the right-wing agenda. The remaining states teetered between the two extremes. In a country of rising polarization, it was scarcely a surprise that issues ranging from abortion rights to DEI divided the states and, in turn, the country.

To explore these divisions, I developed a "right-wing idea factory index," based on each state's policies on the core idea factory issues: whether they delayed locking down at the 2020 outbreak of Covid; whether they had created trigger bans in advance of the 2022 *Dobbs* decision that put abortion decisions in the hands of the states and then banned abortions early in a pregnancy; how aggressively their citizens pursued book bans and their legislatures proposed DEI bans; whether they developed school voucher programs and established themselves as right-to-work states; whether they decided at the beginning of Obamacare whether to take advantage of federal subsidies for additional coverage; and whether they banned care for trans children. Some states were leaders in building idea factories. Other states fought to stop the movement, while others rocked between the extremes (see Table 6.2).

To truly understand the workings of the right-wing idea factory, it is a mistake to track individual policy areas, like abortion or DEI; to presume that the states run similar policy production lines, because each state is in fact very different; or to separate federal and state policymaking, on the assumption that they run on separate tracks. The state political cultures and power systems have fallen into different clusters, just as their policies have. Although federal and state policymaking has certainly been intertwined, the right-wing idea factory at the state level developed independently

TABLE 6.2 States Grouped as Factory Leaders, in the Middle, or Factory Avoiders

Factory leaders	Middle states	Factory avoiders
Oklahoma	Iowa	California
Texas	West Virginia	Colorado
Florida	Arizona	Michigan
Georgia	Kansas	Minnesota
Missouri	Maine	New Jersey
South Carolina	Montana	New Mexico
Tennessee	Wisconsin	Rhode Island
Utah	Ohio	Vermont
Idaho	Virginia	Connecticut
Mississippi	New Hampshire	Delaware
North Carolina	Alaska	Hawaii
South Dakota	Maryland	Illinois
Alabama	Massachusetts	Washington
Arkansas	Nevada	
Indiana	New York	
Kentucky	Oregon	
Louisiana	Pennsylvania	
Nebraska		
North Dakota		
Wyoming		

For the sources and methodology for this table, please see the appendix.

of federal action, often in advance of federal steps, and has often helped generate federal policy stands in turn.

What does this tell us about the genesis of the right-wing idea factories? Policies have become more place-based. Everything from the quality of schools to the success kids have in those schools, from the level of poverty and the ability of family members to climb out of it, from the degree of family stability and the stress people feel within those families, as well as from the role of social networks—all of these things cluster together.

These problems, in turn, make it more likely that people will be angrier where their opportunities are lower and their stress is higher. Not only does their anger feed off the sense that they aren't getting their just piece of the economy. The sources from which they pick up those feelings and then feed off of them tend to be their friends and neighbors, which are different in different parts of the country and which also help fuel the right-wing idea factory. That defines the government that the people want, and, because their drivers are different, so too are the demands they make. As a result, the government that people experience depends fundamentally on where they live. Federalism therefore evolved from the shock absorber that helped accommodate very different visions of what the *United* States ought to be. It also became connected to the great divide at the core of the right-wing idea factory.

The Unitary Executive

The factory also picked up on an idea that flows from the arguments of some of the nation's founders: the "unitary executive" theory of government. The country might have three branches of government, the idea goes, but control of the executive branch isn't shared. The president has sole power over the executive branch. Article II of the Constitution states that the president has the responsibility not only for the executive function but also to "take Care that the Laws be faithfully executed." Therefore, the argument goes, the "take care" clause conveys to the president a particular power: Congress passes laws and the courts administer justice, but when it comes to executing the law, the job is solely the president's, according to the Constitution. Therefore, the argument goes, the Constitution vests in the president a broad, "unitary" power.

The concentration of power was one of the things that the country's founders worried most about. The Federalists who produced the Constitution fretted, more than anything else, about the second branch of government—the presidency—and how best to contain its inherent powers. They had their fill of King George III, and the last thing they wanted after fighting a bloody war of independence was to open the door to a new despot. The founders therefore sandwiched the executive's power in Article II of the Constitution, between the power of Congress—the people's house—in Article I, and the judicial branch, in Article III, whose power was not yet clear.

There was no greater champion of executive power among the founders than Alexander Hamilton, but Hamilton was an even greater champion of the constitutional checks on oligarchy. In Federalist 72, he pointed to the "superior weight and influence of the legislative body in a free government," which would create a "hazard to the executive in a trial of strength of that body." The founders recognized the risk of creating a government with a president charged to "take Care that the Laws be faithfully executed," as Article II of the Constitution states. This is an impressive power, but Article II begins by placing executive power into the context of laws passed Congress. That certainly didn't satisfy the critics of the Federalists, however, who worried the president would become "chief magistrate and generalissimo of the United States," which led them to be "alarmed with the apprehensions of aristocracy."[12] One anti-federalist, known in print as "Philadelphiensis" and outed as Benjamin Workman, a mathematics instructor at the University of Pennsylvania, worried precisely that the president would become an oligarch:

> Who can deny but the president general will be a king to all intents and purposes, and one of the most dangerous kind too; a king elected to command a standing army? Thus our laws are to be administered by this tyrant; for the whole, or at least the most important part of the executive department is put in his hands.[13]

In the end, of course, the Federalists won out. The states ratified the Constitution, established the presidency, and bought into the problem of controlling the executive that they had created.

The fundamental constitutional tension was between those who promoted the concept of a "living constitution," who contended that the Constitution needed to evolve its basic principles to meet the emerging challenges of modern society, and those who argued that the "written Constitution" was what mattered, captured in the plain meaning of the words as they were originally written. The "written constitution" approach had no stronger proponent than Justice Antonin Scalia. The justice excoriated "living constitution" proponents who, he said, made the question of whether something was constitutional depend on "if you care passionately about something." If the constitutional standard is "How passionately do you care?" then there was no standard.[14] Judges had an obligation to avoid following the political winds, Scalia believed, and that was just the danger that the "living constitution" approach raised. He wrote,

> If the law is to make any attempt at consistency and predictability, surely there must be general agreement not only that judges reject one exegetical approach (originalism), but that they adopt another. And it is hard to discern any emerging consensus among the nonoriginalists as to what this might be.[15]

Scalia made this the core of his approach to the law and to the cases that came before him. His relentless effort, coupled with his supreme intelligence and wicked sense of humor, gradually won him support on the Court and an enthusiastic embrace in the conservative legal community. The plain meaning of Article II made the president supreme over the executive branch, they contended, and that in turn built the foundation for an aggressive assertion of presidential power. This was an argument that the Left could obviously use as vigorously as the Right, but it was the right-wing that did so. That was true in part because the Left was temperamentally focused more on a balance of power between the branches. The Left, more-over, had used the "living constitution" to expand rights, ranging from protecting civil rights to establishing a woman's right to choose whether to end a pregnancy. Abortion and the "living constitution" were inseparable. There is no mention of abortion in the Consti-tution or in any of its amendments, and the Court had premised the right to abortion on a woman's assertion of privacy. Only a liv-ing, not a literal, reading of the Constitution made that possible. So Scalia's aggressive pursuit of the "written constitution" approach was an intellectual, political, and policy wedge between the Left and the Right.

It provided Trumpism with the intellectual firepower it needed for a massive—indeed, revolutionary—centralization of govern-ment power at the start of Trump's second term. After Trump's first term, the president's loyalists and the billionaires who supported them concluded they had made one very serious mistake: not mov-ing fast enough. Their reaction time was the product, in part, of a very slow transition, since the Trump team did not really expect to win, and the president scrapped most of the transition planning that was done. In the four years that followed, they determined not to allow that to happen again. After Trump's 2025 inauguration, they were prepared with a tsunami of executive actions: executive orders, agency guidance, agency shutdowns, personnel firings, repeal of reg-ulations, a tariff barrage, and challenges to federal court rulings, all of which happened so quickly that it was impossible for anyone to keep up, let alone track the implications for American policy and institutions.

But one thing was certain: In a remarkably short time, the second Trump administration upset the basic culture and even much of the rule of law undergirding the American political sys-tem. It simultaneously advanced the unitary executive approach to American government and an oligarchical swing of power, in pre-cisely the ways that many of the nation's founders most feared—even though, in doing so, the president's assertion of power rested on powers that, they said, went back to the time of the founders. Trump was the foremost practitioner of the unitary executive in the nation's history, even more than Richard Nixon, whose aggressive use of presidential power led to his resignation. Trump swept aside traditional conservatism and put the right-wing idea factory at the center of political power.

Conservative political thought is as old as political thought itself. The basics have always been clear: Promote individual liberty, keep government small, ensure equality before the law, and grow the economy. In a word endlessly confusing to Americans, this brand of conservatism has its roots deep in "liberalism," a term that comes from the Latin for "free." The Romans, in fact, held a basic precept: *libera res publica, liber populus*—"a free republic, a free people" (although, of course, *liber populus* did not refer to all members of the *populus*, since a substantial number of Romans were slaves, especially in the city of Rome itself).

But searching for the roots of freedom invariably leads to *liber*; liberalism invariably takes them to liberal democracy; and liberal democracy takes them to the fundamental values. The debate over how to establish and preserve these values in government animated Edmund Burke to write his critique of the French Revolution in 1790 and made him the father of conservatism. Those ideas animated conservative philosophy for 225 years, until the 2010s pushed aside the great traditions: Burke, classical conservatism, and ancient ideas about establishing a small government focused on preventing government from aggressively promoting political values—they all disappeared in the work of the right-wing idea factory.

By that point, classical conservatism had lost its zip. William F. Buckley Jr. was no longer alive to drive the movement, and the circulation of his magazine, *National Review*, dropped in half during the 2010s.[16] In 2024, Luke Savage wrote, "With the rise of MAGA in the ranks of the GOP, the Right no longer needs a veneer of intellectualism. It no longer needs National Review."[17] Conservatism had shifted from a movement with powerful intellectual roots to one engaged with what once had been the movement's more primitive fringe. There was a sophistication to Buckley's conservatism, but during the 2010s conservatism moved to a reactionary style with no pretense to ideological purity, intellectual firepower, or intellectual consistency.

Instead, conservatism had become the engine for the right-wing idea factory to produce pragmatic tools for gaining, keeping, and expanding political power. Buckley and other classical conservatives certainly always wanted to see government adopt their views (and reject the views of the Left), but they also put far more weight on the power of ideas that had grown over centuries.

The traditional Republican Party evaporated along with traditional conservatism. The party continued holding conventions, nominating officials, and organizing legislatures, but the Republican Party of the mid-2020s had virtually nothing in common with the Tea Party of 2009 or Republicanism of the 2010s. Gone were the pursuits of free-market competition, small government, fiscal restraint, balanced budgets, and other classical themes. Ideas mattered only to the degree they could harness money and voters. The only constant was the tactical pursuit of political advantage, not the strategic advancement of big ideas. The party continued to venerate Ronald Reagan as a near-sainted figure, and Donald Trump regularly invoked him, but the Reagan of the 1980s had little to do with the Trump of the 2020s. The right-wing idea factory had changed all that, especially in fueling the unitary executive theory.

The theory has enormous practical implications. Toward the end of the first hundred days of Trump's second term, a *Time* magazine reporter pressed him on whether he was expanding the power of the presidency. The president replied, "Well, I don't feel I'm expanding it. I think I'm using it as it was meant to be used."[18] But did the founders really intend to give presidents that level of power? The simple but perhaps surprising answer is this: We simply don't know. The founders didn't pay much attention to the meaning of the "take care" clause; they focused far more on balancing the powers among the branches and, especially, ensuring that the executive was strong enough to administer the laws but never powerful enough to risk repeating the abuses of King George III. The "take care" clause has just ten words. As Sophia Shams points out, how the president chooses to interpret those words—and what constrains both the Congress and the courts—has turned out to be enormously complex.[19]

The Supreme Court has treated "the meaning of the clause as obvious when it is anything but that," explained Jack Goldsmith and John F. Manning.[20] That has given presidents wiggle room to stretch its boundaries, as has a Congress unwilling since Watergate to rein in that executive instinct. Trump repeatedly declared national emergencies to justify expanded federal policies, from a national emergency on his first day aimed at choking off the flow of migrants at the southern border, to another invoking massive increases in tariffs.

He was not the only president to challenge the boundaries of presidential power. After Congress failed to act, Joe Biden invoked presidential power to forgive student debt. During the Korean War, Harry S. Truman declared a national emergency to seize steel plants. In both cases, the Supreme Court ruled that the president had overstepped his legal authority. But Trump was determined to stretch the boundaries of presidential power even further.

In the country's first decades, the "take care" clause defined presidential duties, not the president's powers. In *Marbury v. Madison* (1803), for example, the Supreme Court concentrated on the executive's responsibility to comply with the law, in a decision best known for establishing the principle of judicial review.[21] In 1838 (*Kendall v. United States*), the Court reinforced the president's responsibility to execute the law and rejected the idea that the Constitution provided the president with a source of power.[22] That began to change with the 1926 decision in *Myers v. US*, in which the Court expanded presidential power based on the "take care" clause. At issue was whether the president had the power to remove a postmaster, Frank Myers, who had been appointed by the president and confirmed by the Senate (that was the case for postmasters at large post offices until 1971). President Woodrow Wilson fired Myers without getting approval by the Senate. Myers claimed he had been unconstitutionally fired because Wilson did not have the power to do so, and he sued for back pay. The Court held that Wilson was well within his power in dismissing him. In fact, "In the absence of any express limitation respecting removals, that as his selection of administrative officers is essential to the execution of the laws by him, so must be his power of removing those for whom he cannot continue to be responsible," as Chief Justice Howard Taft put it.[23] Taft, of course, was a former president himself.

The question of just how far a president might stretch executive power remained a lively debate. In 1952, in the middle of the Korean War, the country depended on a steady supply of steel for its war effort. The United Steel Workers, however, threatened to strike. Truman concluded that the strike would produce enormous problems, so he directed the federal government to seize control of the steel mills. The companies countered that, in their view, the president lacked power to do that. In *Youngstown Sheet & Tube v. Sawyer*, the Court sided with the steel companies. There was no law providing the president with the power to seize private companies, and Truman had overstepped his bounds, the Court ruled.[24]

So the president clearly had not only the constitutional power but also the responsibility to carry out the law. The president did not have the power, according to the Court, to act beyond the law that Congress had written, but the president's power increased across policies, Congress's delegations to executive branch agencies multiplied, and the power of the administrative state vastly increased, as Dwight Waldo noted in his 1948 masterpiece, *The Administrative State*.[25] Among many other contributions of his work, Waldo both coined the term "administrative state" and positioned it most fundamentally as a matter of political theory: the role of administration in a modernizing democratic society, and the importance of administrative officials in ethically using their power to promote democratic values.

Until the Reagan administration, however, the notion of the "unitary executive" was primarily a question for debate among historians, as they sought to understand the nation's founding. That changed in the 1980s, with arguments made by the right-wing that went like this. The courts were too elitist. Congress was ineffective. The New Deal administrative state had grown too large, too inefficient, and too independent. Beltway-insider bureaucrats were gaining power but were out of touch with the public, and they needed strong, centralized presidential power to rein them in. Then there was the always simmering Cold War, which demanded a strong presidency.[26]

The right-wing rolled the theoretical argument into a policy blueprint, beginning in 1981 with the Heritage Foundation's Mandate for Leadership policy guide, a sweeping collection of recommendations in a volume of nearly eleven hundred pages.[27] The Heritage volume was, Reagan said a few years later, "a warning shot, telling the liberal establishment that a new sheriff and new deputies had ridden into town and they could not expect to carry on business as usual."[28]

The right-wing's enthusiasm for the idea of a powerful president to rein in a growing administrative state, of course, depended on whether it was a Republican president exercising it. After President Barack Obama said he would use executive orders to sidestep a Congress struggling to pass almost anything, Republicans were horrified. Representative Steve Scalise (R-La) complained, "President Obama has this fantasy that he can just use his pen to write laws." He continued, "We don't have a monarchy in this country—there's an executive branch and the legislative branch, and the president has to work with Congress to get things done."[29] Joe Biden had barely been in the Oval Office for a day when the right-wing began savaging him for executive overreach. "He's signaled that he'll take unilateral steps that usurp Congress' power and leave no room for debate or dissent," complained Kay James, then president of the Heritage Foundation.[30]

The courts, however, were a brake on the Democrats' dreams of empowering the executive. In 2023, the Court struck down the Biden administration's claim it could cancel $400 billion in student loans. Joining the challenge to Biden were Nebraska and five other states with Republican attorneys general (Arkansas, Iowa, Kansas, Missouri, and South Carolina).[31] They said that the Biden administration had violated the Administrative Procedure Act, which laid out specific guidelines for issuing new regulations and protecting the separation of powers, through a conclusion that the president didn't have the power to make such a policy to begin with. That was correct, the 6–3 majority of the John Roberts Court concluded.

However, when Donald Trump said he would be a dictator on day one of a second term, 74 percent of Republicans surveyed said they thought that would be a good idea. Only 13 percent of Democrats agreed.[32] The view of executive power—especially its balance within the rule of law—certainly depended on the eye of the beholder and the hand of its wielder.

The unitary executive approach was important for framing the power of the executive, especially for cases making their way through the courts. It was just as important as a fig leaf to cover the growing assertion of the president's authority, by both Democratic and Republican administrations. The right-wing, however, made the more enthusiastic use of the argument, and it was also the more eager to reach back to the period of the founding to justify the case (even though, as I've pointed out, the founders neither discussed, nor defined, executive reach as a principle).

Nevertheless, the right-wing discovered it could advance its agenda more forcefully the more aggressively it centralized power in the executive. That meant yanking decisions away from career bureaucrats (or what it called the "deep state"). It meant insisting that bureaucrats confine themselves to the law precisely as written by

Congress. Then, thanks to the work of Leonard Leo and his fellow conservatives, it meant relying on an increasingly conservative federal judiciary to rein in administrative power.

Therefore, by the time Trump won the 2024 presidential election, the right-wing idea factory had produced all the raw materials that conservatives needed for a massive assault on the administrative state.[33] All the threads came together: Yarvin's call for an "American Caesar," Marini's theoretical work on the need for a supercharged executive, Vought's holy war coupled with Musk's chainsaw, all supporting the unitary executive theory of government, aimed at providing the president with overwhelming powers. Congressional dithering gave the president few problems in making the case for a unitary executive. The courts proved marginally more effective in slowing the march toward unified power, but the aggressive work by the administration and its legal strategists overwhelmed the courts' capacity to produce timely rulings on the key cases or to move beyond bite-sized issues.

Saikrishna Bangalore Prakash, in *The Living Presidency*, came at the idea of the unitary executive theory from the other perspective. His argument is firmly from the right, rooted in warnings about the expanding view of the presidency and an analysis that holds a different originalist perspective: that the founders intended the power of the presidency to be checked, and that it was the job of the other branches of government to check it. "Our living presidency subverts the idea of an executive subject to the Constitution and to the laws." And he added the sharp warning, "If presidents can unilaterally alter the Constitution, they can alter the document that spells out and limits their authority." The great risk, he warned, is an executive increasingly unfettered by the Constitution.[34] Prakash drew the line between the conservative argument limiting presidential power and the right-wing idea factory liberating it. The division forms along the "take care" clause: just what it means to see that the laws are faithfully executed. This is the line that separates the traditional conservatives from the brand of the Right that emerged during the 2010s.

At the federal level, the fundamental triumph—and the ultimate risk—of the right-wing idea factory was creating the American Caesar, full of power that overwhelmed the other two branches of government, which had been designed to prevent just such an outcome. It was the stuff that Thomas Paine had feared, Yarvin had cheered, and Prakash had warned of. And it paved the road to Trumpism.

Analysts have spilled thousands of gallons of ink and terabytes of pixels trying to explain Donald Trump, his appeal to the electorate, and his personal motivations. One can turn to his own autobiography, *Trump: The Art of the Deal*, a book for which his coauthor, Tony Schwartz, has since expressed regret. Schwartz said, "I never imagined that writing a book for a buffoonish real estate developer could eventually help him get elected president of the United States. That it did is a source of shame and regret I will always carry."[35] The NBC executive in charge of marketing Trump's television show, *The Apprentice*, sang the same tune in 2024, saying, "I want to apologize to America. I helped create a monster."[36] A group of mental health specialists pointedly questioned Trump's fitness to serve in the most important job in the world, although diagnosing a patient one has never treated crosses the line to which most psychiatrists hold—as does crossing the line of personal privacy.[37] His niece, Mary L. Trump, herself a clinical psychologist, tried to root Trump's behavior in his upbringing, in a book titled *Too Much and Never Enough: How My Family Created the World's Most Dangerous Man*.[38]

In seeking to understand the Trump phenomenon, Francis Fukuyama contended that Trump should not be understood in terms of ideas or class or social groups. Psychology, he concluded, was the most powerful spotlight. Fukuyama turned to Nietzsche and his concept of "ressentiment," characterized by "acute resentment of others based on wounded pride, perceived disregard, fears of inadequacy, and a desire to exact revenge on those who had earlier failed to pay adequate respect."[39] If anything is certain, the question of what made Trump into Trump will preoccupy historians, political scientists, psychologists, and legions of journalists for generations, if not longer.

Sorting out Trump's psychology is not my goal here, even if it were possible, which it surely is not. More important, at least for my analysis, is the way that Trump picked up the opportunities created by the right-wing base. Indeed, it was the very fact that, as Fukuyama suggests, Trump did not have a driving philosophy that made it possible for him to pivot from being a left-leaning Democrat to the right-wing Republican he became as president. That tremendous ideological flexibility, in turn, made it possible for Trump to carry forward the aspirations both of ideologues with a right-leaning agenda and of Republicans who saw in Trump the chance to greatly enhance presidential power and to create a genuine "imperial presidency," as longtime columnist Doyle McManus wrote for the *Los Angeles Times*.[40]

In 1973, Arthur M. Schlesinger Jr. explored the rise of presidential imperialism, especially in the use of presidential power in waging war. He wrote, "By the early 1970s, the American president had become on issues of war and peace the most absolute monarch (with the exception of Mao Tse-tung of China) among the great powers of the world."[41] It was a masterful book, but it failed to anticipate what was to come fifty years later. Trump's imperialism—or, at least, the imperial power that Trump asserted in his second term—exceeded what previous presidents might have imagined. He went much farther than Richard Nixon had ever dreamed of going.

Post-Constitutionalism

At the core of Trump's agenda was, at least for the first few months, the unbridled zeal of billionaire Elon Musk and then, as the administration matured, Project 2025. Its leader was Russell Vought—Trump's budget director in the first administration, the only member of his cabinet to come back in the same role in the second term and the person within the Trump administration who knew best how to work the levers of internal bureaucratic power. His goals were clear. "I want to be the person that crushes the deep state," he told *The Economist*. He said that he wanted to "break the bureaucracy to the president's will." His main target was the civil service, the career officials who, he was convinced, were dominated by woke left-leaning ideologues determined to undermine the president's policies. Vought took an apocalyptic view of their role and promised to put them "in trauma."[42]

In addition to his policy zeal he had a strong religious drive. Vought saw himself as a holy warrior in God's service. "We need to trust that the duty is ours and the results are God's," he explained.[43] He believed in using government to advance his deeply held religious values and saw Trump as a "gift of God." America had entered a "post constitutional moment," he explained. This meant that

> our constitutional institutions, understandings, and practices have all been transformed, over decades, away from the words on the paper into a new arrangement—a new regime if you will—that pays only lip service to the old Constitution. Our system is now much more like an unwritten constitution which operates based on precedents, like the English system. No constitutional amendments have been passed to enact this, but new legal paradigms have been introduced—a "living constitution," independent agencies, permanent, "expert" civil servants—that have changed the underlying separation of powers at the core of our system.

"The Left quietly adopted a strategy of institutional change that left the constitutional system of separate powers in place but radically perverted how they operated," he continued. That left the right-wing only one alternative: understanding that "the Constitution we live under is not the one that our Founders gave us," which meant political leaders had to become "radical constitutionalists." That meant going back to the original words of the Constitution and scraping underneath the "scar tissue" that had grown up over time.[44]

Vought built on arguments that several key members of the right-wing idea machine had been generating in the years before. They were a very different collection of thinkers than the economists like Milton Friedman and public intellectuals like William F. Buckley Jr. who had built modern American conservatism. The prescription that Vought and others brought to the Trump administration led naturally to an argument for the aggressive expansion of presidential power. They saw that expansion as essential and inevitable, because the traditional constitutional order had already broken down, as evidenced by the growing power, in their view, of an unelected and unaccountable deep state. For example, senior fellow at the right-leaning Claremont Institute John Marini laid out a case for what ailed American government—the dominance of non-constitutional forces from the left. He saw an increase in the power of the president as the cure.

In 2012, Marini began an essay contending that "America has a problem, not because of our Constitution but because constitutionalism as a theoretical doctrine is no longer meaningful in our politics." He traced his argument back to Thomas Paine, who wrote that "a constitution is a thing antecedent to a government, and a government is only the creature of a constitution. The constitution of a country is not the act of its government, but of the people constituting a government."[45] Therefore, Marini concluded, for a government to be legitimate, the people had to be sovereign, "with government as the people's creation and servant."

Throughout the twentieth century, however, that was less and less the case to the right-wing. The culprit, Marini said, was that "the sovereignty of the people, established by the Constitution, was replaced by the sovereignty of government, understood in terms of the modern concept of the rational or administrative State." That was the natural result of the Progressive movement in general, and of Franklin D. Roosevelt in particular.[46] The power of the state had replaced the power of the people, and the power of the people's politics had given way to the power of administration. For the right-wing, government became too centralized, to the point that by 1975 the prime role of the federal government was regulating the details of the lives of Americans. Congress might pass new laws, but that was "primarily on behalf of the expansion of the administrative state."

This argument became the foundation of the "deep state" argument that conquered the right-wing during the 2010s. The Progressives created a bigger government. A bigger government required a larger administrative apparatus. The larger administrative apparatus concentrated political power, away from the people, and then became focused on growing its own growth and power. The separation-of-powers theory proved worthless in stopping this erosion of the people's sovereignty, because Congress fell into the trap of growing government even more and, when the president stretched the boundaries of executive power, Congress did not push back. Both trends helped fuel the administrative state.

As a result, Marini argued, in *Unmasking the Administrative State*, "The administrative state represents a post-constitutional order, one in which rule by law has been replaced by rule by administration." Since Congress was impotent, "Only the president, by acting forcefully, has the authority and the responsibility to restore self-government."[47] Marini pointed to Thomas Paine's contention in *The Rights of Man* that "nature and reason, not government, established the ground from which those principles [of constitutionalism] arose."[48] Constitutional government thus becomes meaningless if its principles shift with the times or with the ambitions of politicians. That is why, Marini believed, the United States was in a "post-constitutional order," because the basic constitution—between the sovereignty of rights and the sovereignty of the American people— had broken down in favor of a post-constitutional regime, in which policymakers in general—and policy administrators in particular— ran the system to benefit their aims and their power.

That was the undercurrent of the strategy that Russell Vought brought to the second Trump administration. It connected as well with the remarkable if brief sweep of Elon Musk's march through the federal government in taking over its personnel, information technology, and real estate processes.

Musk's strategy came in part from his experience as an entrepreneur, having developed the first truly successful electric vehicle and having created a successful commercial space launch rocket. Smart engineers, he was convinced, would own the future, by creating products that would have a worldwide market. But his strategy also traced in part from the philosophy of a computer engineer, Curtis Yarvin. Musk was more than happy to pick up the baton with the Department of Government Efficiency (DOGE) that he had talked about with Trump before the election, and that Trump launched with his inaugural address in January 2025.

After being savaged in the press and losing his access to key policy decisions, Musk left the administration in May 2025. If Musk faded away, however, his DOGE did not, cutting a wide swathe through the executive branch's personnel, regulatory, budgetary, information technology, and structure—the key policies that defined the steps toward administering the law—and leaving behind a cadre of DOGErs devoted to carrying on his work. That supported Trump's ideas about how to "take care" in the federal government. Musk might have faded away from his government work, but his team continued to broaden the president's power and the administration's concept of how the "take care" responsibility ought to work.

Congress was complicit in this shift of power. Two of the most astute observers of the legislative branch, Thomas E. Mann and Norman J. Ornstein, called Congress *The Broken Branch* in the title of their 2006 book. Six years later, they reassessed their diagnosis and in their next title concluded *It's Even Worse Than It Looks*. They continued to make the same point in a series of lectures and articles, with Ornstein making the blunt assessment in 2018 that the Republicans broke Congress.[49] The founders viewed Congress not only as the first branch of government but also as the essential balance to presidential power. That balance was doomed to be ineffective so long as Congress put little on the scale.

Meanwhile, the federal courts struggled to limit the overreach of executive power. There was a lively judicial debate in the first months of the second Trump administration, with plaintiffs challenging the president's decisions and federal courts weighing the cases, frequently deciding against the president. Trump attacked federal judges who had decided against him as "rogue," with Attorney General Pam Bondi calling judges "deranged." His press secretary, Karoline Leavitt, accused judges of "judicial overreach," attacking judges who "brazenly abused their judicial power." The president's deputy chief of staff, Stephen Miller, said bluntly, "We are living under a judicial tyranny."[50]

A June 2025 decision, *Trump v. Casa*, made it far easier for the Trump administration to resist the rulings by district judges that had bedeviled him. Challenges across the country had led judges to issue universal injunctions on individual cases that applied across the country. That allowed single cases to push back the president's decisions, pending appeals to higher federal courts, which invariably took considerable time.[51] Trump's Justice Department challenged the authority of individual district court judges to create national policy, and its lawyers won. "Universal injunctions likely exceed the equitable authority that Congress has given to federal courts," Amy Coney Barrett wrote for the 6–3 majority. In her dissenting opinion, Ketanji Brown Jackson wrote, "Make no mistake: Today's ruling allows the Executive to deny people rights that the Founders plainly wrote into our Constitution, so long as those individuals have not found a lawyer or asked a court in a particular manner to have their rights protected." She summarized her worries in two words: "Disaster looms." Nevertheless, with *Trump v. Casa*, the Supreme Court made it even easier for Trump to claim post-constitutional powers.

These forces, coupled with the president's own quest for political power, transformed the "unitary executive" model from a historical curiosity to the central strategy of the Trump presidency. Democratic presidents had not pursued power with the same eagerness, but history has shown that, once presidents' power is established, the balance of powers is hard to restore. The unitary executive was a change that undoubtedly would have stirred Madison and many of the other founders to grave concern. A super-powerful president was precisely what they had worked hard to avoid.

Meanwhile, in the states, the right-wing idea factory manufactured policies, leaders to pursue them, and cash to promote them. In 2010, the same year that the Supreme Court decided *Citizens United*, the Republicans used this combination to brush back traditional conservatism and use the Tea Party movement to capture some voters' anger with President Barack Obama in general and the financial bailout in particular. The factory created the drive to capture un unprecedented number of "trifectas"—single-party control of the governorship and of both houses of the state legislature—in twenty-two states (Figure 6.1). Moreover, despite Obama's success in 2012 and Biden's win in 2020, Republicans managed to hold onto trifectas in nearly half of all the states.

In several statehouses, powerful Republican governors championed right-wing policies. Florida's Ron DeSantis was one of the leaders, until his power began ebbing away following his failure

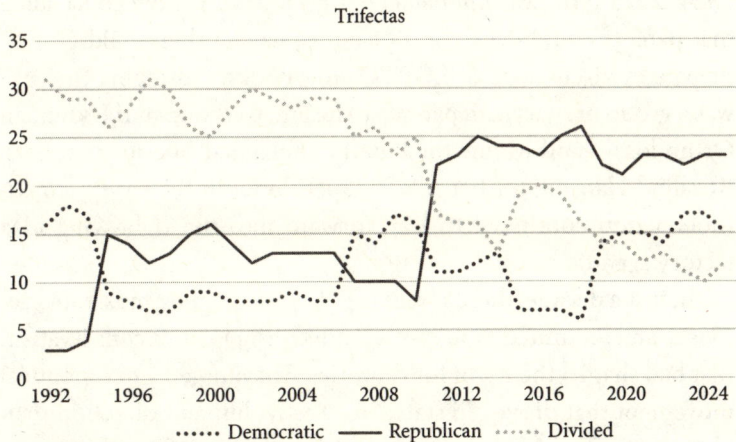

FIGURE 6.1 Republican State Government Trifectas Have Increased

Source: Ballotpedia, https://ballotpedia.org/State_government_trifectas#Historical_trifecta_numbers.

in challenging Trump for the Republican nomination in 2024. In Texas, Governor Greg Abbott led a strategy to build the border wall that Trump had not. That goal quietly slipped away because of the ballooning costs, but he fought ferociously to win one of the country's most aggressive school choice laws in 2024. In Arkansas, Trump's former press secretary, Sarah Huckabee Sanders, won the governorship and used the post to sign a law prohibiting transgender people from using the restroom of their choice in public schools and allowing anyone who had received gender-affirming care while a minor to challenge the doctor who had performed the procedure with a malpractice lawsuit.

Federalism thus became a powerful engine driving the factory at the grassroots. Most of the media attention was on Trump at the federal level, but the state-level policy changes had not only laid the foundation for the federal initiatives but also created a powerful force that guaranteed the right-wing idea factory would continue working hard after Trump's departure from the political scene. For example, one of the landmark cases of the Supreme Court's 2024–2025 term was *Mahmoud v. Taylor*, in which the court ruled that parents could decide to opt out of having their children participate in discussions of LGBTQ storybooks.[52] Bringing the case was a group of Maryland parents (Muslim, Catholic, and Ukrainian Orthodox)—and Moms for Liberty applauded one its members, Rosalind Hanson, for her role as a petitioner in the case.[53] Grassroots action continued to lean forward into the right-wing idea factory agenda.

In just a decade, these forces—policy ideologues, grassroots activists, and unlimited money—upended principles of conservatism that had shaped the Right for centuries. They forged a new political movement that drove red states in a vastly different direction than blue states. The American idea factory produced Donald Trump and crowned its work with Trump's restoration with the 2024 election, but it was much more. The movement was already running when Trump was just a reality-show host. It built a foundation, especially in the states, that ensured its continued success. A Democratic takeover at the federal level was likely to leave the Republican trifectas untouched, thanks to the success of both parties of locking in their state legislative majorities. And that, in turn, ensured the continued success of the right-wing idea factory.

Chapter 7

The Global Right-Wing Idea Factory

Many of the world's nations have struggled with very similar divides. Economic mobility has become more difficult; anger at traditional politicians has grown. Right-wing leaders harnessed that anger, including Italy's Giorgia Meloni, France's Marine Le Pen, Hungary's Viktor Orbán, and Argentina's Javier Milei, whose gift of a gilt chainsaw to Elon Musk became his symbol of federal government budget cutting in 2025 until it became too strong a political weight hanging around both of their necks. But the rise of the global right raises a fundamental question: Was the United States the leader or the follower of this global movement?

Longtime Trump whisperer Steve Bannon argued that Trump was indispensable to America, to the movement, and to the globe. "Like they said about Louis XIV, 'after me the deluge.' There's nobody that can replace Trump. He's a unifying figure and a figure as a deliverer of blunt force trauma that only he can do to the established order," he told a reporter six weeks after Trump's 2024 election triumph.[1] This echoed a constant theme: that Trump had generated the right-wing movement and that without him the movement was bound to founder. Trump himself often admired right-wing rulers in other countries, so the connections and parallels became inescapable.

In fact, the global right-wing movement significantly predated Trump. But although Trump himself did little more than jump on movements already underway, in both the United States and in countries around the world, he became the symbolic head of the global right-wing movement around the world, in both word and deed. The "deep state" language he popularized became universal, even though the term predated his presidential campaign. So did the idea of weakening the deep state by slashing away at the bureaucracy, despite ongoing global campaigns to do just that. In short, there has been a great deal of convergence in style and substance.

Two weeks after Trump's 2024 re-election, Argentine President Javier Milei said he wanted to destroy the country's state from the inside. He told *The Economist* that his contempt for the state was "infinite" and that "anything I can do to remove the interference of the state, I'm going to do."[2] The right-wing around the world had gained ground but won little policy traction until Milei won his race in Argentina, Marine Le Pen led a vote of no confidence in the French government, Giorgia Meloni ran on a nativist plat-form to capture the government, and of course Trump won his 2024 comeback. *The Economist* reported at the end of 2024 that, in more than half of the members of the European Union, hard-right par-ties had the support of at least 20 percent of the electorate. The right-wing "has opportunistically found new topics to drum up fury about," as *The Economist* put it, walking the same pragmatic steps that helped the Right in America get traction.[3] There was a heavy dose of anti-immigrant sentiment, worries about the economy, and (though it is an issue far from the minds of most Americans on the right-wing) opposition to policies designed to mute the effects of climate change. Many voters worried that climate change mitigation could impose big costs at a time when the economy was especially tight.

Milei called himself an "anarcho-capitalist," committed to re-placing public organizations with private markets. His movement built on Hayek's case for market capitalism that was developed in more robust form in Murray N. Rothbard's *Man, Economy, and State* (1962). Rothbard called for a "contractual society," in which voluntary, interpersonal exchanges shape social interactions. Every student of basic economics will recognize the description: "A gives up a good to B in exchange for a good that B gives up to A." Each side is better off by making the exchange that most benefits them. That, Rothbard contends, is the best course for society, and he warns about what he calls the "violent intervention" of government into the free market and the "failure of government" that imperils a free society.[4] This, of course, is the foundation of the first week of introductory economics. Rothbard wanted to make it universal in practice. It was a form of uber-privatization.

Milei sought to boost the private market by cutting thirty thousand government jobs, half of his government's agencies, and many government subsidies, all the while deregulating a broad collection of government services. Reporters called it "shock therapy" for the Argentine government. As the Trump team prepared to take office in late 2024, Milei's strategy seemed the perfect model. Vivek Ramaswamy, who for a short time headed Trump's "Department of Government Efficiency" with Elon Musk, said this was just what the United States needed: "A reasonable formula to fix the U.S. government: Milei-style cuts, on steroids."[5] Their enthusiasm for Milei's strategy, however, weakened as Milei's government wobbled, and the Trump administration weighed whether to intervene with the strength of the Argentine peso on the line.

The simultaneous rise of the right-wing in Argentina, Europe, and the United States followed a remarkably similar course. Economic security decreased. Worries about immigration increased. Conservatives wanted to crack down on migrants and boost private markets. In the United States, there was the flood of migrants across the southern border. For Europe, there was the big surge in migrants coming to the continent across the Mediterranean in shabby boats, through war zones on foot, and across Eastern Europe from climate and political crises in Africa and Afghanistan. Europe also struggled with the flood of more than 6.7 million refugees seeking to escape the war in Ukraine. These issues fueled the rise of right-wing rhetoric. Add to this the electoral success of Narendra Modi in India, Brazil's Jair Bolsonaro, and Israel's Benjamin Netanyahu. Argentina's Milei described himself as a "paleolibertarian," which would translate as "paleoconservative," in spirit of Pat Buchanan, who led an ideological movement in the US during the 1980s.

Behind these vast political movements lies an important fact: The right-wing movements in the United States and Europe ended up in very similar places, but they got there by taking very different paths.

The American right-wing took a circuitous course to the right-wing idea factory of the 2010s. Traditional conservatism had its base in classical liberalism, Burkean-style, with a focus on individual liberty, a belief in free-market capitalism, and a commitment to limited government. It was a foundation laid in the *decentralization of power:* in individuals, in markets, and in small government, with echoes of the cautious approach to governmental power advanced by at least some of the nation's founders. In the United States during the late 1990s, traditional conservatism wobbled and then crashed: in part because of the rising concern of much of the Republican Party faithful that free markets were leaving them behind, and in part because of a simple calculation that they needed different tactics to fight off Bill Clinton's clever efforts to outflank them.

Even in retrospect, it's impossible to disentangle Newt Gingrich's commitment to launching new policies from his blunt effort to wrest political control from Clinton. The rise of the RINO label—"Republicans in Name Only"—was not only a pejorative cast at Republicans espousing the values of the moderate tradition of their party. It was a declaration of independence from the party's free-market ideology, and it provided a runway from which to launch the new brand of the new right that Steve Bannon and others espoused. The right-wing emerged from that foundation. So, too, did a far more enthusiastic embrace of governmental power, even federal and executive power, aimed at advancing the social goals of the new conservatism. From that foundation came Donald Trump.

The right-wing in Europe grew along a different path, especially in rhetoric: a revolt *against the centralization* of power. It also emerged over a far longer time frame. Much of the story of Europe over the last millennium is a tale of efforts to wrest power away from the monarchy and the Catholic Church, which for centuries were often indistinguishable, especially in how they reinforced their efforts to centralize power. Through the Dark Ages, royal rule depended on the church not only because of shared religious beliefs but also because of ecclesiastical expertise. For a very long time, monks were the repository of knowledge. For centuries, they were the ones in society who knew how to read and write. Indeed, the Dark Ages weren't quite so dark as commonly supposed because of the illuminated manuscripts that the monks created and the Church sustained.

Cracks in that tradition began with the nobles who confronted King John at Runnymede in 1215 and forced him to sign the Magna Carta. Civics teachers, for generations, have pointed to the document as a foundation for fundamental rights. And it certainly was that. But more fundamentally, it was about political power, with John—and centralized power—coming out on the short end. That tension continued through the Middle Ages, with monarchs supported by the church (and vice versa). Monarchs allied with the Church and its preaching about eternal salvation. That linked their royal rule with the risk of eternal damnation for those who disobeyed the church's teachings, which made the church extraordinarily useful to monarchies across Europe.

For that matter, the Protestant Reformation was about much more than trying to force change on a reluctant Catholic Church, and King Henry VIII's quest for a divorce was only part of the reason for his break with Rome. The Reformation sought to shake the Church's firm grasp on political power; putting the Bible into the native tongue of the people was a profoundly decentralizing force. The people were no longer dependent on clerics to share the Gospel, and

Henry's creation of the Church of England gave him control over the realm's most powerful institution at a time when the power of the Catholic Church often rivaled that of the monarch, stretching as it did across national boundaries. These battles were about far more than Henry's vanity or the practice of religion. The Reformation, for Henry VIII and Martin Luther and other European-based reformers, was as much about political control as religion. Indeed, the translation of the Bible into the people's languages was vastly decentralizing. The invention of the printing press, which made it possible to put the vernacular Bible into the hands of ordinary people, weakened the control of the clergy and, ultimately, of the monarchies with which they were associated.

The Enlightenment fed on this quest to break the centralized power of the monarchy. Indeed, it was that theme that fed the American zeal for individual liberty. Britain's King George III might have been mad, but he clearly recognized the threat to the monarchy that the unruly American colonists posed. The French had already deposed Louis XVI. In Denmark, Greece, Ireland, Italy, the Netherlands, Poland, Prussia, Spain, and other countries, a restless public forced changes in the monarchy. It was what E. J. Hobsbawm called "the age of revolution."[6]

Europe, of course, had been the home of liberal democracy. Before the Enlightenment, and long before the American colonists declared themselves independent, monarchies dominated rule on the continent. In Britain, anti-royalists beheaded Charles I in 1649. Oliver Cromwell succeeded him, but he did not last long in power and died in 1658. The forces leading the Restoration so despised Cromwell that they dug up his body from Westminster Abbey, hanged it in chains, threw it into a pit, and then beheaded the corpse and put his head on a spike for almost twenty-five years. Exhibitors later purchased his head for public viewing, before it was finally buried again, this time in Cambridge. Americans might distrust their leaders, but they haven't mistreated even their most despised presidents like this.

Following this turmoil came British Enlightenment figures like John Locke and Jeremy Bentham. France had Montesquieu, Voltaire, and Jean-Jacques Rousseau. Together, they made a case for the natural rights of people, the evils of an authoritarian state, and the need for a functional democracy. Montesquieu, in particular, argued the importance of the rule of law, with political power applying to everyone—even kings—and that basic laws ought to guide the conduct of government.[7] These ideas spread throughout Europe and America as the foundation for what a good government ought to look like and the definition of "liberal democracy" ("liberal" because of its connection with liberty and freedom).

About the same time that traditional conservatism began to lose its foundation in the United States, especially during the 1980s, a "neoliberal" movement emerged in Europe based on a pro-private-economy approach. Britain's Margaret Thatcher won a reputation as the continent's "Iron Lady," a label ironically created by a Soviet journalist who certainly knew about iron rulers.[8] She championed a paring back of government and privatization that Ronald Reagan envied. After the global economic collapse in the late 1990s, that movement gained ground. But there were also massive government interventions to shore up the financial system, which, in turn, reinforced the instincts of government leaders to move back to traditional pro-government policies of the postwar era.[9] The public, however, did not share their enthusiasm for the corporate bailouts or for their leaders.

Reflecting what was happening during the 2010s in the United States, there was growing concern in Europe that these policies increased inequality, with benefits for the wealthy at the expense of the middle and working class. After accounting for inflation, wages often stayed flat at best. Poverty increased.[10] In most European countries, the middle class shrank by two-thirds from 2016 to 2021, and more people slid into the lower class.[11] Even in the twenty "happiest countries in the world" for 2024, the "happiness scores" of fifteen of the countries (derived by Gallup from a collection of economic, social, health, government corruption, and freedom indicators) fell from the year previous (and two of the countries could not be compared because there was no prior-year data).[12] These economic trends both mirrored and reinforced the broader right-wing movement around the world.

There was an erosion of faith in the legitimacy of democracy, a rise in identity politics, growing worries about immigration, and an increase in racism. Italy and Greece, which already had some of the continent's weaker economies, found themselves pressed to accommodate tens of thousands of migrants. In Eastern Europe, migrants desperate to reach new homes—at least to get into one European country to obtain the right to travel to others—entered through the long land border. In the UK, distant from the points of African migration, coastal towns worried about coping with the arrivals of small boats. And in the United States, as Steven Hahn pointed out in his sweeping review of the issue, waves of illiberalism have swept the country virtually since its beginning.[13]

The BBC reported that one bishop was "appalled" by a bill introduced in Parliament that would give the government power to remove anyone entering the UK illegally and to move them to a "safe country," according to the plan. The proposal, the bishop said, was devised because of the influx of "brown people."[14] Meanwhile, after a Saudi migrant plowed his car through a Christmas market in the German town of Magdeburg, the far-right party known as AfD (Alternative für Deutschland, or Alternative for Germany) held a rally that attracted thirty-five hundred people (and the support of Trump adviser Elon Musk). The party's leader said, "Anyone who despises—even kills—the citizens of the country that grants them asylum, anyone who despises everything we stand for, everything we love, does not belong to us." The crowd agreed, chanting "deportation" during the event.[15]

All these forces stimulated the rise of far-right parties. They pulled centrist parties to the right as well. In just the last months of 2024, the French National Assembly ousted Prime Minister Michel

Barnier in a vote of no confidence, and President Emmanuel Macron teetered on the edge as his longtime far-right opponent, Marine Le Pen, picked up support. Germany's government collapsed amid a national struggle over how to deal with a stagnant economy. The AfD gained ground as well. With support from neo-Nazis and a more radical position, the party was working against "the principle of democracy," German intelligence services concluded.[16] In Britain, the Tories suffered historic losses in the 2024 election, but the Reform UK party, led by Nigel Farage and taking an anti-immigrant stand, picked up support. The pro-democracy watchdog Freedom House said that "illiberalism established itself as the new normal in the region that stretches from Central Europe through Eurasia."[17]

Governments in Brazil, Hungary, India, and Poland saw the rise of radical right parties. The movement spread to Denmark, Bulgaria, Estonia, Italy, Slovakia, and the United Kingdom; from there, support for the right rose in Croatia, the Czech Republic, Finland, France, Germany, Hungary, Italy, the Netherlands, and Slovakia between the mid-2010s and the mid-2020s.[18] As Dutch scholar Cas Mudde pointed out, "The far right is closely connected to the political mainstream; and in more and more countries it is becoming the political mainstream." It's part of "the mainstreaming and normalization of the far right in general, and the populist radical right in particular."[19]

The European right did not have any think tanks as powerful as the Heritage Foundation, but it did have the Groupement de Recherche et d'Études pour la Civilisation Européenne (GRECE, for short, the Research and Study Group for European Civilization, founded in France). Under the leadership of Alain de Benoist, it carved out a philosophy for the *nouvelle droit* (the new right). GRECE championed opposition to European forms of woke policy, including multiculturalism; and opposition to more traditional forms of conservatism, including free-market capitalism and liberal democracy. De Benoist and others associated with GRECE, like Guillaume Faye, worked hard to establish a European far right, in ways like some far-right American organizations. They argued the case for "ethnopluralism," or protecting regional identities as defined by traditional cultures. This, of course, was a direct attack on the unity principles of the European Union. The European far right is very, very different from the American far right in other ways, too, including an explicit rejection of Christianity and even an embrace of "neopaganism." If the American right argued for Christianity as a way of promoting what it saw as traditional American values, the anti-religious foundation of GRECE could be seen as a rejection of traditional European values, especially the traditional power of the Catholic Church and the monarchy.

From this base, the European far right advanced. Klaus von Beyme traced the story from the end of World War II through three waves of far-right politics.[20] From 1945 to 1955, there was neo-fascism, as elements of the movement that helped drive Europe to war fought a rear-guard action in a fight to avoid being marginalized. In the second wave, between 1955 and 1980, right-wing groups struggled to oppose the elites that arose in the postwar world. From 1980 to 2000, a third wave emerged, driven by worries about immigration and unemployment and worries about jobs. Populist right-wing movements began to emerge, Mudde explained, especially with authoritarian, nativist, and populist themes. It was at this point that the far right in the United States began to connect with the far-longer, much-deeper movement in Europe, especially in Pat Buchanan's "paleoconservatism."

Mudde outlined the fourth phase, which developed after 2000. Many of the old issues bubbled up, especially the immigration-authoritarian-populism themes. What most distinguishes this fourth wave, he says, "is the mainstreaming of the far right." Ideas that would have been barely acceptable in the decades before came to drive the ideas of major political parties. Moreover, he said, the movement has seen "a dizzying array of new far-right parties" that gained leverage over public policy, especially in a tough stand against immigration. The boundaries between the far right and the more traditional right have become far more fuzzy and much less meaningful.[21] As he notes, the rise of the right-wing has seen a rejection of the traditional values of liberal democracy, of the pursuit of an egalitarian society, and of the embrace of international alliances. It even opposes the democratic election of leaders based on majority vote. It has focused on nationalism, authoritarianism, order, and discipline. However, it did not do so with a movement toward homogenization. It splintered into groups, all heading in roughly the same direction but without strong coherence or coordination.[22] It piled up significant electoral successes around the world, topped, of course, by the Trump restoration in 2024.

The European far-right activists leapt to their position long before those in the United States, who coalesced around the Tea Party and other early members of the far right in the early 2010s. As the decade moved along, however, the paths of the European and American far right converged. Big themes emerged: the complaints from the middle and lower classes about being left behind; the blame and xenophobia heaped on migrants; the rejection of the quest for equality as a failed proposition of the "woke" left; dismissal of engagement with other countries; and streaks of authoritarianism, coupled with refusal to embrace the rule of law and the separation of governmental powers. Themes were similar, but the groups behind them were often very different, especially in Europe.

Americans came late to the far right, but they soon dominated it. Alice Weidel, co-chair of AfD, called Trump's 2024 election a repudiation of "woke Hollywood" and the left-leaning policies its actors embraced. For Hungarian Prime Minister Viktor Orbán, Trump's win was "a much-needed victory for the World!"[23] The far right had become like the Hydra, the multi-headed monster from Greek mythology, which proved almost impossible to kill (until Hercules brought in reinforcements from his nephew). Analysts began to worry about "democratic backsliding" in Europe, which expanded into "a rapid, wholesale unraveling of the post-1989 political order in Europe" that saw the fall of communism in Eastern Europe.[24]

The modern European right-wing movement began to form much earlier, immediately after World War II. It was a continuing echo of the fascism that rocked the continent during the 1930s and 1940s. The roots of its rebellion were deep, going back to the centralization of power in monarchs and religion during the Dark Ages. It explicitly rejected the internationalism that was an initial goal and major contribution of postwar Europe. And, unlike the predominance of major right-wing think tanks in the United States, idea factories were relatively rarer and weaker in Europe. In the United States, by contrast, the right-wing movement did not gain a solid political foothold until the early 2010s, with an explicit rejection of the decentralizing forces of market power and individual freedom derived from the Enlightenment. As mentioned earlier, it also rejected traditional Republicans—RINOs—and "woke" Democrats, although it came to share the anti-internationalism of the European right-wing movement (see Table 7.1).

Rising Populism and Declining Trust

Two trends emerged in the 2010s: rising populism, which disrupted long-lasting traditions and deep-seated values; and declining trust in government, not just in the United States but around the world. The decline of trust in American government is legendary, but the problem became a global one, a trend often missed by Americans.

The global communications firm Edelman has conducted an annual assessment of trust across twenty-five countries since 2000. In its 2012 survey, Edelman found that trust in the twenty-five large countries it surveyed suffered an unprecedented decline.[25] In half of the countries, government had become less trusted than business, media, and nongovernmental organizations, and more countries became "distrusters" than "trusters." The surveys showed that citizens did not trust government to do what was right. The economic collapse in 2008–2009 led to a global recession as well as to the collapse

TABLE 7.1 A Comparison of the Right-Wing Agenda in Europe and the United States

	Europe	United States
Areas of divergence		
Emergence of the right wing	Shortly after World War II	In the 2010s
Rejected historical tradition	Dark Ages	Enlightenment
Rejected philosophical tradition	Centralization of power in monarchs and religion	Decentralization of power in markets
Rebellion against	Post-world war internationalism	Traditional Republicans, "woke" Democrats, and internationalism
Think tank support	Weak, but ideas from GRECE	Strong, including organizations like Heritage Foundation
Areas of convergence		
Traditional policies rejected	Liberal democracy, egalitarian society, international alliances, checks and balances	Liberal democracy, egalitarian society, international alliances, checks and balances
New idea emerging	Paleoconservatism	Paleoconservatism
Motivating problems	Pocketbook issues, immigration	Pocketbook issues, immigration
Outcome	Mainstreaming of far right	Mainstreaming of far right
Emerging risk	Authoritarianism	Authoritarianism

of global companies like Lehman Brothers and AIG. Governments everywhere stepped in with bailouts. "But in 2011," Edelman concluded, "government became paralyzed by the politics of extremism and endless haggling—and the public lost confidence."[26] Distrust was also shaking American politics, but, as Edelman found, in surveys of distrust the United States fell in the middle in 2012, below Brazil and Sweden but just above South Korea and Poland. (In a finding sure to stun most Americans, China was at the top, being the most trusted, and was followed by the United Arab Emirates, Singapore, and India.)

By 2024, government across the world was seen as far less competent and ethical than business. Nearly two-thirds of people feared that "government leaders [were] purposely trying to mislead people by saying things they know are false or cross exaggerations."[27] The United States had fallen further, sandwiched below Ireland and Spain and above Germany and South Korea—twenty-third of twenty-eight countries in that year's survey on governments' competence and ethics. China, meanwhile, remained at the top, with its trust index score even rising three points, while the US score dropped three points.[28]

Mixing with declining trust in government was shrinking trust in experts, especially government experts. In 2024, governments around the world were seen as much less ethical and competent than business, with its "competence" scoring twice as poorly as its "ethics." When Edelman conducted its survey, it asked individuals across the globe how much they trusted different groups to tell the truth. For government, 45 percent trusted government, and only 47 percent trusted journalists. Trust in scientists was much better— 74 percent. But, in a true surprise, precisely the same share of respondents said that they trusted "someone like me" just as much as scientists. Authority had become so dispersed—or, perhaps, so weakened—that friends and neighbors had acquired as much trust as scientific experts.

Much of the problem flowed from the people's conviction that science had become politicized, with 53 percent around the globe agreeing with that statement. In the United States, the number was 67 percent, the same as in China. Around the world, 59 percent of respondents thought that government regulators did not have enough understanding of emerging technologies to regulate them effectively. Here, the United States was worse yet again, with 63 percent believing that government didn't have enough capacity. When it came to rejection of innovation (for issues like green energy, AI, gene-based medicine, and GMO foods), 27 percent of those on the right around the world rejected innovation. There was a seven-point spread between the Left and the Right. In the United States, the problem yet again was worse, with the spread between Right and Left almost twice as great as the next-highest country, Australia. In the United States, 12 percent of those on the left distrusted innovation, compared with 20 percent of those on the left around the world. On the right, more than half—53 percent—rejected innovation. That was twice as high as rightists around the world.

The American sense of profound distrust, which often seems large and unique, is in fact a near-universal problem. Trust in government was at 51 percent across the twenty-eight countries in Edelman's 2024 survey. On the other hand, broadly shared trust problems are often significantly worse in the United States, especially in the spread across ideological lines. Trust in American government was at 40 percent, eleven points below the global average and just half the level of the most-trusted governments (Saudi Arabia, China, and the United Arab Emirates). In a faint bit of good news, however, the United States wasn't at the bottom of the surveys.

A second longitudinal survey, conducted by the Organization for Economic Cooperation and Development (OECD), produced similar results, with 39 percent of those surveyed in 2023 trusting their national government.[29] Those who felt financially insecure, who had lower levels of education, as well as women and the young, tended to have lower levels of trust. The most important factor by far, however, was "having a say in government actions."[30]

The OECD concluded that this lack of trust damaged democracy because "democracies require citizen trust in government to function effectively." The report also suggested that the problem was worsening. "Countries face a crisis of trust which becomes increasingly concerning amid economic downturns, health emergencies and other crises." Indeed, the OECD argued, "Low trust environments are a threat to effective democratic governance in light of evolving global challenges."[31] If democracy is a goal—and strengthening democracy has been a central goal for the United States since its founding and for many of the world's countries for generations—trust is essential. Crises—health, economic, social—have eroded that trust, as has confidence in government's ability to tackle them successfully. No country has escaped. It's little wonder, therefore, that no country has been able to escape the crisis of trust. Moreover, the problems of mistrust have spilled over into the basics of government capacity, including reliance on experts. Trust has become a partisan issue, eroding on the right faster than on the left, for countries around the world.

Leaking Trust

In the United States, this has led to surprising votes of no confidence in democracy itself. In April 2024, the convention of Washington State Republicans debated a resolution to repeal the Seventeenth Amendment, passed in 1913, and take away voters' power to elect US senators. Such a move would return Washington to the days when the state legislature chose senators. Those supporting the resolution cited the Federalist Papers, contending that this was what James Madison had in mind.[32]

But then things got weird. "We are devolving into a democracy, because congressmen and senators are elected by the same pool," one delegate said. "We do not want to be a democracy." This wasn't a slip of the tongue—the platform really did warn about the devolution of the United States into a "democracy." The party passed a resolution that said, "The Republican Party is the party of limited, Constitutional government, and the Democratic Party promotes progressivism and socialism." (This point ignores the fact, of course, that most of the early Progressives, including leaders like Theodore Roosevelt, were Republicans. This was a time before "progressive" flipped its meaning from "good government" to "liberal government" and when its leaders became Democrats instead of Republicans.) Then, the resolution continued, "Every time the word 'democracy' is used favorably it serves to promote the principles of the Democratic Party, the principles of which we ardently oppose." So, the resolution resolved, "We encourage Republicans to substitute the words 'republic' and 'republicanism' where previously they have used the word 'democracy.'" They opposed "legislation which makes our nation more 'democratic' in nature." To back up their argument, they quoted John Adams: "Democracy . . . while it lasts is more bloody than either aristocracy or monarchy. Remember, democracy never lasts long. It soon wastes, exhausts, and murders itself. There is never a democracy that did not commit suicide."[33]

How did the party end up opposed to *democracy*, with a conscious effort to wrap itself in quotations from Adams to support a position he had fought with all his vigor to reject? In the twenty-first century, democracy had been taking its lumps on social media. One Instagram post, for example, contended that "the ideal of a democracy is universal equality. The ideal of a constitutional republic is individual liberty."[34] Another stated, "The United States is a constitutional republic not a democracy. There is a difference." To which another user replied, "True—Today DNC/CCP goal is to strip of us of our individual liberty and make we the people serfs" (with DNC presumably standing for the Democratic National Committee and CCP referring to the Chinese Communist Party).[35] Many members of the right-wing reject some of the country's most fundamental values.

And as for the invocation of John Adams, they don't quite get his worries right. In a letter he wrote in 1814 to John Taylor, he relied on the lessons of history, going from the ancients to the more recent struggles of French democracy, to contend that no form of government could eliminate the pathologies that flow from human nature. In fact, he took on Taylor's suggestion that "Democracy is more pernicious than Monarchy or Aristocracy," asking in the letter, "Is this fair, sir?" He went on to say that violence had often troubled democracies, from the plebians sacrificed in ancient times, to the Inquisition, the burning of the US Capitol by British Army General Robert Ross during the War of 1812, and the French Revolution. "Oh! my soul!" he wrote. "I am weary of these dismal Contemplations! When will Mankind listen to reason, to nature or to Revelation?" The problem came from the very nature of man, because "Those Passions are the same in all Men under all forms of Simple Government, and when unchecked, produce the same Effects of Fraud Violence and Cruelty." Adams wasn't attacking democracy but bemoaning the sad instinct of humans to resort to destructive violence, no matter the form of government over them.[36] But that fuller reading of Adams and his letter escaped the conventioneers in Washington State back in 2024.

The state party's stand against democracy brought it ridicule. The *Seattle Times* ran a story with the headline, "The WA GOP put it in writing that they're not into democracy."[37] On the left, Rachel Maddow said on her MSNBC television show that "taking an overt anti-democracy stance kind of with an exclamation point is among other things going to get you national headlines."[38]

But the Washington Republican 2024 platform was in sync with arguments that had been appearing on the right for several years. A 2016 post from the conservative Hoover Institution was titled "The Mob Is Coming for You: Our Society Is Transforming from an Orderly Republic into a Wild and Radical Democracy." The author, Victor Davis Hanson, traced the debate back to the ancients. "The Romans knew enough about mercurial ancient Athens," he wrote, "to appreciate that they did not want a radical democracy. Instead, they sought to take away absolute power from the people and redistribute it within a 'mixed' government." He added, "Transitory manias are also common in democratic society."[39] More broadly, however, research by James Druckman, Samara Klar, Yanna Krupnikov, Matthew Levendusky, and John Barry Ryan concluded that partisan hostility was eroding the fundamentals of democracy and, over time, could erode democratic institutions.[40] Druckman said he was fearful of "the normalization of what can devolve into dehumanizing, inciting rhetoric." He warned, "It has consequences for what people think of democracy."[41]

That led to a fundamental tension between the quest for political power and the pursuit of democratic values. To what degree was the right-wing willing to sacrifice—or distort—those values in the pursuit of its ideological agenda and of the policy preferences of its members? To what degree were those values more important than the rule of law and the broader, more fundamental view of accountability—an approach to accountability that went beyond personal loyalty to the leader of a party or the political values that leader represented? That is part of the much larger story of the erosion of traditional conservatism, which I'll take up in the next chapter.

Chapter 8

The Death of Traditional Conservatism

Barack Obama might have challenged the Democratic Party with his rousing "Yes We Can" campaign in 2008 but as, David DiSalvo contended in *Forbes*, that turned into "Let's take a nap."[1] The left-wing had a big success with the 2010 passage of Obama's Affordable Care Act but many of its most thoughtful members quietly admitted that the movement had gradually lost its mojo until, ultimately, it collapsed in the 2024 presidential election. The downward slide of the Left helped the upward glide of the Right.

Within the Right, there was a constant struggle for the steering wheel. There was Bannon's social conservatism, Musk's hardcharging capitalism, Deneen's regime change, Vance's economic nationalism, and Vought's Christian nationalism. That made it hard to describe just what the right-wing ideology truly was. This fuzziness of core beliefs, however, was truly a feature, not a bug. The right-wing idea factory did not try to build just one boat but a fleet of related ones, often (but not always) sailing in the same direction. They shared their antipathy for the Left and their eagerness to upset the reign of progressive ideas since the administration of Franklin D. Roosevelt. They also shared some surprising common ground, both in religious (often Catholic) roots and their evangelical fury in rooting out the power of the "woke" left, which they believed had burrowed deeply into the nation's social and political institutions.

Traditional conservatives, nurtured in the long tradition from Cato through Burke to Buckley and Reagan, had withered away.[2] Indeed, if the Reagan administration marked the high point of classical liberalism and free-market economics, the second Trump administration was the triumph of the populist forces that (mostly) rejected these fundamentals of conservatism.

Is There a Bedrock Base to Conservatism?

For a long time, conservatives pointed to history both to shape and to justify their beliefs. When the US Supreme Court upturned the precedent legalizing abortion in the 2020 case, *Dobbs v. Jackson*, Justice Samuel Alito's majority opinion argued that the original case, *Roe v. Wade* (1973), was "wrongly decided," because "The Constitution makes no express reference to a right to obtain an abortion." In fact, he said, until shortly before *Roe*, abortion was a crime in all the states. Therefore, he contended, "A right to abortion is not deeply rooted in the Nation's history and traditions." But in a stinging dissent, Justice Elena Kagan wrote for two other colleagues in suggesting that Alito was selective in quoting from history.

> The majority could write just as long an opinion showing, for example, that until the mid-20th century, "there was no support in American law for a constitutional right to obtain [contraceptives]." So one of two things must be true. Either the majority does not really believe in its own reasoning. Or if it does, all rights that have no history stretching back to the mid-19th century are insecure. Either the mass of the majority's opinion is hypocrisy, or additional constitutional rights are under threat. It is one or the other.

She pointed to precedents in medical practice and legal argument that went back to the thirteenth century. Even though they had a long history, she was not convinced they should have any power over the treatment of disease today.[3]

To the Left's dismay, the right-wing increasingly answered this question by wrapping its approach around the founders, as they saw it. The right-wing sought to identify basic traditions that could guide its movement—or, more often, to identify its social and economic values and find basic traditions to support them. In shoring up its case, the right-wing read selectively into history to find words to support its position even though the original words of the founders often defy efforts to derive clear meaning. They deliberately built ambiguity in as a way of cobbling together a fragile unity. The founders, moreover, would surely be stunned at the pace of innovation that has occurred since, although it is easy to imagine Benjamin Franklin as an earlier adopter of every new smartphone produced.

But it is equally difficult to imagine Franklin and the other founders being alarmed with Elon Musk's chainsaw at a rally for obliterating large parts of American government? Argentine President Javier Milei had the chainsaw engraved, "Viva la libertad, carajo," which translates to "Long live liberty, damn it." Musk replied, "This is the chainsaw for bureaucracy."[4] The founders were revolutionaries, but they did not take glee in wielding dangerous garage tools. Even more important, they fought with a deep reverence for government and its value for securing values on behalf of "we the people."

Neither the chainsaw metaphor nor Musk's enthusiasm was accidental. Two years before, Alana Newhouse had written about what she called "brokenism." The fundamental divisions in American society, she said, were no longer between Democrats and Republicans or liberals and conservatives. Rather, "The most vital debate in America today is between those who believe there is something fundamentally broken in America, and that it's an emergency, and those who do not." She suggested that what might have developed was a manifestation of the "horseshoe theory," in which the left and right extremes share more with each other than with centrists. Covid had helped fuel this line of thought, and it was driving major changes in American politics.[5]

Newhouse was mostly right. There was indeed a large collection of people on both the right and the left convinced that America was broken. The Right, however, proved far more successful in building a political case around it, in supporting Donald Trump's argument for "American carnage," and then using brokenness to drive the second-term agenda of disrupting much of American government and, under Musk's leadership, destroying whole parts of it. The approach resonated with many Americans, who did not like much of what they saw and were willing to burn government down. In a 2024 Ipsos poll, 62 percent of Americans said they believed that the system was broken, a higher rate than in Great Britain and an average of twenty-eight other countries in its survey. Satisfaction with how democracy worked was lower in the United States than in the UK, France, Italy, Poland, and Sweden, and barely higher than in Croatia. In its index of polarization, the United States had gone from a score of 6 in 1977 to 34 in 2021.[6] The result for the country, as political scientist David Dagan contended, was "the great demolition," with Trump seeking "to tear it down to a degree that has no parallel in American history."[7]

Behind the stunning rise of Trumpism was a shadowy world of tech bros and a collection of venture capitalists like Marc Andreessen, who helped create Mosaic, the first web browser that allowed creators to insert graphics on a web page instead of bouncing users to a separate window. He later co-founded Netscape, which replaced Mosaic before Microsoft's Internet Explorer replaced it, only to have Google Chrome replace them all. Andreessen went on to co-found Andreessen-Horowitz, one of the top venture capital firms in the world. There was Sriram Krishnan, who left his partnership at Andreessen-Horowitz to become a senior adviser on artificial intelligence in the Trump White House in 2025, and Erik Torenberg, a high-tech entrepreneur. The coalition of these tech bros was "the single most important place in which a stunning realignment toward Donald Trump was shaped and negotiated," according to Ben Smith on Semafor.[8] They created the "power group chats" that became part "Republic of Letters," as one participant called it, referring to the seventeenth-century culture of intellectual discourse through long pieces of correspondence, much like the exchanges between Jefferson and Madison—except in real time and at lightning speed.

The tech bros, along with most of Silicon Valley, had always leaned hard to the left and supported Democratic causes. That changed in the early 2020s as "the tech community was feeling alienated" by New York City left-leaning critics of tech. "Tech was now an island, with few friends in either the red or blue tents, yet its expansion continued and soon it owned the world," wrote one self-described "San Francisco geek."[9] The Left was opposed to the accumulation of big power that came with great size and wealth. Robby Soave concluded in right-leaning *Reason*, "The tech bros love Trump because the Democrats pushed them away."[10] That led to the remarkable sight of a large group of tech bros at Trump's 2025 inauguration, including Meta's Mark Zuckerberg, Amazon's Jeff Bezos, Google's Sundar Pichai, and Elon Musk, who ran Tesla, SpaceX, and the social media site X.

The Signal group "Chatham House" was the center of most of the conversations, "which have fueled a new alliance of tech and the US right," Smith explained. Named after the famed British think tank, the Chatham House Signal group grew out of the debates over Covid-19, when the Left tended to dominate social media as well as the policy debates about how best to manage the pandemic. Those not part of the progressive mainstream felt isolated, Andreessen and others explained, so they took their conversations underground on Signal, with settings that often deleted chats in a very short period. As Erik Torenberg, a tech entrepreneur, explained, "People during 2020 felt that there was a monoculture on social media, and if they didn't agree with something, group chats became a safe space to debate that, share that, build consensus, feel that you're not alone." There was a sense of censorship, participants agreed, in which those with other views were neither respected nor heard. That ignited the tech bro conversations on Signal, where the Chatham House group grew to three hundred members.

Noah Smith, a Substack author, posted on X, which had formerly been the social media site Twitter, "Group chats are now where everything important and interesting happens."[11] Discussions included Joe Lonsdale, an entrepreneur, venture capitalist, and co-founder of the University of Austin, a small, private university focused on a "great books" curriculum and resistance to what he believed was the dominance of universities by the Left. Participants in other debates were Vivek Ramaswamy, who worked with Elon Musk on DOGE for a time; Mark Cuban, minority owner of the National Basketball Association's Dallas Mavericks and one of the "sharks" on the television show *Shark Tank*; Chris Rufo, who led the intellectual movement against woke education; and Curtis Yarvin, whose ideas reinforced those of Russell Vought and Elon Musk.

Smith described a manic pace to many of these Signal chats, with Andreessen following scores of chats simultaneously. "How does he have the time?" one participant asked, only half-jokingly wondering how many hours of keeping up with the chats left for sleep. Private group chats became singularly important, Krishnan wrote before joining the White House, because "group chats rule the world." He blogged, "Being part of the right group chat can feel like having a peek at the kitchen of a restaurant but instead of food, messy ideas and gossip fly about in real time, get mixed, remixed, discarded, polished before they show up in a prepared fashion in public."[12] As political journalist Mark Halperin said, "The left seems largely unaware that some of the smartest and most sophisticated Trump supporters in the nation from coast to coast are part of an overlapping set of text chains that allow their members to share links, intel, tactics, strategy, and ad hoc assignments."[13]

Traditional conservatism grew, indeed thrived, on public debates. They often politically played from behind, but some like William Buckley seemed to thrive on it. In part, that flowed from the fact that they were convinced, deep down, that they had the winning hand, and it flowed, in part, from their taste for intellectual combat, a sport at which they often were very good. Traditional conservatives invariably were out front with their views. The new right-wing conservatives, however, were happy to cede the public limelight to the Left, whose members often seemed to them humorless, overly earnest, and tiresome, focused on what Rufo said was "infinite discourse" instead of action. The tech bros, in contrast, had developed an "illiberal worldview," one "more concerned with power than speech," as Smith put it.[14]

The new right-wing spent a great deal of its time developing new policy ideas, sharing and debating them with each other, and honing them to the point of a spear that could be used in acquiring power. They already were masters of the tech universe, as captains of great private companies and holders of more money than they could reasonably spend. The core tenets of illiberalism were impatience with the separation of powers, distrust of the media, and a view of elections as a tactic to rationalize the consolidation of power.

The tech bros systematically disassembled Francis Fukuyama's contention in *The End of History and the Last Man* that globalization made liberal democracy ascendant, pushing aside illiberal forces.[15] Instead, the tech bros and their invitation-only Signal chats created a powerful but largely invisible engine driving the shift from traditionalism to Trumpism.

The Elements of the Right-Wing Idea Factory

Behind this shift were eight basic elements.

1. *Big dark money.* The new right-wing would have been impossible without the US Supreme Court's 2010 decision in *Citizens United.* The premise was simple: Money was speech, speech could not be limited, and so, therefore, campaign contributions to political campaigns and public issues could not be limited either. The promise was balanced: It applied to both left-leaning groups like

unions and right-leaning groups like corporations. And since people engaged in speech did not have to post a notice in advance, except perhaps to get a parade permit when their speech might interfere with traffic, organizations involved in campaign or issue spending should not have to do so either. The only limits on expenditures could come through a clear (or apparent) quid pro quo deal, where an organization extracted a promise of policy action in exchange for a contribution. In turn, that meant the easiest way to stay on the safe side of the line was to ensure that the contributions had no coordination with a political campaign. And although it created a game anyone could play, conservatives proved far better at it: They had more donors with deep pockets, and those donors were willing to give big and often.

But the game was not just *big* money. It was also *dark* money. The Court's contortions in *Citizens United* exempted all donors from reporting the source, amount, or purpose of their contributions. That not only created a powerful influence on big policies. It helped fuel the big right-wing think tanks, including the groups that had sprung up after Trump's 2020 election defeat. It also made possible large-scale funding to influence state policy. For example, in 2021, two anonymous gifts to the Donors Trust of more than $425 million each in turn supported conservative groups like Leonard Leo's "The 85 Fund." The money went to promote restrictions on abortion, reduce voter fraud, redistricting that favored Republican candidates, and a variety of other conservative causes.[16] In Texas, Governor Greg Abbott received large contributions to support his school choice program from Jeff Yass, a Pennsylvania billionaire.[17] Billionaires from West Texas's oil country, Tim Dunn, Farris Wilks, and Dan Wilks, poured millions more into the fight.[18] The contributions paid off when the Texas legislature approved the choice plan in its 2025 session. Money prodigiously flowed, but the only pathway to determining where the money came from was deep digging by reporters. Not only did big ideas emerge, but the fuel driving them on was impossible to measure at scale.

2. *Policy pivots.* One notable feature of traditional conservatism was the relative stability of its big issues. The Republican Party Platform of 1980, for example, featured proposals for tax cuts, deregulation, more defense spending, a balanced budget, and rolling back communism. Reagan's platform was similar in many ways to what Dwight D. Eisenhower's Republican Party laid out in 1952. Some of those old chestnuts remained in the 2010s and 2020s—most notably, proposals for more tax cuts—but the right-wing idea factory often pivoted as new issues promised new opportunities for new political wins.

In the last weeks of a very close US Senate campaign in 2024, for example, incumbent Ted Cruz (R-Texas) began a television ad campaign telling voters, "Boys and girls: They're different." Cruz said that his Democratic opponent, Collin Allred, wanted to put boys on girls' sports teams. Allred put up his own ad denying the charge. Republicans were very happy with the outcome; Cruz opened a lead that lasted through Election Day. "Republicans have not figured out how to win parts of the culture war where Democrats are out of step with the American people," proclaimed the head of the American Principles Project, a right-wing advocacy group. It was not a big issue in Texas, since the number of Americans who identified as trans constituted less than 1 percent of the population and, in any event, the state legislature had already made the issue moot with a ban on athletes playing on teams with teammates who were not all of the same sex assigned at birth. Terry Schilling, the head of the American Principles Project, was pleased with the outcome. There had been a battle in North Carolina over trans access to bathrooms, but the issue didn't work any longer when conventions walked away and the Republican governor lost. "So then we pivoted to the sports issue," Schilling said. "It's been wildly successful."[19] The right-wing increasingly sought to figure out which issues produced political strength and went to them. The pivot defined the core tactical approach.

3. *Acceleration.* Following closely on the policy pivots was the acceleration of the right-wing assembly line. The pattern was clearest

at the federal level with Trump's second term, where new policies flew out of the White House at a stunning pace, in part to avoid the administration's fear of running out of time as it did in the first term and in part to feed Musk's "move fast/break things" instinct from Silicon Valley, at least during his brief time there. The idea factories at the state and local levels did not move nearly so fast; their political environments were very different. But at the federal level during Trump's second term, one of the strongest imperatives was ensuring that nothing was left undone at the end of the presidency. The administration felt the ultimate need for speed.

Social media helped drive the movement forward, and Facebook proved especially attractive to the rank and file, while X was the platform for the movement's leaders. Compared with the Left, the right-wing had a distinct social media advantage. It stimulated "hashtag activism," which favored right-wing causes and which, in turn, spread right-wing ideas more rapidly because ideas tended to be viewed and shared more often. In fact, the authors of one 2022 study found there was a consistent pattern of "amplification of the right" that favored the faster spread of right-wing ideas.[20] Social media helped rioters organize for the January 6, 2021, assault on the US Capitol. Social media helped radicalize the rioters and then, when they discovered that law enforcement officials had begun to penetrate their social media platforms, they migrated to less-well-known or more private platforms to evade monitoring.[21] All of these factors accelerated the development of the right-wing idea factory.

4. *Clusters.* Differences in policy among the American states are older than the states themselves. Slavery was obviously the premier example, but the states also diverged between mercantile and agricultural interests, between coastal and inland towns, and between large and small communities. These differences almost prevented the colonies from becoming the United States and very nearly drove the North and South into irreconcilable countries. Big differences persisted through the twentieth century, especially on matters of race.

The right-wing idea factories of the 2010s, however, clustered states very differently. Ideas sometimes bubbled into the states from think tanks but, more often, they came from the populist and grass-roots energy of residents, often after problems created rage that demanded response. This energy often began from the most local of steps, from local school boards and businesspeople, but residents often found allies in other communities. These clusters fed the new movement, in very different ways than the old splits among the states. In many states, shared interests among activists spilled across the states, from abortion to book banning to school choice. These issues clustered within states, and then issues spilled across state boundaries, and that generated new clusters. The issue clusters, in turn, made the United States less united.

The United States lagged other countries in launching the right-wing idea factory, but once the movement got rolling, right-wing leaders in other countries looked to the United States for leadership. These global clusters, in turn, fed a far broader movement.

5. *Quality control.* The right-wing idea factory produced a host of new policy thoughts and a great deal of new policy actions. If ideas were the plan and money was the fuel, was there any real quality control in the factory? A consequence of the speed with which the idea factory produced new work—and often changed it—was that those running the factory rarely stopped to assess the results it produced. Ideas mattered more than impact. Process, not product, was sovereign. The incentives were to generate new ideas and to use those ideas to build political support. It was a movement, therefore, without quality control and where the measure of impact lay in the political power it produced—not the policy results it generated.

6. *Anti-intellectualism.* There was, in addition, a heavy anti-expert tone to most of the right-wing idea factory's rhetoric. From the earliest days of the country, populists have never trusted experts. In making the case for the national assumption of state Revolutionary War debts, Hamilton had to fight against populists who were convinced that his plan was just a move to fatten big-city bankers.

Agrarians constantly struggled for cheap money on easy terms, which was the last thing their lenders wanted. When it came to the grassroots activists, all that mattered was the problem on the doorstep, whether it was a Covid shutdown that didn't make sense or books that ran against deep-seated values. In both threads, the underlying theme was that people did not want experts telling them what to do: Because they did not trust the experts, they believed that the experts were more interested in enhancing their own power at the people's expense, or because they believed more in their own common sense, however uninformed.

The anti-intellectual core of Trumpism ran even deeper. It grew from a fundamental rejection of traditional conservatism, since right-wingers were unconvinced it had served them or their party well. And it blossomed from a rejection of elites and knowledge workers who seemed to be winning the economic game when they were not. It was class warfare, twenty-first-century style. "The target of the administration's campaign is a stratum of society sometimes called the professional managerial class," as Franklin Foer put it.[22]

The professional class found itself on Trump's hit list: scientists doing esoteric research with grants funded through the public dole; journalists who seemed to be peddling ideas that didn't match the views of news consumers, except for those watching Fox; high-powered law firms with highly paid attorneys; university professors who seemed distant from the reality of the lives of too many Americans and who supposedly spent their time indoctrinating children in woke-left opinions; and Ivy League universities in particular, with deep endowments and too many haughty administrators (all, at least, in the view of those in MAGA world). The revolt of the masses against the elites, of course, is a well-practiced part of political revolution, from the Protestant Reformation and its battle against the Catholic Church to Mao Zedong's Great Proletarian Cultural Revolution of the 1960s and 1970s, which sent intellectuals to work in the fields and factories. The right-wing has counterattacked the intellectual class at major universities by creating new centers of citizenship, including those at Arizona State University, the University of Florida, the University of North Carolina at Chapel Hill, the University of Tennessee, Knoxville, and the University of Texas at Austin

The revolt against intellectuals made the right-wing idea factory even more powerful because it pushed back against the elites and simultaneously offered a broad collection of big new ideas that gained substantial public traction.

7. *Trickle-up*. The Reagan tax cuts of 1981 and 1986 gained the unflattering label of "trickle-down economics," although the label itself came from the Hoover administration and its hope that money in the economy would flow down to the neediest people in society just as water flowed downhill, as Hoover, an engineer, knew very well. The ideas of the right-wing idea factory, however, tended to trickle up. Both the populists and grassroots tried out new ideas, kept what resonated, and tossed the others out. The well-financed national conservative organizations set their radar screens to deep scan, looking for new ideas they could champion.

There was no better way of developing these ideas than to see what market tests in local communities found. Big fast-food chains test new products in smaller markets to see what sells and how they can best tweak new sandwiches and sides. Communities like Cincinnati, Indianapolis, Nashville, and Jacksonville sometimes give consumers a taste of what's coming across the rest of the country. So, too, this has been the case for products from the right-wing idea factory. Of course, these test markets don't always produce good results. "New Coke" and "Crystal Pepsi" both tested well but failed nationally. Wow! potato chips offered less fat and fewer calories, but their manufacturer pulled them from the market when too many consumers developed serious indigestion from eating the chips. Some products from local right-wing idea factories had similar problems. Repeated calls to reform the Federal Emergency Management Agency (FEMA) by pushing its functions to the state government have failed when states did not have the capacity to deal with big disasters like Hurricane Katrina's assault on the Gulf Coast in 2005. In the United Kingdom, Brexit in 2020 failed to live up to the promise of pro-growth anti–European Union Britons. But local market tests, especially through American federalism, proved invaluable for stimulating a new conservative agenda.

8. *The trust trap*. There's a difficult paradox hardwired into the workings of the right-wing idea factory. On one hand, the public's declining trust in public institutions not only became legendary but also helped fuel the factory. A 2013 poll couldn't resist having some fun with this deadly serious problem. It found that Congress was less popular than Brussels sprouts, used-car salesmen, Genghis Khan, colonoscopies, and head lice, although it was nearly a tossup with cockroaches.[23] Research has shown, however, that popularity and trust tend to build from the experiences people have in their interactions with things and others—and government programs. At the *retail* level of interaction, people judge government by how well it works for them, on a case-by-case, program-by-program basis.[24] The management consulting firm McKinsey found that a 1 percent increase in the satisfaction of people in their interactions with government led to a 2 percent increase in trust.[25] That's a positive sign that smart government officials can make progress against one of the government's most important yet difficult problems.

However, the most important products of the factory were the big ideas, from a pushback against Covid closures to the creation of government-funded school choice programs. Virtually none of the ideas, however, focused on the results that they produced. It was the concept that mattered—new votes or new programs that ratified the underlying ideas of the right-wing. The factory relied on public distrust to feed its work, but its operations did very little to increase trust, and, in fact, by ignoring the link between ideas and results, it always risked making distrust worse.

TABLE 8.1 Right-Wing Think Tanks

	Founded	Type of nonprofit	Revenue $millions (2022)
Heritage Foundation	1973	501(c)(3)	106.0
Cato Institute	1975	501(c)(3)	57.7
America First Legal	2021	501(c)(3)	44.4
Federalist Society	1983	501(c)(3)	33.9
America First Policy Institute	2021	501(c)(3)	23.6
Heritage Action	2010	501(c)(4)	20.9
American Cornerstone Institute	2021	501(c)(3)	8.5
Center for Renewing America	2021	501(c)(3)	4.7
American Movement	2022	501(c)(4)	3.2
American Moment	2021	501(c)(3)	1.1
American Accountability Foundation	2021	501(c)(3)	0.9
Election Integrity Foundation	2020	501(c)(3)	0.7
State Freedom Caucus Foundation	2023	501(c)(3)	0.6

Source: ProPublica Nonprofit Explorer, https://projects.propublica.org/nonprofits/. Data for the Center for Renewing America comes from its 2023 annual report, https://americarenewing.com/wp-content/uploads/2024/02/CRA_Annual-Repor t_2023_Final.pdf.

Although the bottom-up movement was far more important to the right-wing idea factory than typically recognized, the brain trust of conservative think tanks had a powerful role. They not only assessed the market testing at the grassroots. They served as a funnel for conservative money, a recruitment operation for the broader effort, and the curator of big ideas. Some of these right-wing think tanks had been in business for a very long time, with the Heritage Foundation and the Cato Institute dating to the 1970s. Many of them, however, sprang up quickly after Trump's 2020 defeat in the presidential election, as Table 8.1 shows.

Most of these groups are 501(c)(3) nonprofit organizations, created as public charities to pursue public purposes and eligible for tax-deductible contributions. A few are 501(c)(4) social welfare organizations, eligible to participate in political campaigns but not eligible for tax-deductible contributions. A big part of the "dark money" universe, these 501(c)(4)s can engage in political activity and need not disclose the source of their donations. Both kinds of groups were realistic: They hoped to grab back the presidency but, even if they didn't, they were prepared for a long-term battle, and they were very confident about the outcome. As a senior staff member of one of these groups, who disdained the pushback from the left-wing, told me, "We'll win, sooner or later."[26]

Chapter 9

The Pathology of Power

The central argument of this book is that the Right in America has shifted from traditional conservatism to Trumpism, and that Trumpism—driven by its state-based variants—seeks to accumulate and use power. That change, at its core, is about a swing from enduring truths to pragmatic opportunities aimed squarely at the pursuit of political pull. It has been a clever movement, built on transactions—seeking ideas that could be cashed in for clout. This isn't a new strategy. Machiavelli wrote about it in 1532, in *The Prince*, where he described how leaders could push values aside in the pursuit of power. The right-wing idea factory has been busy at work manufacturing tools of division, designed to break apart the country's ruling coalitions and, in particular, to shatter the power of the left. The difference between Trumpism and previous presidencies is stark. Dwight D. Eisenhower, for example, funded the interstate highway system that quite literally wove the country together and built bridges between states. Lyndon B. Johnson created programs designed to pull up the country's neediest people. Donald Trump, in contrast, committed to the politics of division and proclaimed, "I am your retribution."

But this shift in the right-wing has two important pathologies built within it. One is the erosion of trust in government. The more political leaders push the pursuit of results aside for the pursuit of power, the harder it is for the public to see every one of the leader's actions any way but with cynicism. That, in turn, ultimately erodes the leader's ability to speak on behalf of any but a single sliver of society. That erodes their legitimacy.

The other is that when values become negotiable in the pursuit of power, the harder it is to define and hold onto society's central values. The country's founders faced—and, against all odds, beat—the most powerful army in the world. What sustained them through harsh winters, battlefield losses, near bankruptcy, and internal tensions was a shared belief in the profound ideas of the Declaration of Independence. That's Jon Meacham's point about the enduring power of America's great documents.

How leaders and their people navigate through the great challenges of collective action ultimately has more to do with shared trust in core values than anything else, because it defines their conscience and the conscience of their nation. That's not only the lesson of the nation's founders. It's also the theme of a 1941 classic Western movie, *The Ox-Bow Incident*, starring Academy Award winner Henry Fonda. He had just witnessed a posse hanging a rancher named Donald Martin, who was rumored to have stolen a man's cattle before murdering him. Only after the posse had strung up Martin and his two companions did they realized they had made a terrible mistake: Martin had a legal bill of sale for the cattle, and the person from whom he had purchased the herd was alive and well. But the posse had granted Martin one last mercy before they killed him: They allowed him to write a farewell letter to his wife. One bit of that letter said, as Henry Fonda's character read it aloud to everyone else:

> A man just naturally can't take the law into his own hands and hang people without hurtin' everybody in the world, 'cause then he's just not breaking one law but all laws. Law is a lot more than words you put in a book, or judges or lawyers or sheriffs you hire to carry it out. It's everything people ever have found out about justice and what's right and wrong. It's the very conscience of humanity. There can't

be any such thing as civilization unless people have a conscience, because if people touch God anywhere, where is it except through their conscience?[1]

And just what was the conscience of conservatism, to paraphrase the title of former presidential candidate Barry Goldwater's book? Ambrose Bierce wrote a sardonic definition of a conservative back in 1911: "a statesman who is enamored of existing evils, as distinguished from the Liberal, who wishes to replace them with others."[2] There was more than a giggle in Bierce's observation. From the traditional conservative's point of view, the political system would suffer profound evil if it pushed big changes. The best way to avoid that evil was to build the political system on principles proven over time. That, in fact, was the foundation of Edmund Burke's conservatism. Conservatives were not so much anti-change as pro-principle. They sought to identify the bedrock ideas that, they believed, had been effective in guiding society. Rapid changes in those ideas risked having the ship of state wander from a proven course. And that defined their conscience.

The Left had no such aversion to change. From the New Deal to the Great Society to the big expansion in government-funded healthcare in the 2010s, liberals devised a string of government solutions for social problems. That was their conscience. But the more the problems grew, the faster was the pace of governmental change and the quicker the growth of government, which stirred even more concern from the right-wing. Reaganesque conservatism was no longer enough either to motivate the right-wing or stop the Left. The right-wing idea factory emerged as the way to stop the ever-expanding breadth of government.

The factory had three big drivers: *ideas*, with new positions aimed squarely at upsetting established powers on the left and on the right; *environment*, with big disruptions throughout politics and society; and *institutions*, with big shifts in the underlying political systems. Figure 9.1 shows how these drivers emerged over time.

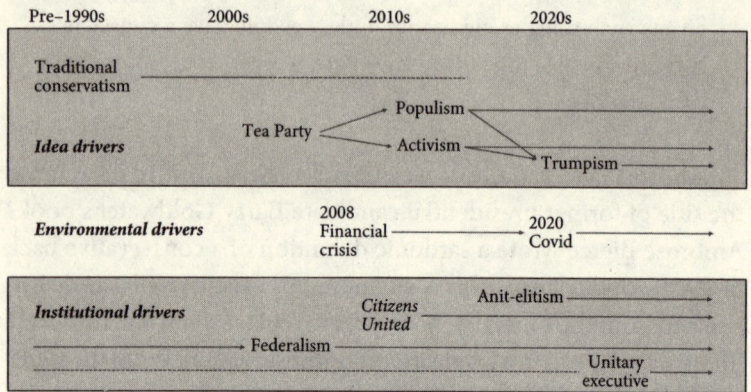

FIGURE 9.1 Plan for the Right-Wing Idea Factory

Traditional conservatism never completely disappeared, but it could not withstand the high-speed pace of the right-wing idea factory. There were different branches of this factory. There was the traditionalism of Steve Bannon and, ultimately, of Donald Trump. On its right flank was Christian nationalism, which sought to establish Christianity as the fundamental moral order and which Katherine Stewart, writing from the left, called "the movement to destroy American democracy."[3] Then there was the more fulsome version of the right-wing in the Heritage Foundation's Project 2025. But together, these branches combined to uproot, in remarkably short order, centuries of free-market economics and the bedrock of conservatism.

Two large shocks drove the right-wing forward. The 2008 economic collapse triggered a crisis that quickly traveled the world. Policymakers concluded they had little choice but to intervene, but their intervention triggered fury among middle- and lower-class taxpayers whose wealth shrank to pay for the bailouts. Then Covid sparked another major governmental intervention, and, yet again, people were unhappy about the expansion of governmental power at the expense of their liberty and the well-being of their kids. A big increase in immigration, the rise of DEI, and other forms of what became viewed as "woke" policies further convinced large numbers of American voters that government simply wasn't serving their interests. That ripened the grounds for the right-wing revolution in the United States—and around the world.

Then there were big changes in the institutional balance of powers. The 2010 *Citizens United* decision by the Supreme Court provided high-octane fuel for the right-wing: large amounts of unaccountable cash supporting the driving ideas of the new conservativism. State governments, always the "laboratories of democracy," became the proving ground for many of the big ideas—new strategies and tactics, tests of whether they could gain political support, and engagement with the populists at the grassroots—as well as the wedge that deepened polarization in America. These groups weakened trust in experts and fed the rising tide of anti-bureaucratic fervor that came from the "deep state" rhetoric. The more the right-wing saw threats to its liberty in the government's growing power, the more it was determined to push forward the unitary executive approach to transform government, which moved the right-wing's approach to "a mechanism for holding power," as Anne Applebaum wrote in *Twilight of Democracy*.[4]

This is why the right-wing idea factory became such an important part of twenty-first century American life. We can ignore the existence of the machine; that would miss one of the most important features shaping (and reshaping) American politics. We can look at it as a collection of fascinating philosophical ideas; it is that, but it is so much more. We can view it as a series of public policy problems and a plan for governments' responses to them; it is that, but this perspective neglects the way it is reshaping American political institutions. And, finally, we can see it as the driving force redefining those institutions, but that is too anodyne a vision. The right-wing idea factory is all of these—ideas, policies, institutions—and it refashions them into a mechanism to fundamentally transform political power and redefine the American conscience.

Then there's Donald Trump. It can be tempting to focus squarely on his remarkable tale, but the right-wing idea factory is more than his political rise—and fall—and rise yet again. It existed before Trump. It helped to fuel him but existed separately from him. And it is destined to outlive him.

The right-wing idea factory is a complex machine devoted to po-litical power: identifying new sources of leverage and new goals to pursue. The temptation is to be drawn into its component parts; the great risk is not to see the big picture that exists behind those parts until it becomes inescapable; the even larger risk is to neglect the broader implications for politics and the rule of law until it redefines the system into something that fundamentally damages America's political health and sweeps aside traditional conservatism.

If Edmund Burke was the *father* of modern conservatism, the philosopher and author Russell Kirk was perhaps its most impor-tant *explainer*.[5] In 1993, Kirk identified ten principles that, he said, represented "the first principles of the conservative persuasion." Table 9.1 lays out Kirk's principles of the centuries of traditional conservatism—and the contrast with Trumpism as it developed in the 2010s. In every respect, Trumpism brushed them aside, in just a few years. Permanent, enduring truths gave way to policies that could—and did—change on a dime. Most important, conserva-tives' commitment to a small government based on principle shifted to a big government that aimed at acquiring, growing, and using po-litical power. Now, it certainly was not the case that conservatives, over the course of more than two centuries, had focused solely on principles to the exclusion of its results or the power it sought to build.

Trumpism was radically different. It focused unabashedly at getting and wielding political power for its own sake.

There was a second principle that separated Trumpism from the traditional positions of both the Right and the Left. These tradi-tions, each in their own way, had a profound respect for the rule of law—the system of laws, institutions, and processes that defined and pursued accountability, transparency, justice, and impartiality in government.

Trumpism was radically different. It paid little attention to the rule of law, to the point it felt unencumbered in arresting Americans off the streets and shipping migrants to other countries without due process.

TABLE 9.1 Traditional Conservatism Versus Trumpism

Traditional conservatism	Trumpism
Recognize permanent moral truths	Assume moral truths change, vary
Adhere to custom, convention, continuity	Pivot as values change
Guide policy through precedent	Shape policy through power
Weigh policy by long-run consequences	Focus on decisions without regard to implementing results
Avoid government efforts to impose equality	Concentrate decision-making over key values
Keep government small to avoid overreach	Use government power to advance values
Link policy and property	Use policy to strengthen the rich
Build society in local communities	Use local communities to test national policies
Limit, balance political power	Concentrate political power in the executive
Change slowly to avoid devouring principle	Pivot quickly to avoid wasted opportunities

Source: The ten ideas under "traditional conservatism" are derived from Russell Kirk, "Ten Conservative Principles" (1993), https://kirkcenter.org/conservatism/ten-conservative-principles/.

Elites suffered greatly at the hands of Trumpism, including state universities (from governors and state legislatures), scientists (like funding for the federal National Institutes of Health), and Ivy League universities (for research grants). For example, in 2023, Florida Governor Ron DeSantis appointed six new trustees to New College, including MAGA activist Chris Rufo, in what he called a "hostile takeover," ready to leap "over the walls and ready to transform higher education from within," as a "hostage rescue operation."[6] It was perhaps the strongest assault against what the right-wing viewed as the woke takeover of American college campuses. But there were also efforts to remake the culture of many other colleges, especially through the establishment of schools or centers focused on citizenship. There was the Hamilton Center at the University of Florida, the School of Civic Life and Leadership at the University of North Carolina, and the School of Civic Leadership at the University of Texas at Austin. Indeed, in advance of Trump's campaign against universities, the Texas state government ensured a strong political hand controlling the leaders of its state-supported institutions and a powerful intervention in everything from what happens in the classroom (which sparked a controversy that cost the job of the president of Texas A&M in 2025) to permissible speech during any demonstration. These efforts spilled over to the assault on the Ivy League universities in 2025 by the Trump administration, including the withholding of $9 billion in grants to Harvard. Then agents for the federal government's agency for Immigration and Customs Enforcement pulled people off the streets, locked them up, sometimes deported them without due process of law, and led to troops dispatched to Democratic cities across the country.

Trumpism was radically different. Unlike both traditional conservatives, who venerated intellectuals like William F. Buckley Jr., and unlike traditional progressives, who had their own stable of intellectuals like John Kenneth Galbraith, Trumpism had no respect for intellectuals and sowed distrust of experts.

Then there was the constant push to make all policies national— or at least those policies that the right-wing believed could amplify its political strength. Uncompromising pursuit of social policy, from book bans to elimination of DEI, rose to the top of the policy agenda in many state governments, which flowed into federal policy. Consider Defense Secretary Pete Hegseth's policy to eliminate DEI in federal agencies, which led to a decision in April 2025 to ban nearly four hundred books held by the US Naval Academy's Nimitz Library. Among the banned books were Maya

Angelou's *I Know Why the Caged Bird Sings* and *Memorializing the Holocaust*, by Janet Jacobs. There were profound paradoxes in the books that remained on the shelves. While officials pulled these books, Adolf Hitler's *Mein Kampf* was still available. *The Bell Curve*, a controversial 1994 book by Richard J. Herrnstein and Charles Murray contending that Blacks had genetically lower levels of intelligence than white people, could still be found. But a critique of the book, *Measured Lies: The Bell Curve Examined*, by Aaron Gresson, Joe L. Kincheloe, and Shirley R. Steinberg, could not. It was one of the books pulled in the purge.[7] The anti-DEI movement that had begun in the states flowed uphill to DOD and, from there, to the library of one of its distinguished service academies.

And then in Massapequa, Long Island, the local school board resisted the New York State mandate to change mascots that drew on Native American culture. Massapequa residents, where the town's name itself was derived from a Native American word, were furious and filed suit to stop the state order. But school officials took one additional step: appealing to Trump. "Perhaps the secretary of education or President Trump might feel that they might have some authority here to step in," said the president of the school board.[8] In deciding to shutter the US Department of Education, Trump had said he wanted to return decisions to state and local governments. But that did not stop Trump from trying to intervene selectively in state and local decisions. He wrote on social media, "I agree with the people in Massapequa, Long Island, who are fighting furiously to keep the Massapequa Chiefs logo on their Teams and School. Forcing them to change the name, after all of these years, is ridiculous and, in actuality, an affront to our great Indian population." He told his Education secretary to support the school district's opposition to the state law. "LONG LIVE THE MASSAPEQUA CHIEF," he concluded in all caps.[9] The right-wing idea factory believed in local control, except when national control might advance their appeal to their base.

Trumpism was radically different. It had no use for the traditional conservative small-government position, and it was willing to use the tools of progressive big government while savaging the principles for which the progressives argued. Trumpism might have sung from the small-government, pro-federalism songbook, but it had no problem in switching to a centralization tune when that might help its cause.

Trumpism thus bore very little resemblance to traditional conservatism. Trumpism was primarily utilitarian; whatever built strength in the political base was the position that Trump and his allies advanced. Traditional conservatism built on principle. It likewise could not have been more different from the perspective of the far left, which it dismissively pushed aside. The principle of Trumpism was simple: the accumulation and protection of political power.

The Engine of Trumpism

As I noted at the beginning of the book, Trumpism developed before Trump emerged as a political force. Traditional conservatism first pivoted to the right-wing values that Bannon advanced. Related ideas bubbled up in the states, where they were tested and refined before the right-wing idea factory sent them national. Trump built on this powerful and growing base, because Trumpism existed before Trump.

The clues for the next wave of Trumpism, moreover, began to develop in the states even before he moved back into the White House in 2025. There was the Florida war against DEI in colleges. There was the decision in both Florida and Utah to ban fluoride in drinking water along with similar decisions in more than fourteen hundred other communities, far in advance of the decision by Secretary of Health and Human Services Robert F. Kennedy Jr. to tell the Centers for Disease Control and Prevention to stop recommending the treatment.[10] Red states began reining in their public health departments before Kennedy did that with the Centers for Disease Control and Prevention.

Without much public notice, some states began advancing Christianity-based, family-friendly policies. In Texas, for example, the state's child welfare system brought Christian churches into partnership as a strategy to strengthen families. As one Texas state program administrator explained, "Texas has a faith-based program within its child welfare system," with an initiative to provide "a nice warm bed with a fluffy mattress" and a "Clergy in the Court for Kids" program. Ministers come to the courtroom "to see, hear, pray, and then respond." The administrator explained that God "has a plan for your life," so "Let Him use YOU, and place you where you need to be."[11] The group with which she worked, Focus on the Family, developed materials on everything from building a healthy marriage to providing "good Christian parenting." Its pro-life program embraced everything from strategies to eliminate abortion to strengthening foster care to developing programs to protect the "preborn" and the "unborn." It was all part of the effort for "helping families thrive in Christ."[12]

In Idaho, Nebraska, South Dakota, and Utah, states created family stability programs. Indiana created a tax credit for newborn children. The House Ways and Means Committee reported that support for family-friendly policy had grown 17 percent from 2021 to 2024, compared with just a 2 percent increase among Democrats. In fact, Republicans saw family-friendly policies as a potential wedge issue, with support for family policy rising among moderates and conservatives but not among progressives.[13]

It was all part of a shift in the right-wing idea factory from the campaign to ban abortions, although that continued to work its way through right-leaning state legislatures, to a new and broader effort to promote family-friendly policies. Elon Musk reaped derision following a *Wall Street Journal* story in which the author profiled the billionaire's prodigious procreation. He referred to his kids as "legion" and told a Saudi Arabian audience, "I do have a lot of kids, and I encourage others to have lots of kids."[14] But the right-wing picked up on family issues generated and tested in states like Texas. In a post-2024 election analysis in the *New Yorker*,

Emma Green wrote, "Social conservatives within Trump's coalition have been workshopping a new playbook."[15] They did this far in advance of Trump's own policy positions, through strategies and tactics that remade Trumpism before the president himself did.

The Heritage Foundation opened its own "Marriage and Family" initiative. "Marriage, the union between one man and one woman, and family," it says, "are the building blocks of all human civilization and the primary institutions of civil society." It included analyses on infertility treatment, and analysis of Daniel Patrick Moynihan's 1965 warning on the collapse of black families, the dangers coming from Americans not having enough children, and the role of dads in shaping society.[16]

It was no surprise, therefore, that Trump signed an executive order just a month into his administration recognizing "the importance of family formation and that our Nation's public policy must make it easier for loving and longing mothers and fathers to have children."[17] Other executive actions pledged more "educational freedom and opportunity for families," help for families struggling to pay their bills, and how his deregulation had already saved families thousands of dollars. His message announcing his attendance at the 2025 Super Bowl even touched on family issues. "This annual tradition transcends our differences and personifies our shared patriotic values of family, faith, and freedom," he said.[18]

Trump made headlines by deporting migrants, but Texas Governor Greg Abbott had worked for years to choke the flow of migrants across the Rio Grande. He launched "Operation Lone Star" in 2021 and sent strike teams from the state police and the Texas National Guard, deputized to have the power to make immigration arrests. Abbott worked on his own parts of the border wall and collected tens of millions of dollars to support the effort. Texas taxpayers spent $11 billion on Abbott's campaign, rivaling Trump's program. An important element of Trump's strategy to shut down the Mexican border was deploying more of the buoys blocking passage that Abbott had shown were effective.

Meanwhile, Moms for Liberty pivoted from their work re-opening schools and their efforts to ban books to organizing in support of a US Supreme Court decision that would allow parents to opt their children out of reading "LGBTQ and gen-der identity-themed books." Moms applauded some of their own members who campaigned in favor of parental choice. "This isn't about banning books—it's about protecting parental rights and respecting religious beliefs," they told participants in their email group. They were campaigning against what they said were efforts from the left to push "an agenda that strips parents of their say in their children's education."[19]

So not only did Trumpism exist before Trump. New forms of the movement were constantly evolving, on the front lines in the states, in advance of what Trump did in the White House and which, in turn, laid the groundwork for the next phase of Trumpism. That guaranteed that the factory would continue to have great impact long after Trump vanished from the political scene. To understand the new right-wing, therefore, it is essential to understand the prod-ucts the factories were building in the states, without which Trump-ism could not have come into being to begin with. That guaranteed that Trumpism would continue long past Trump.

It would be a big mistake, however, to look on the MAGA world and Trumpism as a unified force, a political monolith march-ing together to define the new right. It is more a loose alliance of related ideas and groups and leaders, typically with the same enemy—the woke left—but also with very different tactics in wag-ing the campaign. Many of the state-based efforts had little con-nection to the Washington MAGA world. They moved forward briskly and independently on their own. Even in MAGA Washing-ton, there often were big divisions, such as how best to engage in the mid-2025 turmoil in Iran. Trump loyalists Steve Bannon and Tucker Carlson, former Fox News host, waged a tough campaign to convince Trump to stay out of Iran, as part of their "America First" philosophy. Others in the Trump orbit argued for American involvement, at least to the point of preventing Iran from developing nuclear weapons. On Truth Social, Trump attacked "kooky Tucker Carlson," saying "IRAN CAN NEVER HAVE A NUCLEAR WEAPON."[20]

In fact, *The Economist* contended that "factionalism is growing among the new breed of conservative thinkers as they try to translate anti-wokeness into governing." The magazine wondered whether the country had developed a "woke right," which distilled its campaign into a more rigid philosophy—and which set one part of the right-wing against another.[21] The more Trump dealt with the tough questions of governing, the more those questions created fissures among members of his right-wing coalition.

In terms of the right-wing idea factory, however, that did not matter. The factory continued to produce both big ideas and new leaders. That, in turn, only fed, not diminished, its political strength, because it created a bigger tent under which members of the emerging right-wing could gather. Groups like Moms for Liberty celebrated their strength with a June 2025 "Day at the White House," along with a private tour of the Capitol and a celebration of the Supreme Court's actions in support of their causes. While MAGA elements fought over American engagement in Iran, Moms focused in Illinois on fighting vaccine clinics in schools, restrictions on home schooling, and what they said were "tampon mandates in boys' bathrooms."[22]

Unlike traditional conservatism, which created unity around its teachings, the right-wing idea factory generated related movements, aimed at different targets. They shared a tactical devotion for political organizing and advancing social issues and, occasionally, targeting foreign policy. But because the movement was always based fundamentally in acquiring and using political power, there was no need for the overhanging strategic orthodoxy that had dominated traditional conservatism. They were successful in generating that political power without the need for a central idea, in the spirit of someone like Edmund Burke, to drive the movement.

Who Are We?

That leads to the core question. Is the system that the right-wing idea factory built the system that Americans want, with the accountability they expect and the Constitution that the founders created? Does it capture the rule of law, as legal scholars understand it? What answer does it provide to the questions that Admiral McRaven framed in Chapter 1: Who are we? What is our conscience?

The new right-wing conservatives say they are restoring the Constitution and accountability by giving the president more control. But this isn't the Constitution that most people want, the accountability they expect, or the Constitution that the founders wrote, according to a survey done in 2024 for the National Academy of Public Administration. The people want a government that is transparent, responsible, and competent. They want and expect results that are delivered by expert government workers in a nonpartisan way. They want a system that can "preserve, protect and defend the Constitution of the United States," as the president swears in the oath of office, a system that brings the Constitution's aspirations to life in the work that government agencies do, with the expertise to ensure it's done right.[23]

What they don't want is twisting the Constitution to serve narrow interests by politicizing federal agencies, in ways that are not transparent. They don't want federal agencies robbed of their competence by putting partisan loyalty—to either side—ahead of the competence of the agencies. They don't want to put the performance of programs they care about at risk for the sake of partisan control, and nothing undermines their trust in government more than the suspicion that their hard-earned tax dollars are being twisted by politicization in ways hidden from view.

And, above all, the last thing they want is to have their already deep suspicion of government be fueled by worries that the Constitution is being used to promote narrow partisan ideas. This isn't what "We the People" means for most Americans. "We" has always meant everyone, since New York's Gouverneur Morris penned those words for the Preamble of the Constitution in 1787. The right-wing idea factory has been remarkably successful in producing a new brand for the Republican Party and in reframing ideas about how government ought to work. However, the movement isn't creating either the competence or transparency that most Americans expect in their government.

Gone is Reagan's optimism, replaced by a dystopian view of American society. Gone is the focus on government's results, replaced with a quest for power by bulldozing government's institutions. Gone is the principle of competence, replaced with partisanship. Gone is the founders' delicately constructed balance among the three grand institutions of American government, replaced with a not-so-thinly-veiled effort to enshrine a unitary executive as *uber-primus inter pares*—a first among equals with tactics designed to sideline the other two branches, especially by moving faster than they can ever keep up. For the right-wing, there was great comfort in its single-minded focus on acquiring and using power. "Out of intense complexities intense simplicities emerge," Winston Churchill wrote.[24] Executive power was the intense simplicity of the right-wing idea factory.

The right-wing has filled the courts—the US Supreme Court, the lower federal courts, and state courts—with judges willing to accept the right-wing's original intent argument, even though that intent is usually anything but clear. That's due in part to the long centuries between then and now, which make it hard to read today into the past. And it's also due to the founders' deliberate ambiguity in crafting political institutions, because they were struggling with many of the same issues we face today. It would be a mistake to use their ambiguity then to weave a cloak of certainty today, in the interest of "We, Some of the People," especially to create an even more robust executive with powers not balanced by those in the other branches.

In putting the president into a vastly superior position, the right-wing seeks to hobble government agencies and render them unable to provide the advice—"frank and fearless" advice, as Australian civil servants put it—that administering the country's laws requires. Right-wingers demanded that Congress write laws that are clearer and less subject to interpretation by administrators, but they have asked Congress to do what it has sadly demonstrated it cannot do— spelling out matters of immense complexity with great legislative precision, defining the finest details of policy that are only bound to incite greater polarization, and calling on Congress to speedily pass these detailed laws despite Congress's manifest inability to actually pass much of anything. But the unitary executive approach envisions even further enfeebling the Constitution's first branch of government, the Congress.

This would have chilled the nation's founders. Alexander Hamilton famously wrote in Federalist 70 about the need for "energy in the executive" as an essential part of good government. He explored the idea of "unity," but that was to counter other founders who wanted a multi-headed executive like the dual consuls of ancient Rome. His previous paper, Federalist 69, argued the need for the delicate balance between the president's substantial powers and the constraints that the counterbalancing institutions rightly put on him. The most enthusiastic proponent of executive power among the founders would not have supported the arguments for the unitary executive promoted by the right-wing idea factory.

Meanwhile, grassroots zealots generated an energetic federalism increasingly polarizing in both philosophy and policy. Not only had more power flowed to the states because federal-level polarization pushed more decisions to state governments. Elected state leaders, especially governors, were all too willing to grab ideas, fuel their own national reputations, and enhance their own power. Blue states resisted the move to the right in the red states and that, in turn, created a growing divide among the states. What programs the people got depended on where the people lived. Some states allowed abortions, while others prohibited them. There were some school districts eager to ban books while others fought to ensure free access to publications. There were states who championed parental choice, with the advancement of religious principles, while others created a more level playing field among religions or steered clear of religiously leaning education altogether.

The founders, of course, intended the states to have flexibility to go their own way. In Federalist 10, James Madison famously wrote about "the mischiefs of faction." He worried about two kinds of "mischiefs": efforts by a minority to push the country in an unhealthy direction, and efforts by a majority to impose its will on a minority of the people. In the case of the former, Madison believed that the majority could prevent a minority from taking over. When it came to ensuring a majority could not harm the interests of minorities, Madison was sanguine because of the great variations among the states. "The influence of factious leaders may kindle a flame within their particular States, but will be unable to spread a general conflagration through the other States," he wrote.[25] The government as a whole, especially the federal government, would prevent such a "conflagration." None of the founders imagined or wanted a collection of states fundamentally divided and moving down different tracks.

It is the goal of the right-wing idea factory, however, to remove the barriers to such a "conflagration" and to keep at least their own train moving down their own track. The founders certainly never imagined that the values of the states would remain static. They were convinced, as Chief Justice John Marshall wrote in *Marbury v. Madison* in 1803, that the Constitution was "forming the fundamental and paramount law of the nation," and that governance would grow to meet each challenge of a new age.[26] The ambiguity in the founders' language allowed the Constitution to breathe over the centuries. The founders, in fact, aimed "not to keep the Constitution in tune with the times, but, rather, to keep the times, to the extent possible, in tune with the Constitution," as Walter Berns put it.[27]

That's the central tension in the right-wing movement: whether to keep the times in sync with the Constitution or to adjust the reading of the Constitution to fit the times. The right-wing idea factory contends that they're trying to pull society, governance, and the interpretation of the Constitution back to what the founders intended. In fact, it is just the reverse of what the founders wanted: imposing their interpretation of what ought to govern the process at the expense of any competing idea. This is certainly not reading the Constitution to fit the times. To promote the rule of law and the fundamentals of democratic responsiveness—that is what it means to assert the Constitution.

The Future of Liberal Democracy

Throughout the book, I've tried to explain the dramatic revolution that has upended American policy and politics. What does it all add up to? What are the implications for the future of government and, in particular, for liberal democracy?

Not *that* liberalism, of course—not the liberalism of the Left before it abandoned the label for "progressive" under the incessant bombardment from the Right, but the enduring values of liberal democracy that have guided the country since its beginning: a rule of law shaping the society's pursuit of suffrage, civil rights, civil liberties, political freedom, and protection from the abuse of governmental power. Here's the core question: Is the right-wing idea factory filled with workers who believe in classical liberalism, especially the rule of law? Are they true conservatives?

The answer is no, as I've shown in the book. Populists have risen on the right to push—hard—the policies in which they believe. They have pushed out-of-the-mainstream positions on everyone, first locally and then by seeking to centralize those policies through the federal government and the courts. The grassroots zealots have manufactured new policy issues that matter a great deal to them and that they hope will redefine American politics. Once they gained positions of influence in Trumpism, they upset Madison's delicate balance of powers by using the judiciary to elevate the role of the executive and, especially, of the president. Most of all, as I have demonstrated in the earlier chapters of the book, they have pushed aside the long tradition of the rule of law in favor of finding tactics and strategies to enhance their own political power, for the sake of gaining that power.

The right-wing idea factory attempts to trace its strategy back to the nation's founders. But when it comes to the rule of law, the words of John Adams carry special weight:

> The very definition of a republic is "an empire of laws, and not of men." That, as a republic is the best of governments, so that particular arrangement of the powers of society, or, in other words, that form of government which is best contrived to secure an impartial and exact execution of the laws, is the best of republics.[28]

That rule of law—based on natural rights and rules to promote liberty—lies at the very core of the Constitution and the system of government that the founders created.[29] The right-wing idea factory has sought to redefine that core, even at the risk of creating two countries. The founders warned about tyrannies, and the risk that one relatively narrow part of society might try to impose its values on the rest of the country is precisely one of the fears they warned against. Franklin warned of the risks with his cartoon "Join, or Die."

The nation's founders were wary about creating unbalanced institutions that produced jolting shifts. The nation's political parties hadn't been invented yet, but the founders clearly saw the inevitable rise of that interests that have happened since. Of course, they already had invested much time balancing interests in the South and the North. Having staged an against-all-odds rebellion against the English king and the world's greatest army, they weren't about to risk creating an executive that would immediately recreate the same problems and cripple the country's democratic aspirations before the ink dried on the document. That's why they borrowed so heavily on Enlightenment thinkers and their rule of law in building the new country, writing its governing document, and constructing its institutions. As Michael Glennon, a Tufts University law professor, put it, "If conservatives trash long-held political norms to move against liberals, what will protect them when liberals retake power?"[30] That's why the erosion of the basic principle of the rule of law within the right-wing idea factory is so fundamentally dangerous. It underlines the concerns of the founders, not so much about protecting the Left from the Right but protecting the country from opposing forces that could shred it apart.

That was the danger that Justice Sonia Sotomayor raised in her stinging dissent to the US Supreme Court's 2024 ruling in *Trump v. United States*, which held the president has immunity from criminal prosecution for official acts. The decision of the 6–3 majority, she wrote, "makes a mockery of the principle, foundational to our Constitution and system of Government, that no man is above the law." Yet, given the majority's decision in support of presidential immunity, she concluded, "In every use of official power, the President is now a king above the law."[31] In laying out the president's powers, Alexander Hamilton wrote in Federalist 77 about the essential need for "the requisites to energy," so that the president could serve the will of the people. But he quickly added, "The remaining inquiry is: does it also combine the requisites to safety, in a republican sense, a due dependence on the people, a due responsibility?"[32] In sweeping away the long tradition of constitutional law that held the president accountable for "prosecution in the common course of law," Hamilton wrote, the answer was yes. After the Court's decision to expand presidential immunity, Sotomayor concluded, the answer was no.

But the majority of the Supreme Court disagreed and, in *Trump v. United States*, it held that presidents had absolute immunity for actions taken as part of their official duties and "presumptive immunity" for actions outside the president's constitutional powers. This decision was the natural result of the right-wing idea factory, the product of the Court majority that Leonard Leo helped put into place. It was part of long links assembled by the right-wing machine, including the *Wall Street Journal*, whose editorial page said that the case reinforced the "ability of all Presidents—not merely the last one—to act in the national interest free from prosecution for official acts."[33] Regardless of where one stands on the question of whether a president should have that level of immunity, free from oversight by the courts for alleged crimes committed while in office, it's clear that the right-wing's idea factory had produced a triumph. It re-engineered the rule of law by boosting the power of the executive and stripping away protections against the abuse of power.

The rule of law—a set of expectations by which citizens agree to be governed and through which they can hold their public officials accountable—is fundamental to the function of American democracy. The right-wing has pushed aside hundreds of years of the American rule of law tradition in exchange for changing the rules of the political game to elevate its voice and power to enforce its values.

That is a fundamental challenge to the basic principles of government, a challenge stretching back hundreds of years to days before the Enlightenment. In Robert Bolt's Oscar-winning screenplay for *A Man for All Seasons*, he wrote about the ferocious battle between Sir Thomas More and King Henry VIII over divorcing his first wife, Catherine of Aragon. Bolt set up an angry quarrel between More and his son-in-law, William Roper, an ambitious man eager to knock down the long tradition of law in pursuit of power and position. More said he'd give even the Devil the benefit of the rule of law to ensure that the rule of law is intact for everyone. Roper could not stomach the idea and said, "I'd cut down every law in England" to get after the Devil. More replied,

> Oh? And when the last law was down, and the Devil turned 'round on you, where would you hide, Roper, the laws all being flat? This country is planted thick with laws, from coast to coast, Man's laws, not God's! And if you cut them down, and you're just the man to do it, do you really think you could stand upright in the winds that would blow then?[34]

That is the singular risk of the right-wing idea factory: uprooting the long tradition of the rule of law in the quest for power and, in the process, destabilizing democracy. It also means fundamentally redefining the very conscience of our nation. Changing the strategies and tactics of governance is one thing. But we owe ourselves a frank conversation with ourselves—each of us with all of us—about the conscience of America that we'd recreate.

In their last years, this was the big question that brought together again two old rivals, Thomas Jefferson and John Adams, following their bitter 1800 election contest. "What a Colossus shall we be," Jefferson mused in a late-night letter to Adams. "I like the dreams of the future better than the history of the past. So good night!" A few days later, Adams replied, "May We be 'a Barrier against the Returns of Ignorance and Barbarism'! 'What a Colossus Shall We be'! But will it not be of Brass Iron and Clay? Your Taste is judicious in likeing better the dreams of the Future, than the History of the Past. Upon this Principle I prophecy that you and I Shall Soon meet and be better Friends than ever."[35] To become "better friends than ever," however, required decades, during which they struggled to put aside their profound differences: Adams, a Federalist, who lost to Jefferson in 1800, and Jefferson, a Democratic-Republican whose vice president, Aaron Burr, killed Alexander Hamilton, one of the most prominent Federalists, in a duel.

In these days, having crafted its ideology to acquire political power and spent billions of dollars to do so, the right-wing is not likely to easily let go of what it has gained. And having lost battle after battle, the Left is certainly not likely to give up on efforts to regain power and, when it does so, to clean house of the right-wing zealots that the Trump administration has installed.

Even in its first months, Trump officials made clear they were using short-term ideological screens to make the federal workforce more to their liking. In 2025, the average federal employee had served for a dozen years. In its 2025 hiring plan, however, the administration announced it would require all applicants for federal jobs to respond to an essay question asking, "How would you help advance the President's Executive Orders and policy priorities?"[36] Political pressure forced the administration to back away from that requirement, but the underlying theme remained. The Trump administration sought to use an ideological screen to hire only loyalists into the civil service, and then to ensure they were in place for subsequent administrations. Faced with such an obvious effort to politicize the civil service, left-leaning presidents in future administrations would certainly do their best to counterattack.

One great risk here is that the dreams of the Left will be squashed by the strategies of the Right—and vice versa. A second great risk is that the trust of the public that people will be treated fairly and impartially will evaporate if they came to see a political motive behind every move. Facts and truth will undoubtedly fall victim to the "ignorance and barbarism" about which Jefferson and Adams worried. This would seriously, perhaps even fatally, wound America's grand experiment in democracy.

But the hopeful sign, in the surprising late-in-life reconciliation of Jefferson and Adams, is that this isn't inevitable. They shared hopes for an American colossus that triumphed, of friendships deepened through that pursuit despite their profound differences. Their electoral campaigns for the presidency in 1800 were, by any measure, among the nastiest in American history. If they could emerge from that contest with a joint commitment to the "dreams of the future," there is indeed hope. We, in turn, can hope that it will not take the decades that the healing of their personal rift required. In the accelerating pace of global change of the twenty-first century, we might not have that long.

The Right-Wing Idea Factory Index

The "Right-Wing Idea Factory Index" is a scale that ranges from 0 to 10. Each state is scored with one point for each of the following: whether it delayed locking down at the 2020 outbreak of Covid until after March 27, 2020; whether it had created trigger bans in advance of the 2022 *Dobbs* decision that put abortion decisions in the hands of the states and then banned abortions early in a pregnancy; how aggressively its citizens pursued book bans; whether the state legislature created DEI bans; whether it developed school voucher programs; whether it established itself as a right-to-work state; whether it decided at the beginning of Obamacare to take advantage of federal subsidies for additional coverage; and whether it banned care for trans children.

Sources for the data were, on Covid lockdowns, data collected by the author; on abortion trigger laws: Elizabeth Nash and Isabel Guarnieri, "13 States Have Abortion Trigger Bans—Here's What Happens When Roe Is Overturned," Guttmacher Institute (June 6, 2022), https://www.guttmacher.org/article/2022/06/13-states-have-abortion-trigger-bans-heres-what-happens-when-roe-overturned; on book bans, Pen America, "The Normalization of Book Banning: Banned in the USA, 2024–2025" and previous years (Octoberr 1, 2025), https://pen.org/report/the-normalization-of-book-banning/; on school voucher plans, Education Commission of the States, "Private School Choice: Vouchers 2024), https://reports.ecs.org/comparisons/private-school-choice-vouchers-2024; on right-to-work states, https://worldpopulationreview.com/state-rankings/right-to-work-states; on Medicaid expansion before 2016, https://www.macpac.gov/subtopic/medicaid-expansion/; and on banning care for trans children, https://www.kff.org/other/dashboard/gender-affirming-care-policy-tracker/.

NOTES

Preface

1. Quoted by Sam Jones, "Donald Trump considers running for president," *The Guardian* (October 6, 2010), https://www.theguardian.com/world/blog/2010/oct/06/donald-trump-considers-bid-president.

2. Jim VandeHei and Mike Allen, "Behind the Curtain: The most unprecedented presidency in 250 years," *Axios* (September 23, 2025), https://www.axios.com/2025/09/23/trump-unprecedented-presidency-behind-the-curtain.

Chapter 1

1. John Winthrop, " City Upon a Hill, 1630" (New York: Gilder Lehman Institute of American History), https://www.gilderlehrman.org/sites/default/files/inline-pdfs/Winthrop%27s%20City%20upon%20a%20Hill.pdf.

2. Edmund Burke, *Reflections on the Revolution in France*, ed. Frank M. Turner (1790; New Haven: Yale University Press, 2003).

3. Ronald Reagan, "Inaugural Address 1981" (Ronald Reagan Presidential Library and Museum), https://www.reaganlibrary.gov/archives/speech/inaugural-address-1981.

4. "Public Trust in Government: 1958–2024" (Pew Research Center, June 24, 2024), https://www.pewresearch.org/politics/2024/06/24/public-trust-in-government-1958-2024/.

5. Rana Foroohar, "What Ever Happened to Upward Mobility," *Time* (November 14, 2011), https://time.com/archive/6640610/what-ever-happened-to-upward-mobility/.

6. Dennis Jacobe, "Six in 10 Oppose Wall Street Bailouts" (Gallup, April 3, 2008), https://news.gallup.com/poll/106114/six-oppose-wall-street-bailouts.aspx.

7. Arun Gupta, "The Tea Party: The New Populism" (Political Research Associates, August 1, 2011), https://politicalresearch.org/2011/08/01/tea-party-new-populism.

8. TV Internet Archive, https://archive.org.

9. Russell Kirk, "Ten Conservative Principles" (1993), https://kirkcenter.org/conservatism/ten-conservative-principles/.

10. See Google Trends, at https://trends.google.com/trends/explore?cat=19&date=2005-01-01%202025-06-26&geo=US&q=balanced%20federal%20budget&hl=en; Stephen Slivinski, "The Grand Old Spending Party: How Republicans Became Big Spenders," Policy Analysis (Cato Institute, May 3, 2005), https://www.cato.org/sites/cato.org/files/pubs/pdf/pa543.pdf; and William A. Niskanen, "Limiting Government: The Failure of 'Starve the Beast,'" Cato Journal 26:3 (2006), 553–558, https://www.cato.org/sites/cato.org/files/serials/files/cato-journal/2006/11/cj26n3-8.pdf.

11. Leo Sands, "The History of GOP: How Republicans Became the Grand Old Party," Washington Post (November 9, 2022), https://www.washingtonpost.com/history/2022/11/09/gop-meaning-republicans/.

12. Maggie Astor, "Heritage Foundation Head Refers to 'Second American Revolution,'" New York Times (July 3, 2024), https://www.nytimes.com/2024/07/03/us/politics/heritage-foundation-2025-policy-america.html.

13. Fareed Zakaria, "The Rise of Illiberal Democracy," Foreign Affairs (November–December 1997), 22–43.

14. See George H. Nash, The Conservative Intellectual Movement in America Since 1945 (New York: Basic Books, 1976); and Paul Gottfried, The Conservative Movement (Boston: Twayne, 1988).

15. Eric Bradner, "Alt-Right Leader: 'Hail Trump! Hail Our People! Hail Victory!,'" CNN (November 22, 2016), https://edition.cnn.com/2016/11/21/politics/alt-right-gathering-donald-trump/?utm_source=substack&utm_medium=email.

16. "Steve Bannon: The Trump-Whisperer's Rapid Fall from Grace," BBC (August 20, 2020), https://www.bbc.com/news/world-us-canada-42636667.

17. René Guénon, *The Crisis of the Modern World*, trans. Marco Pallis, Arthur Osborne, and Richard C. Nicholson, 4th ed. (Hillsdale, NY: Sophia Perennis, 2004); and Joshua S. Lupo, "The Political Theology of Traditionalism: Steve Bannon, the Far Right, and the End of Days" (January 16, 2024), https://contendingmodernities.nd.edu/theorizing-modernities/political-theology-traditionalism/.

18. David Marchese, "Curtis Yarvin Says Democracy Is Done. Powerful Conservatives Are Listening," *New York Times Magazine* (January 18, 2025), https://www.nytimes.com/2025/01/18/magazine/curtis-yarvin-interview.html.

19. More generally, see Ramon Lopez, "A Taxonomy of the New Right," *Persuasion* (June 19, 2025), https://www.persuasion.community/p/a-taxonomy-of-the-new-right?utm_source=post-email-title&publication_id=61579&post_id=166253828&utm_campaign=email-post-title&isFreemail=false&r=su09y&triedRedirect=true&utm_medium=email.

20. *Citizens United v. Federal Election Commission*, 558 U.S. 310 (2010), https://www.oyez.org/cases/2008/08-205.

21. Neil J. Smelser, *Theory of Collective Behavior* (Glencoe, IL: Free Press, 1963); Ted Robert Gurr, *Why Men Rebel* (Princeton: Princeton University Press, 1970).

22. John D. McCarthy and Mayer N. Zald, "Mobilization and Social Movements: A Partial Theory," *American Journal of Sociology* 82:6 (1977), 1212–1241. See also Charles Tilly, *From Mobilization to Revolution* (Boston: Addison-Wesley, 1977); and Doug McAdam, *Political Process and the Development of Black Insurgency, 1930–1970* (Chicago: University of Chicago Press, 1982).

23. Sidney Tarrow, *Power in Movement: Social Movements and Contentious Politics*, 4th ed. (Cambridge: Cambridge University Press, 2022), 7–9. Compare John W. Kingdon, *Agendas, Alternatives, and Public Policies* (New York: Longman, 2002).

24. James MacGregor Burns, *Leadership* (New York: Harper, 1978), 19, 20; see also James V. Downton, *Rebel Leadership: Commitment and Charisma in the Revolutionary Process* (New York: Free Press, 1973).

25. Barry Goldwater, *The Conscience of a Conservative* (Shepherdsville, Ky.: Victor Publishing Company, 1960), Foreword, https://books.google.com/books/download/The_Conscience_of_a_Conservative.pdf?id=9NeFAAAAMAAJ&output=pdf.

26. Russell Kirk, "Ten Conservative Principles" (1993), https://kirkcenter.org/conservatism/ten-conservative-principles/.

27. Admiral William McRaven, "We Are the Good Guys," at Garry Kasparov substack (April 9, 2025), https://thenextmove.substack.com/p/admiral-william-h-mcraven-we-are.

28. John Kenneth Galbraith, "Address to Meeting of the National Policy Committee on Pockets of Poverty, December 13, 1963," republished in *Congressional Record* (December 18, 1963), 25042, https://www.congress.gov/88/crecb/1963/12/18/GPO-CRECB-1963-pt19-5-2.pdf.

29. Jon Meacham, "Introduction," *The Declaration of Independence and the Constitution of the United States* (New York: Modern Library, 2025), viii–ix.

Chapter 2

1. Institute for Health Metrics and Evaluation, "COVID-19: What's New for April 1, 2020," https://www.healthdata.org/sites/default/files/files/Projects/COVID/Estimation_update_040120.pdf.

2. Jakub Hlávka and Adam Rose, " COVID-19's Total Cost to the U.S. Economy Will Reach $14 Trillion by End of 2023" (Leonard D. Schaeffer Institute for Public Policy and Government Service, University of Southern California, May 16, 2023), https://schaeffer.usc.edu/research/covid-19s-total-cost-to-the-economy-in-us-will-reach-14-trillion-by-end-of-2023-new-research/.

3. Rose Khattar and Lily Roberts, " 5 Reasons Why the Labor Market Recovery Was Historic" (Washington, DC: Center for American Progress, November 2, 2023), https://www.americanprogress.org/article/5-reasons-why-the-labor-market-recovery-was-historic/.

4. Adam Kamrandt-Scott, "The Politics of Pandemic Influenza Preparedness," in Colin McInnes, Kelley Lee, and Jeremy Youde (eds.), *The Oxford Handbook of Global Health Politics*, Oxford Handbooks (2020; online ed., Oxford Academic, January 11, 2018), https://doi.org/10.1093/oxfordhb/9780190456818.013.32.

5. Aysha Qamar, "At Least 5 States Report an Increase in Calls to Poison Control after Trump's 'Disinfectant' COVID-19 Remarks" (Michigan Poison and Drug Information Center, 2021), https://www.poison.med.wayne.edu/updates-content/kstytapp2qfstf0pkacdxmz943u1hs.

6. Kacper Niburski and Oskar Niburski, "Impact of Trump's Promotion of Unproven COVID-19 Treatments and Subsequent Internet Trends: Observational Study," *Journal of Medical Internet Research* 22:11 (2020), https://doi.org/10.2196/20044.

7. Megan Brenan, "Americans' Trust in Media Remains at Trend Low" (Gallup, October 14, 2024), https://news.gallup.com/poll/651977/americans-trust-media-remains-trend-low.aspx.

8. Elisa Shearer and Kirsten Eddy, "Republicans Have Become More Likely Since 2024 to Trust Information from News Outlets, Social Media" (Pew Research Center, May 8, 2025), https://www.pewresearch.org/short-reads/2025/05/08/republicans-have-become-more-likely-since-2024-to-trust-information-from-news-outlets-social-media/.

9. Roy H. Perlis, Katherine Ognyanova, Ata Uslu, et al., "Trust in Physicians and Hospitals During the COVID-19 Pandemic in a 50-State Survey of US Adults," *JAMA Network* 7:7 (July 31, 2024), https://doi.org/10.1001/jamanetworkopen.2024.24984.

10. 2024 Edelman Trust Barometer—Special Report: Trust and Health (2024), https://www.edelman.com/trust/2024/trust-barometer/special-report-health.

11. Rachel Minkin, "About Half of Americans Say Public K-12 Education Is Going in the Wrong Direction" (Pew Research Center, April 4, 2024), https://www.pewresearch.org/short-reads/2024/04/04/about-half-of-americans-say-public-k-12-education-is-going-in-the-wrong-direction/.

12. Denise Royal, Carlos Suarez, and Ray Sanchez, "Moms for Liberty Faces New Challenges and Growing Pushback over Its Conservative Education Agenda," CNN (February 3, 2024), https://www.cnn.com/2024/02/03/us/moms-for-liberty-scandal-opposition/index.html.

13. Mitch Perry, "Moms for Liberty Now Has 310 Chapters in 48 States; What Will They Do Now?," *Florida Phoenix* (February 2, 2024), https://floridaphoenix.com/2024/02/02/moms-for-liberty-now-has-310-chapters-in-48-states-what-will-they-do-now/.

14. "Former BPS Board Member Tina Descovich Co-Founds 'Moms for Liberty'; Defends Parental Rights in Education," *Space Coast Daily* (February 9, 2021), https://spacecoastdaily.com/2021/02/former-bps-board-member-tina-descovich-co-founds-moms-for-liberty-defends-parental-rights-in-education/.

15. Tim Craig, "Moms for Liberty Has Turned 'Parental Rights' into a Rallying Cry for Conservative Parents," *Washington Post* (October 15, 2021), https://www.washingtonpost.com/national/moms-for-liberty-parents-rights/2021/10/14/bf3d9ccc-286a-11ec-8831-a31e7b3de188_story.html.

16. Tunku Varadarajan, "Moms for Liberty: 'We Do Not Co-Parent with the Government,'" *Wall Street Journal* (September 1, 2023), https://www.wsj.

com/articles/we-do-not-co-parent-with-the-government-justice-descovich-education-rights-d9609fc6.

17. Varadarajan, "Moms for Liberty."

18. Finch Walker, "'End DEI' Portal Is 'Culmination' of Her Efforts, Says Moms for Liberty Co-Founder Justice," *Florida Today* (March 5, 2025), https://www.floridatoday.com/story/news/2025/03/05/moms-for-libertys-justice-played-role-in-dept-of-eds-end-dei-portal/81167730007/.

19. M4MU, https://m4lu.org/?vcrmeid=xAzbsMXh0uPhzjK5NY4rg&vcrmiid=zxn17M08bkCkWTbz0eXKQg.

20. Moms for Liberty, "Moms for Liberty Speak Out," https://www.momsforliberty.org/mom-videos/.

21. Moms for Liberty, "Celebrating Women's History Month" (2025), https://www.momsforliberty.org/summit-awards/?vcrmeid=bTI1P1dpE0mErTFk7n7LA&vcrmiid=zxn17M08bkCkWTbz0eXKQg.

22. Moms for Liberty, "We Do Not Co-Parent with Government" (email, June 26, 2025).

23. PEN America, "Banned in the USA: Rising School Book Bans Threaten Free Expression and Students' First Amendment Rights" (April 2022), https://pen.org/banned-in-the-usa/.

24. "Central York Banned Book List," https://cpb-us-w2.wpmucdn.com/blogs.socsd.org/dist/0/461/files/2021/09/YC-Banned-List-Infographic_REVISED.pdf.

25. Editorial, "Central York Unifies Behind Banned Books—but Stay Vigilant," *York Dispatch* (October 1, 2021), https://advance-lexis-com.proxy-um.researchport.umd.edu/document/?pdmfid=1,516,831&crid=5daf24af-c67a-4a25-9a78-7e48f589521a&pddocfullpath=%2Fshared%2Fdocument%2Fnews%2Furn%3AcontentItem%3A63SM-F1J1-DYMD-603Y-00000-00&pdcontentcomponentid=304,479&pdteaserkey=sr23&pditab=allpods&ecomp=kmnyk&earg=sr23&prid=3724649d-4d2a-452e-b4d4-e892676e720c.

26. Alex Chaet, "Watch the Entire CNN/Sesame Street Racism Town Hall" (June 6, 2020), https://www.cnn.com/2020/06/06/app-news-section/cnn-sesame-street-race-town-hall-app-june-6-2020-app/index.html.

27. Evan McMorris-Santoro, Linh Tran, Sahar Akbarzai, and Mirna Alsharif, "Students Fight Back Against a Book Ban That Has a Pennsylvania Community Divided," CNN (September 16, 2021), https://www.cnn.com/2021/09/15/us/book-ban-controversy-pennsylvania/index.html.

28. McMorris-Santoro et al., "Students Fight Back."

29. Tina Locurto, "'Afraid to Teach': School's Book Ban Targeted Black, Latino Authors," *York Dispatch* (September 1, 2021), https://www.yorkdispatch.com/story/news/education/2021/09/01/afraid-teach-schools-book-ban-targeted-black-latino-authors/5601980001/.

30. Nyle Vialet, "Stand Up to Censorship In Schools," *Publisher's Weekly* (October 1, 2021), https://www.publishersweekly.com/pw/by-topic/columns-and-blogs/soapbox/article/87505-stand-up-to-censorship-in-schools.html.

31. Mirna Alsharif and Liam Reilly, "Pennsylvania School District Reverses Ban on Books by Authors of Color After Students Fought Back," CNN (September 23, 2021), https://www.cnn.com/2021/09/23/us/pennsylvania-school-book-ban-reversed.

32. Editorial, "Do the Homework on Moms for Liberty–Affiliated School Initiatives," *York Dispatch* (June 11, 2023), https://www.yorkdispatch.com/story/opinion/editorials/2023/06/11/do-the-homework-on-moms-for-liberty-affiliated-school-initiatives/70310990007/.

33. Meredith Willse, "On Eve of Considering Book Policy, Central York Docs Show School Board Candidate Requested Removals," *York Dispatch* (June 9, 2023), https://www.yorkdispatch.com/story/news/education/2023/06/09/will-central-pass-the-library-resource-policy/70304030007/.

34. Gabriela Martinez, "Central York's School Board Will Vote on Updating Its Book Review Policy," WITF Public Television (March 21, 2023), https://www.witf.org/2023/03/21/central-yorks-school-board-will-vote-on-updating-its-book-review-policy/.

35. Hannah Natanson, "Objection to Sexual, LGBTQ Content Propels Spike in Book Challenges," *Washington Post* (June 9, 2023), https://www.washingtonpost.com/education/2023/05/23/lgbtq-book-ban-challengers/.

36. Elizabeth A. Harris and Alexandra Alter, "A Fast-Growing Network of Conservative Groups Is Fueling a Surge in Book Bans," *New York Times* (December 12, 2022), https://www.nytimes.com/2022/12/12/books/book-bans-libraries.html.

37. Jonathan Friedman, "Banned in the USA: The Growing Movement to Censor Books in Schools," PEN America (September 19, 2022), https://pen.org/report/banned-usa-growing-movement-to-censor-books-in-schools/

38. Friedman, "Banned in the USA."

39. MassResistance (April 11, 2022), https://www.massresistance.org/docs/gen4/22b/Mississippi-parents-stop-graphic-books/

index.html?fbclid=IwAR1M9ivcBpdFrgXKWnBvmmRB45BmaH-uL1hg1Rctiz0badFtwYrM7AI-9Ig.

40. "Safe Ed K-12 Task Force Asks for Full Elimination of Sex Ed Due to Abuse and Ongoing Violation of Florida Law" (September 18, 2020), https://menafn.com/1100819161/Safe-Ed-K-12-Task-Force-Asks-for-Full-Elimination-of-Sex-Ed-Due-to-Abuse-and-Ongoing-Violation-of-Florida-Law.

41. Friedman, "Banned in the USA."

42. Friedman, "Banned in the USA."

43. *Jacobellis v. Ohio*, 378 U.S. 184 (1964), https://supreme.justia.com/cases/federal/us/378/184/.

44. Moms for Liberty (undated), https://drive.google.com/file/d/1BNfax73kzqWwMMfkjcopgEXMDBD-fr4O/view.

45. No Left Turn for Education, "Books" (undated), https://www.aclu.org/wp-content/uploads/legal-documents/12-27_noleftturn_blacklisted_books_list.pdf.

46. No Left Turn in Education, "Welcome to Rated Books" (undated), https://www.ratedbooks.org/nlte.

47. RatedBooks, "Know Before You Read" (undated), https://www.ratedbooks.org/.

48. Mead Gruver, "From Masks to Book Banning, Conservatives Take On Educators," Associated Press (September 19, 2021), https://apnews.com/article/conservatives-educators-coronavirus-masks-book-banning-cfe02e318d95070d468c88e7294d8aa9.

49. Anthony Zurcher, "Why Are Certain School Books Being Banned in US?," BBC (February 7, 2022), https://www.bbc.com/news/world-us-canada-60261660.

50. Zurcher, "Why Are Certain School Books Being Banned in US?"

51. Damien Cave, "'Out of Darkness,' by Ashley Hope Pérez," *New York Times* (November 6, 2015), https://www.nytimes.com/2015/11/08/books/review/out-of-darkness-by-ashley-hope-perez.html.

52. Ashley Hope Péreza, "A Texas School District Banned My Book. Then Things Got Really Ugly," *Texas Monthly* (December 2, 2021), https://www.texasmonthly.com/news-politics/texas-school-district-banned-my-book/.

53. Friedman, "Banned in the USA"; Eesha Pendharkar, "Who's Behind the Escalating Push to Ban Books? A New Report Has Answers," *EducationWeek*

(September 19, 2022), https://www.edweek.org/leadership/whos-behind-the-escalating-push-to-ban-books-a-new-report-has-answers/2022/09.

54. Lois Mai Chan, "The Burning of the Books in China, 213 B.C.," *Journal of Library History* 7:2 (1972), 101–108.

55. Barak Blum, "Banned from the Libraries? Ovid's Books and Their Fate in the Exile Poetry," *American Journal of Philology* 138:3 (2017), 488–526.

56. "'Wizard of Oz' Banned from Detroit Libraries," *Toledo Blade* (April 5, 1957), https://news.google.com/newspapers?nid=1350&dat=19,570,405&id=FldIAAAAIBAJ&sjid=wgAEAAAAIBAJ&pg=4518%2C6308190&fbclid=IwAR33Bl23DSrqqApYJ92LxnXPcQojV3Kt1K-IHCL6FB0uhQQvzCCO1ckEvII.

57. Virginia Tech Special Collections, University Archives, "Challenging and Banning Literary Classics" (September 29, 2016), https://scuablog.lib.vt.edu/2016/09/29/banned-book-week-2016/#:~:text=The%20Sun%20Also%20Rises%2C%20by,overall%20decadence%20of%20its%20characters.

58. "LGBTQ Fiction Sales Are Surging in the U.S., NPD Says," NPD (June 15, 2022), https://www.npd.com/news/press-releases/2022/lgbtq-fiction-sales-are-surging-in-the-u-s-npd-says/.

59. Pen America, "Banned in the USA: Beyond the Shelves" (November 1, 2024), https://pen.org/report/beyond-the-shelves/.

60. Praveena Somasundaram, "School Board Censures Trustee After She Allegedly Sneaked into Library," *Washington Post* (August 25, 2023), https://www.washingtonpost.com/nation/2023/08/25/granbury-texas-trustee-censure-library/.

61. Sarah Mervosh, "Who Runs the Best U.S. Schools? It May Be the Defense Department," *New York Times* (October 10, 2023), https://www.nytimes.com/2023/10/10/us/schools-pandemic-defense-department.html; and Kenneth K. Wong, "Public School Systems Can Learn a Lot from the Department of Defense Education Activity" (Washington, DC: Brookings Institution, July 15, 2024), https://www.brookings.edu/articles/public-school-systems-can-learn-a-lot-from-the-department-of-defense-education-activity/#:~:text=The%20Department%20of%20Defense%20Education%20Activity%20(DoDEA)%20reached%20a%20historic,both%204th%20and%208th%20grade.

62. Ed Pilkington, "Pentagon Schools Suspend Library Books for 'Compliance Review' Under Trump Orders," *The Guardian* (February 13, 2025), https://www.theguardian.com/us-news/2025/feb/13/pentagon-schools-closed-libraries-trump

63. John Ismay and Kate Selig, "Naval Academy Takes Steps to End Diversity Policies in Books and Admissions," *New York Times* (March 28, 2025), https://www.nytimes.com/2025/03/28/us/politics/naval-academy-diversity-affirmative-action.html; the full list of books removed from the shelves can be found at https://media.defense.gov/2025/Apr/04/2003683009/-1/-1/0/250404-LIST%20OF%20REMOVED%20BOOKS%20FROM%20NIMITZ%20LIBRARY.PDF.

Chapter 3

1. Ross Douthat, "Steve Bannon on 'Broligarchs' vs. Populism," *New York Times* (January 31, 2025), https://www.nytimes.com/2025/01/31/opinion/steve-bannon-on-broligarchs-vs-populism.html.

2. Cas Mudde and Cristobel Rovira Kaltwasser, *Populism: A Very Short Introduction* (Oxford: Oxford University Press, 2017), 5–6.

3. Michael Wolff, *Fire and Fury: Inside the Trump White House* (New York: Henry Holt, 2018).

4. David Smith, "Trump Tower Meeting with Russians 'Treasonous,' Bannon Says in Explosive Book," *The Guardian* (January 3, 2018), https://www.theguardian.com/us-news/2018/jan/03/donald-trump-russia-steve-bannon-michael-wolff.

5. Douthat, "Steve Bannon."

6. Rotten Tomatoes, "Generation Zero" (2010), https://www.rottentomatoes.com/m/generation_zero.

7. "Steve Bannon: The Trump-Whisperer's Rapid Fall from Grace," BBC (August 20, 2020), https://www.bbc.com/news/world-us-canada-42636667.

8. René Guénon, *The Crisis of the Modern World*, trans. Marco Pallis, Arthur Osborne, and Richard C. Nicholson, 4th ed. (Hillsdale, NY: Sophia Perennis, 2004); and Joshua S. Lupo, "The Political Theology of Traditionalism: Steve Bannon, the Far Right, and the End of Days" (January 16, 2024), https://contendingmodernities.nd.edu/theorizing-modernities/political-theology-traditionalism/.

9. Isaac Arnsdorf, "How Steve Bannon Guided the MAGA Movement's Rebound from Jan. 6," *Washington Post* (April 4, 2024), https://www.washingtonpost.com/politics/2024/04/04/steve-bannon-maga-january-6/.

10. Bari Weiss, "Leonard Leo—The Man Who Rebuilt the Supreme Court," *Free Press* (March 27, 2025), https://www.thefp.com/p/full-transcript-

leonard-leo. See *Roe v. Wade*, 410 U.S. 113 (1973), https://supreme.justia. com/cases/federal/us/410/113/.

11. Phyllis Schlafly, *A Choice Not an Echo: The Inside Story of How American Presidents Are Chosen* (Alton, IL: Pere Marquette Press, 1964).

12. Anna Massoglia and Karl Evers-Hillstrom, "'Dark Money' Topped $1 Billion in 2020, Largely Boosting Democrats," OpenSecrets (March 17, 2021), https://www.opensecrets.org/news/2021/03/one-billion-dark-money-2020-electioncycle.

13. Anna Massoglia and Kaitlin Washburn, "2017 Financials of the Koch's Dark Money Network," OpenSecrets (November 29, 2018), https://www.opensecrets.org/news/2018/11/2017-financials-of-the-kochs-dark-money-network/.

14. John Gramlich, "How Trump Compares with other Recent Presidents in Appointing Federal Judges," Pew Research Center (January 13, 2021), https://www.pewresearch.org/short-reads/2021/01/13/how-trump-compares-with-other-recent-presidents-in-appointing-federal-judges/; and "Factbox: Donald Trump's Legacy—Six Policy Takeaways," Reuters (October 30, 2020), https://www.reuters.com/article/us-usa-trump-legacy-factbox/factbox-donald-trumps-legacy-six-policy-takeaways-idUSKBN27F1GK.

15. "2023 Year-End Report on the Federal Judiciary," https://www.supremecourt.gov/publicinfo/year-end/2023year-endreport.pdf.

16. Andy Kroll, Andrea Bernstein, and Ilya Marritz, "We Don't Talk About Leonard: The Man Behind the Right's Supreme Court Supermajority," *ProPublica* (October 11, 2023), https://www.propublica.org/article/we-dont-talk-about-leonard-leo-supreme-court-supermajority.

17. Kroll et al., "We Don't Talk."

18. "Trump Administration Judicial Nominees and the Administrative state," Ballotpedia, https://ballotpedia.org/Trump_administration_judicial_nominees_and_the_administrative_state#:':text=About%20half%20of%20Trump's%20judicial,that%20focuses%20on%20legal%20issues.

19. John Hayward, "More In Sorrow Than in Anger: Trump Calls Romney 'Sad and Pathetic," Breitbart News Daily (June 13, 2016), https://www.breitbart.com/radio/2016/06/13/sorrow-anger-trump-calls-romney-sad-pathetic/.

20. Steven M. Teles, *The Rise of the Conservative Legal Movement* (Princeton: Princeton University Press, 2008).

21. "Friends of the Court: SCOTUS Justices' Beneficial Relationships with Billionaire Donors," *ProPublica* (undated), https://www.propublica.org/series/supreme-court-scotus.

22. *Dobbs v. Jackson Women's Health Organization*, 597 U.S. 215 (2022), https://supreme.justia.com/cases/federal/us/597/19-1392/#tab-opinion-4600822.

23. Brian Schwartz, "Nonprofit Financed by Billionaire George Soros Quietly Donated $140 Million to Political Causes in 2021," CNBC (January 4, 2023), https://www.cnbc.com/2023/01/04/nonprofit-financed-by-billionaire-george-soros-donated-140-million-to-political-groups-in-2021.html.

24. Kenneth P. Vogel and Shane Goldmacher, "An Unusual $1.6 Billion Donation Bolsters Conservatives," *New York Times* (August 22, 2022), https://www.nytimes.com/2022/08/22/us/politics/republican-dark-money.html.

25. Maggie Severns, Josh Dawsey, and John Jurgensen, "This Conservative Is Doing Just Fine, Thank You, After Getting Dumped by Trump," *Wall Street Journal* (June 3, 2025), https://www.wsj.com/business/media/leonard-leo-trump-2cd729c8?mod=hp_lead_pos7.

26. Donald Trump, post on Truth Social (included in @TrumpDailyPosts, May 29, 2025), https://x.com/TrumpDailyPosts/status/1928292159397998661.

27. Jesus Jiménez and Nicholas Bogel-Burroughs, "What Are Abortion Trigger Laws and Which States Have Them?," *New York Times* (June 24, 2022), https://www.nytimes.com/2022/06/25/us/trigger-laws-abortion-states-roe.html#:~:text=The%20Supreme%20Court's%20decision%20to,states%20that%20have%20trigger%20laws; and Elizabeth Nash and Lauren Cross, "26 States Are Certain or Likely to Ban Abortion Without Roe: Here's Which Ones and Why," Guttmacher Institute (October 28, 2021), https://www.guttmacher.org/article/2021/10/26-states-are-certain-or-likely-ban-abortion-without-roe-heres-which-ones-and-why.

28. Benjamin Rader et al., "Estimated Travel Time and Spatial Access to Abortion Facilities in the US Before and After the Dobbs v Jackson Women's Health Decision," *Journal of the American Medical Association* 328:20 (November 22, 2022), 2041–2047, https://doi.org/10.1001/jama.2022.20424.

29. National Conference of State Legislatures, "State Abortion Laws: Protections and Restrictions" (January 29, 2024), https://www.ncsl.org/health/state-abortion-laws-protections-and-restrictions.

30. Americans United for Life, "2020 State Legislative Sessions Report: Annual Report on Government Affairs from America's Leader in Life-Affirming Law and Policy" (undated), https://aul.org/wp-content/uploads/2020/10/2020-State-Legislative-Sessions-Report.pdf.

31. Ximena Bustillo, "Who and What Is Behind Abortion Ban Trigger Law Bills? Two Groups Laid the Groundwork," NPR Morning Edition (July 8, 2022), https://www.npr.org/2022/07/08/1110299496/trigger-laws-13-states-two-groups-laid-groundwork.

32. Americans United for Life, "Pro-Life Model Legislation and Guides" (undated), https://aul.org/law-and-policy/; and Anne Ryman and Matt Wynn, "For Anti-Abortion Activists, Success of 'Heartbeat' Bills Was 10 Years in the Making," Center for Public Integrity (June 20, 2019), https://publicintegrity.org/politics/state-politics/copy-paste-legislate/for-anti-abortion-activists-success-of-heartbeat-bills-was-10-years-in-the-making/.

33. Kavitha Surana, "Some Republicans Were Willing to Compromise on Abortion Ban Exceptions. Activists Made Sure They Didn't," *ProPublica* (November 27, 2023), https://www.propublica.org/article/abortion-ban-exceptions-trigger-laws-health-risks.

34. Helen Christophi, "For Christ's Sake," *The Progressive* (April 27, 2021), https://progressive.org/magazine/for-christ-sake-christophi/.

35. Heidi Schlumpf, "Leonard Leo, Architect of Conservative Supreme Court, Takes on Wider Culture," *National Catholic Reporter* (January 4, 2024), https://www.ncronline.org/news/leonard-leo-architect-conservative-supreme-court-takes-wider-culture. See also Mary Jo McConahay, *Playing God: American Catholic Bishops and the Far Right* (Brooklyn: Melville House, 2023).

36. See https://crcadvisors.com/ (accessed May 19, 2024).

37. Schlumpf, "Leonard Leo."

38. Schlumpf, "Leonard Leo."

39. Anna Massoglia and Andrew Perez, "Secretive Conservative Legal Group Funded by $17 Million Mystery Donor Before Kavanaugh Fight," OpenSecrets (May 17, 2019), https://www.opensecrets.org/news/2019/05/dark-money-group-funded-by-17million-mystery-donor-before-kavanaugh/.

40. Heidi Schlumpf, "Trump's Catholic Cabinet: How Will Their Faith Shape Their Work?," *National Catholic Reporter* (February 13, 2025), https://www.ncronline.org/news/trumps-catholic-cabinet-how-will-their-faith-shape-their-work.

41. "Russ Vought: Donald Trump's Holy Warrior," *The Economist* (January 3, 2025), https://www.economist.com/united-states/2025/01/03/russ-vought-donald-trumps-holy-warrior.

42. Antonio Spadaro and Marcelo Figueroa, "Evangelical Fundamentalism and Catholic Integralism," La Civilta Cattolica (undated), https://www.laciviltacattolica.it/articolo/evangelical-fundamentalism-and-catholic-integralism-in-the-usa-a-surprising-ecumenism//.

43. "Stephen Bannon Criticizes the Catholic Church for Joining the Debate on DACA, Broadcast on 'CBS This Morning'" (September 7, 2017), https://www.paramountpressexpress.com/cbs-news-and-stations/releases/?view=48442. See also Conor Gaffey, "Steve Bannon's Long Struggle with the Catholic Church," *Newsweek* (September 22, 2017), https://www.newsweek.com/steve-bannon-60-minutes-pope-francis-catholic-church-663021; and Neil Howe, "Where Did Steve Bannon Get His Worldview? From My Book," *Washington Post* (February 24, 2017), https://www.washingtonpost.com/entertainment/books/where-did-steve-bannon-get-his-worldview-from-my-book/2017/02/24/16937f38-f84a-11e6-9845-576c69081518_story.html.

44. Rebecca Shabad, "Donald Trump Names His Favorite Bible Verse," CBS News (April 14, 2016), https://www.cbsnews.com/news/donald-trump-names-his-favorite-bible-verse/.

45. Billy Hallowell, "'It Changed Something in Me': Trump Admits Attempted Assassination Transformed His Belief in God," Christian Broadcasting Network (February 7, 2015), https://cbn.com/news/us/it-changed-something-me-trump-admits-attempted-assassination-transformed-his-belief-god.

46. Spadaro and Figueroa, "Evangelical Fundamentalism."

47. "Letter of the Holy Father Francis to the Bishops of the United States of America" (February 10, 2025), https://www.vatican.va/content/francesco/en/letters/2025/documents/20250210-lettera-vescovi-usa.html.

48. Allison Prang, "JD Vance 'Surprised' by Pushback from Pope Francis, US Bishops on Immigration," *National Catholic Reporter* (February 28, 2025), https://www.ncronline.org/news/vance-surprised-pushback-pope-us-bishops-new-immigration-policies.

49. David Crary and Amelia Thomson-Deveaux, "AP VoteCast Shows Trump Boosted His Level of Support Among Catholic Voters," AP (November 13, 2024), https://apnews.com/article/election-2024-trump-catholic-voters-f73f2c74b1e21cc96ff42a671220dbdb.

50. For a review of academic studies about populism, see John Abromeit, "A Critical Review of Recent Literature on Populism," *Politics and Governance*

5:4 (2017), http://dx.doi.org.proxy-um.researchport.umd.edu/10.17645/pag.v5i4.1146; Cas Mudde and Cristobal Rovira Kaltwasser, *Populism: A Very Short Introduction* (New York: Oxford University Press, 2017); Ruth Wodak, *The Politics of Fear: What Right-Wing Populist Discourses Mean* (Los Angeles: Sage, 2016); Jan-Werner Müller, *What Is Populism?* (Philadelphia: University of Pennsylvania Press, 2016); Benjamin Moffitt, *The Global Rise of Populism: Performance, Political Style and Representation* (Stanford, CA: Stanford University Press, 2016); Federico Finchelstein, *From Fascism to Populism in History* (Berkeley: University of California Press, 2017); and John Abromeit, Bridget María Chesterton, Gary Marotta, and York Norman, eds., *Transformations of Populism in Europe and the Americas: History and Recent Tendencies* (New York: Bloomsbury, 2016).

Chapter 4

1. David Brooks, "Roe's Birth, and Death," *New York Times* (April 21, 2005), https://www.nytimes.com/2005/04/21/opinion/roes-birth-and-death.html?smid=nytcore-ios-share&referringSource=articleShare.

2. Guttmacher Institute, "13 States Have Abortion Trigger Bans—Here's What Happens When Roe Is Overturned" (June 6, 2022), https://www.guttmacher.org/article/2022/06/13-states-have-abortion-trigger-bans-heres-what-happens-when-roe-overturned; "26 States Are Certain or Likely to Ban Abortion Without Roe: Here's Which Ones and Why" (October 28, 2021), https://www.guttmacher.org/article/2021/10/26-states-are-certain-or-likely-ban-abortion-without-roe-heres-which-ones-and-why.

3. Brooks, "Roe's Birth, and Death."

4. Robert Post and Reva Siegel, "Roe Rage: Democratic Constitutionalism and Backlash," *Harvard Civil Rights–Civil Liberties Law Review* 42 (2007), 373–433.

5. Jerry Brewer, "The Panic over Trans Sports Inclusion," *Washington Post* (June 6, 2024), https://www.washingtonpost.com/sports/interactive/2024/transgender-sports-debate-politics/.

6. Casey Parks, "How a Grandma Became the Focus of a 'Misinformed' Trump Ad on Trans Athletes," *Washington Post* (November 5, 2024), https://www.washingtonpost.com/nation/2024/11/05/election-trans-sports-trump-campaign/.

7. Rachel Bachman, Laura Kusisto, and Kris Maher, "The Trump Ads That Pushed Transgender Rights to Center Stage," *Wall Street Journal* (November

7, 2024), https://www.wsj.com/politics/elections/trump-ads-transgender-rights-harris-election-b287c9d8.

8. Eleanor Klibanoff, "How 'Wildly Successful' Anti-Trans Ads Fired Up Texas Voters for Republicans," *Texas Tribune* (November 8, 2024), https://www.texastribune.org/2024/11/08/transgender-ads-motivate-texas-republicans/.

9. Gloria Steinem, "A Bunny's Tale, Part I," *Show* (May 1963), 97ff; and "A Bunny's Tale, Part II," *Show* (June 1963), 66ff.

10. Ronald Dworkin, *Life's Dominion: An Argument about Abortion, Euthanasia, and Individual Freedom* (New York: Vintage Books, 1994), 102.

11. Linda Greenhouse and Reva B. Siegel, "Before (and After) Roe v. Wade: New Questions About Backlash," *Yale Law Journal* 120 (2011), 2028–2097, esp. 2028.

12. "State Bans on Abortion Throughout Pregnancy," Guttmacher Institute (May 1, 2024), https://www.guttmacher.org/state-policy/explore/state-policies-abortion-bans.

13. Lisa H. Harris, "Navigating Loss of Abortion Services—A Large Academic Medical Center Prepares for the Overturn of Roe v Wade," *New England Journal of Medicine* 386:22 (May 11, 2022), 2061–2064, https://doi.org/10.1056/NEJMp2206246.

14. Mabinty Quarshire, "What to Know About Texas Abortion Law That Bans the Procedure Once Heartbeat Is Detected," *USA Today* (September 2, 2021), https://www.usatoday.com/story/news/politics/2021/09/01/texas-abortion-law-what-to-know/5679581001/.

15. Alison Gemmill, Claire E. Margerison, Elizabeth A. Stuart, et al., "Infant Deaths After Texas' 2021 Ban on Abortion in Early Pregnancy," *JAMA Pediatrics* (June 24, 2024), doi:10.1001/jamapediatrics.2024.0885.

16. Madeleine Rubin, "Texas Medical Board to consider issuing guidance on abortion laws' medical exceptions," *Texas Tribune* (March 14, 2024), https://www.texastribune.org/2024/03/14/texas-medical-board-doctors-abortion-guidance/#:~:text=Texas%20laws%20ban%20nearly%20all,a%20serious%20risk%20of%20substantial.

17. Cassandra Jaramillo and Kavitha Surana, "A Texas Woman Died After the Hospital Said It Would Be a Crime to Intervene in Her Miscarriage," *Texas Tribune* (October 30, 2024), https://www.texastribune.org/2024/10/30/texas-abortion-ban-josseli-barnica-death-miscarriage/#:~:text=Three%20days%20after%20she%20delivered,the%20heartbeat%20of%20a%20fetus.

18. Kavitha Surana, "Abortion Bans Have Delayed Emergency Medical Care. In Georgia, Experts Say This Mother's Death Was Preventable," *ProPublica* (September 16, 2024), https://www.propublica.org/article/georgia-abortion-ban-amber-thurman-death.

19. https://www.nytimes.com/2023/12/14/podcasts/the-daily/texas-abortion-ban.html?showTranscript=1.

20. Sabrina Tavernise, "The Woman Who Fought the Texas Abortion Ban," *New York Times* (December 14, 2023), https://www.nytimes.com/2023/12/14/podcasts/the-daily/texas-abortion-ban.html?showTranscript=1.

21. https://fundtexaschoice.org/get-help/.

22. https://powertodecide.org/get-involved/abortion-access-for-all.

23. https://www.abortionfinder.org/.

24. https://needabortion.org/.

25. https://www.reproductiveservices.com/.

26. See https://fundtexaschoice.org/get-help/#:~:text=Fund%20Texas%20Choice%20helps%20Texans,lodging%2C%20and%20other%20practical%20needs.&text=Our%20helpline%20and%20online%20support,Mondays%20to%206pm%20on%20Thursdays;   https://powertodecide.org/get-involved/abortion-access-for-all; https://www.abortionfinder.org/; Need Abortion.org; and https://www.reproductiveservices.com/.

27. Sara Cline and Geoff Mulvihill, "Warrant Cites Abortion Pill Prescription," *Arkansas Democrat Gazette* (February 1, 2025), https://www.arkansasonline.com/news/2025/feb/01/warrant-cites-abortion-pill-prescription/.

28. https://www.elevatedaccess.org/.

29. https://www.elevatedaccess.org/.

30. Kimya Forouzan, Amy Friedrich-Karnik, and Isaac Maddow-Zimet, "The High Toll of US Abortion Bans: Nearly One in Five Patients Now Traveling Out of State for Abortion Care," Guttmacher Institute (December 2023), https://www.guttmacher.org/2023/12/high-toll-us-abortion-bans-nearly-one-five-patients-now-traveling-out-state-abortion-care.

31. Grace Benninghoff, "OB-GYN Residents Are Required to Receive Clinical Abortion Training. They Can't Do That in Texas," *Texas Monthly* (May 23, 2023), https://www.texasmonthly.com/news-politics/abortion-training-ob-gyn-medical-residents-leaving-texas/.

32. Nadine El-Bawab, "Doctors Face Tough Decision to Leave States with Abortion Bans," ABCNews (June 23, 2023), https://abcnews.go.com/US/doctors-face-tough-decision-leave-states-abortion-bans/story?id=10016 7986#:~:text=In%20interviews%20with%20ABC%20News,best%20 care%20possible%20for%20patients.

33. Kyle Pfannenstiel, "Idaho Is Losing OB-GYNs After Strict Abortion Ban. But Health Exceptions Unlikely This Year," *Idaho Capital Sun* (April 5, 2024), https://idahocapitalsun.com/2024/04/05/idaho-is-losing-ob-gyns-after-strict-abortion-ban-but-health-exceptions-unlikely-this-year/#:~:text= Idaho%20lost%2022%25%20of%20practicing,has%20created%20uncert ainty%20and%20fear.

34. PBS News, "Interactive: How Key Groups of Americans Voted in 2024" (November 7, 2024), https://www.pbs.org/newshour/politics/interactive-how-key-groups-of-americans-voted-in—2024-according-to-ap-votecast.

35. Rachel K. Jones and Amy Friedrich-Karnik, "Medication Abortion Accounted for 63% of All US Abortions in 2023—An Increase from 53% in 2020" (March 2024), https://www.guttmacher.org/2024/03/medication-abortion-accounted-63-all-us-abortions-2023-increase-53-2020#:~:text= New%20Guttmacher%20Institute%20research%20from,nationally%20be tween%202020%20and%202023.

36. Caroline Kitchener, Robert Barnes, and Ann E. Marimow, "The Controversial Article Matthew Kacsmaryk Did Not Disclose to the Senate," *Washington Post* (April 15, 2023), https://www.washingtonpost.com/politics/2023/04/15/matthew-kacsmaryk-law-review/. For the article, see Justin E. Butterfield and Stephanie N. Taub, "The Jurisprudence of the Body: Conscience Rights in the Use of the Sword, Scalpel, and Syringe," *Texas Review of Law and Politics* 21:3 (September 20, 2017), 409—421.

37. Amanda Becker, "Dark Money Is Flowing to Groups Trying to Limit Medication Abortion. Leonard Leo Is Again at the Center," *The 19th News* (January 4, 2024), https://19thnews.org/2024/01/leonard-leo-center-medication-abortion-restriction-efforts/.

38. https://nwaafund.org/.

39. https://www.indigenousidalliance.org/.

40. https://idahoabortionrights.com/.

41. Daniel C. Vock, "Why the Fight over Abortion Pills Isn't over Yet," Route Fifty (June 14, 2014), https://www.route-fifty.com/management/2024/06/why-fight-over-abortion-pills-isnt-over-yet/397402/; Molly Cook Escobar,

Amy Schoenfeld Walker, Allison McCann, Scott Reinhard, and Helmuth Ros-ales, "171,000 Traveled for Abortions Last Year. See Where They Went," *New York Times* (June 13, 2014); and David W. Chen, "In Isolated Guam, Abortion Is Legal. And Nearly Impossible to Get," *New York Times* (June 26, 2023), https://www.nytimes.com/2023/06/26/us/guam-abortion.html.

42. Clarence Thomas, Concurring, *Thomas E. Dobbs v. Jackson Women's Health Organization*, 597 U.S. 215 (2022), https://www.supremecourt.gov/opinions/21pdf/19-1392_6j37.pdf.

43. Paul F. Hemez, "Spouses in Opposite-Sex and Same-Sex Married Couples and Their Households: 2022," American Community Survey Briefs, US Census Bureau, ACSBR-020 (June 2024), 8, https://www2.census.gov/library/publications/2024/demo/acsbr-020.pdf.

44. Greenhouse and Siegel, "Before (and After) Roe," 2086.

45. Williams Institute, UCLA School of Law, "The Impact of 2024 Anti-Transgender Legislation on Youth" (April 2024), https://williamsinstitute.law.ucla.edu/publications/2024-anti-trans-legislation/; and Human Rights Campaign, "Map: Attacks on Gender Affirming Care by State" (2024), https://www.hrc.org/resources/attacks-on-gender-affirming-care-by-state-map.

46. Quoted by Lisa Lerer and Elizabeth Dias, "Hillary Clinton Has Some Tough Words for Democrats, and for Women," *New York Times* (May 25, 2024), https://www.nytimes.com/2024/05/25/us/politics/hillary-clinton-abortion.html?smid=nytcore-ios-share&referringSource=articleShare.

47. Donald F. Kettl, *The Divided States of America: Why Federalism Doesn't Work* (Princeton: Princeton University Press, 2020).

Chapter 5

1. *New York Times Magazine*, "The 1619 Project" (August 14, 2019), https://www.nytimes.com/interactive/2019/08/14/magazine/1619-america-slavery.html.

2. Pulitzer Center, 2019 Annual Report, https://reports.pulitzercenter.org/pulitzer-center-2019-annual-report/index.html.

3. Timothy Sandefur, "The 1619 Project: An Autopsy," Cato Institute (October 27, 2020), https://www.cato.org/commentary/1619-project-autopsy.

4. Sarah Schwartz, "Lawmakers Push to Ban '1619 Project' from Schools," *Education Week* (February 3, 2021), https://www.edweek.org/teaching-learning/lawmakers-push-to-ban-1619-project-from-schools/2021/02#:~:text=

The%20Arkansas%20and%20Mississippi%20bills,the%20United%20S
tates%20was%20founded.%E2%80%9D.

5. Barbara Roderiguez, "Republican State Lawmakers Want to Pun-
ish Schools That Teach the 1619 Project," *USA Today* (February 10,
2021), https://www.usatoday.com/story/news/education/2021/02/10/
slavery-and-history-states-threaten-funding-schools-teach-1619-project/
4454195001/.

6. Juan Perez, $1 Nicole Gaudiano, "Trump Blasts 1619 Project as Devos
praises alternative black history curriculum," *Politico* (September 17, 2020),
https://www.politico.com/news/2020/09/17/devos-black-history-1776-
unites-417186.

7. KK Ottesen, "An ARCHITECT of Critical Race Theory: 'We Cannot
Allow All of the LESSONS from the Civil Rights Movement Forward to Be
Packed Up and Put Away for Storage,'" *Washington Post* (January 19, 2022),
https://www.washingtonpost.com/lifestyle/magazine/an-architect-of-
critical-race-theory-we-cannot-allow-all-of-the-lessons-from-the-civil-rights-
movement-forward-to-be-packed-up-and-put-away-for-storage/2022/01/
14/24bb31de-627e-11ec-a7e8-3a8455b71fad_story.html. For an early
foundation of CRT, see Max Horkheimer, republished in *Critical Theory:
Selected Essays*, trans. Matthew J. O'Connell et al. (New York: Continuum,
1982).

8. "Quick Facts," City of Colleyville, Texas, https://www.colleyville.com/
colleyville/about-colleyville-quick-facts.

9. Wayne Carter, "District Calls Anniversary Photo of High School Principal
and His Wife 'Questionable,'" NBC DFW (August 2, 2021), https://www.
nbcdfw.com/news/local/carter-in-the-classroom/district-calls-anniversary-
photo-of-high-school-principal-and-his-wife-questionable/2704613/.

10. Joelle Goldstein, "Principal Speaks Out After School District Brands
His Anniversary Pic with Wife 'Questionable,'" *People* (August 3, 2021),
https://people.com/human-interest/texas-hs-principal-speaks-out-after-
questionable-anniversary-photos-with-wife/.

11. Brian Lopez, "How a Black High School Principal Was Swept into a
'Critical Race Theory' Maelstrom in a Mostly White Texas Suburb," *Texas
Tribune* (September 18, 2021), https://www.texastribune.org/2021/09/18/
colleyville-principal-critical-race-theory/.

12. Greater Grapevine-Colleyville Independent School District, "Former
School Board Candidate Calls for Firing of Colleyville Heritage HS Principal,"

Fort Worth Star-Telegram (August 3, 2021), https://www.star-telegram.com/news/local/article253238543.html.

13. Lopez, "Black High School Principal."

14. "Lt. Gov. Dan Patrick: Statement on the Passage of Senate Bill 3" (July 16, 2021), https://www.ltgov.texas.gov/2021/07/16/lt-gov-dan-patrick-statement-on-the-passage-of-senate-bill-3/. On the *New York Times* project, see https://www.nytimes.com/interactive/2019/08/14/magazine/1619-america-slavery.html.

15. TX School Choice, Twitter (June 16, 2021), https://twitter.com/TX_SchoolChoice/status/1405217413277306885.

16. Christopher F. Rufo, Twitter (March 2, 2021), https://twitter.com/realchrisrufo/status/1366820252252733446?ref_src=twsrc%5Etfw%7Ctwcamp%5Etweetembed%7Ctwterm%5E1366823034187702273%7Ctwgr%5Edea86972fd24011ad1e0738f67b99e5410a68b4d%7Ctwcon%5Es2_&ref_url=https%3A%2F%2Fwww.washingtonexaminer.com%2Fnews%2F2593946%2Farizona-education-department-encourages-talking-to-babies-about-racism-says-3-month-olds-can-be-racist-report%2F.

17. "Governor DeSantis Announces Legislative Proposal to Stop W.O.K.E. Activism and Critical Race Theory in Schools and Corporations" (December 15, 2021), https://www.flgov.com/2021/12/15/governor-desantis-announces-legislative-proposal-to-stop-w-o-k-e-activism-and-critical-race-theory-in-schools-and-corporations/.

18. Christopher F. Rufo, "'Antiracism' Comes to the Heartland," *City Journal* (January 19, 2021), https://www.city-journal.org/article/antiracism-comes-to-the-heartland.

19. Josie Ensor, "He Is America's 'Most Effective Conservative'. This Is His Blueprint for Trump," *The Times* (December 5, 2024), https://www.thetimes.com/world/us-world/article/christopher-rufo-department-education-2025-trump-28j6p3djb.

20. Jack Stripling and David Jesse, "He Wanted a Presidency. He Became a Pariah," *Chronicle of Higher Education* (June 13, 2025), https://www.chronicle.com/article/he-wanted-a-presidency-he-became-a-pariah; and Maria Avlonitis, "The Top Choice for UF President Was Rejected. What's Next?," Independent Florida Alligator (June 9, 2025), https://www.alligator.org/article/2025/06/top-choice-for-uf-president-was-rejected-whats-next.

21. Victor Garcia, "Journalist Declares 'One-Man War Against Critical Race Theory' After Nuke Lab Holds 'White Privilege' Training," Fox News (August 13, 2020), https://www.foxnews.com/us/chris-rufo-one-man-war-race-theory.

22. Sam Dorman, "Chris Rufo Calls on Trump to End Critical Race Theory 'Cult Indoctrination' in Federal Government," Fox News (September 1, 2020), https://www.foxnews.com/politics/chris-rufo-race-theory-cult-federal-government.

23. Laura Meckler and Josh Dawsey, "Republicans, spurred by an unlikely figure, see political promise in targeting critical race theory," *Stars and Stripes* (June 19, 2021), https://www.stripes.com/theaters/us/2021-06-19/Republicans-spurred-by-an-unlikely-figure-see-political-promise-in-critical-race-theory-1740970.html.

24. Christopher F. Rufo, "Critical Race Theory Briefing Book" (February 14, 2023), https://christopherrufo.com/p/crt-briefing-book?mc_cid=340fbeafe6&mc_eid=f645157ebf.

25. Parents Defending Education, "Parents Defending Education National Poll: Americans Overwhelmingly Reject 'Woke' Race and Gender Policies in K-12 Education" (May 10, 2021), https://defendinged.org/commentaries/parents-defending-education-national-poll-americans-overwhelmingly-reject-woke-race-and-gender-policies-in-k-12-education/.

26. "Executive Order on Combating Race and Sex Stereotyping" (September 22, 2020), https://trumpwhitehouse.archives.gov/presidential-actions/executive-order-combating-race-sex-stereotyping/#:~:text=The%20contractor%20shall%20not%20use,her%20race%20or%20sex%2C%20is.

27. Twitter (May 11, 2021), https://twitter.com/iandprior/status/1392292044975087617.

28. School Board meeting, Carmel, NY, https://www.youtube.com/watch?v=zxu3wdiXRF0.

29. Julia Carrie Wong, "From Viral Videos to Fox News: How Rightwing Media Fueled the Critical Race Theory Panic," *The Guardian* (June 30, 2021), https://www.theguardian.com/education/2021/jun/30/critical-race-theory-rightwing-social-media-viral-video.

30. William H. Frey, "Anti-CRT Bills Are Aimed to Incite the GOP Base—Not Parents," Brookings Institution (March 30, 2022), https://www.brookings.edu/articles/anti-crt-bills-are-aimed-to-incite-the-gop-base-not-parents/.

31. Pia Deshpande et al., "Critical Race Theory and Asymmetric Mobilization," *Political Behavior* 46 (2024), 1677–1699, https://doi.org/10.1007/s11109-023-09889-4.

32. Alauna Safarpour et al., "Divisive or Descriptive? How Americans Understand Critical Race Theory," *Journal of Race, Ethnicity, and Politics* 9:1 (2024), 157–181, doi:10.1017/rep.2023.39.

33. Matt Gertz, "Fox's Anti-Critical Race Theory' Parents Are Also GOP Activists," Media Matters (June 17, 2021), https://www.mediamatters.org/fox-news/foxs-anti-critical-race-theory-parents-are-also-gop-activists.

34. Warren Fiske, "Youngkin Offers Little Proof Critical Race Theory Is in 'All' Virginia Schools" (July 9, 2021), https://www.politifact.com/factchecks/2021/aug/10/glenn-youngkin/youngkin-offers-little-proof-critical-race-theory-/.

35. Eva McKend and Dan Merica, "Virginia Republicans Seize on Parental Rights and Schools Fight in Final Weeks of Campaign," CNN (October 7, 2021), https://www.cnn.com/2021/10/07/politics/glenn-youngkin-parental-rights-education-strategy/index.html.

36. Zach Montellaro and Brittany Gibson, "Youngkin Wins, Flipping Virginia Red," *Politico* (November 3, 2021), https://www.politico.com/news/2021/11/02/virginia-governor-race-polls-close-518625.

37. Theodoric Meyer, Maggie Severns, and Meridith McGraw, "'The Tea Party to the 10th Power': Trumpworld Bets Big on Critical Race Theory," *Politico* (June 23, 2021), https://www.politico.com/news/2021/06/23/trumpworld-critical-race-theory-495712.

38. Lis Power, "Fox News' Obsession with Critical Race Theory, by the Numbers," Media Matters (June 15, 2021), https://www.mediamatters.org/fox-news/fox-news-obsession-critical-race-theory-numbers.

39. Heritage Action for America, Reject Critical Race Theory (undated), https://hafa.nyc3.cdn.digitaloceanspaces.com/assets/REJECT-CRT-E-Book.pdf.

40. Citizens for Renewing America, https://citizensrenewingamerica.com/issue_topic/critical-race-theory/.

41. Citizens for Renewing America, "Combatting Critical Race Theory in Your Community: An A to Z Guide on How to Stop Critical Race Theory and Reclaim Your Local School Board," https://citizensrenewingamerica.com/issues/combatting-critical-race-theory-in-your-community/.

42. America First Legal Foundation, IRS Form 990 (ProPublica), https://projects.propublica.org/nonprofits/organizations/862190372/202323199349307967/IRS990.

43. 1776 Project PAC, https://1776projectpac.com/.

44. Safarpour et al., "Divisive or Descriptive?"

45. Andrea Zelinsky, "Lone Star Parent Power: How One of the Nation's Toughest Anti-Critical Race Theory Laws Emboldened Angry Texas Parents Demanding Book Banning, Educator Firings," The 74 (November 4, 2021), https://www.the74million.org/article/lone-star-parent-power-how-one-of-the-nations-toughest-anti-critical-race-theory-laws-emboldened-angry-texas-parents-demanding-book-banning-educator-firings/.

46. Harini S. Shah and Julie Bohlen, "Implicit Bias," National Library of Information (March 4, 2023), https://www.ncbi.nlm.nih.gov/books/NBK5 89697/#:~:text=Implicit%20bias%20includes%20the%20subconscious,% 2C%20affect%20their%20decision%2Dmaking.

47. J. Brian Charles, "Can Shaun Harper Save DEI?," *Chronicle of Higher Education* (June 20, 2024), https://www.chronicle.com/article/can-shaun-harper-save-dei?sra=true.

48. Bianca Quilantan, "The New Red Scare for Red States: Diversity Programs," *Politico* (March 19, 2023), https://www.politico.com/news/2023/ 03/19/gop-culture-war-college-dei-florida-texas-00087697.

49. Executive Order, "Ending Radical and Wasteful Government DEI Programs and Preferencing" (January 20, 2025), https://www.whitehouse.gov/ presidential-actions/2025/01/ending-radical-and-wasteful-government-dei-programs-and-preferencing/; Executive Order, "Ending Illegal Discrimination and Restoring Merit-Based Opportunity" (January 21, 2025), https://www.whitehouse.gov/presidential-actions/2025/01/ending-illegal-discrimination-and-restoring-merit-based-opportunity/.

50. The White House, "Fact Sheet: President Donald J. Trump Ends DEI Madness and Restores Excellence and Safety within the Federal Aviation Administration" (January 22, 2025), https://www.whitehouse.gov/fact-sheets/ 2025/01/fact-sheet-president-donald-j-trump-ends-dei-madness-and-restores-excellence-and-safety-within-the-federal-aviation-administration/.

51. Isaac Stanley-Becker, "The Trump Administration Is Spending $2 Million to Figure Out Whether DEI Causes Plane Crashes," *The Atlantic* (June 5, 2025), https://www.theatlantic.com/politics/archive/2025/06/ government-investigating-whether-dei-causes-plane-crashes/683038/.

52. David E. Sanger, "Trump Blames D.E.I. and Biden for Crash Under His Watch," *New York Times* (February 1, 2025), https://www.nytimes.com/ 2025/01/30/us/politics/trump-plane-crash-dei-faa-diversity.html.

53. "DEI Legislation Tracker," *Chronicle of Higher Education* (updatedAugust 22, 2025), https://www.chronicle.com/article/here-are-the-states-where-lawmakers-are-seeking-to-ban-colleges-dei-efforts?sra=true.

54. Erin Gretzinger and Maggie Hicks, "Tracking Higher Ed's Dismantling of DEI," *Chronicle of Higher Education* (May 6, 2024), https://www.chronicle.com/article/tracking-higher-eds-dismantling-of-dei.

55. Press Release, "Governor Ron DeSantis Hosts Roundtable Exposing the Diversity Equity and Inclusion Scam in Higher Education" (March 13, 2023), https://www.flgov.com/2023/03/13/governor-ron-desantis-hosts-roundtable-exposing-the-diversity-equity-and-inclusion-scam-in-higher-education/.

56. Scott Yenor, "Florida Universities: From Woke to Professionalism" (March 11, 2023), https://dc.claremont.org/florida-universities-from-woke-to-professionalism/.

57. Yenor, "Florida Universities," 4.

58. Claremont Institute Center for the American Way of Life, "Americans Deserve to Know Who Funded BLM Riots," *Newsweek* (March 14, 2023), https://www.newsweek.com/americans-deserve-know-who-funded-blm-riots-opinion-1787460

59. Claremont Institute, "Give the Gift of Freedom," https://www.claremont.org/donate/. Claremont is a 501(c)(3) organization.

60. Andy Kroll, "Revealed: The Billionaires Funding the Coup's Brain Trust," *Rolling Stone* (January 12, 2022), https://www.rollingstone.com/politics/politics-news/devos-bradley-claremont-trump-election-fraud-insurrection-1274253/.

61. Kaanita Iyer and Chris Boyette, "Texas Governor Signs Bill to Ban DEI Offices at State Public Colleges," CNN (June 25, 2023), https://www.cnn.com/2023/06/15/politics/greg-abbott-texas-dei-office-ban-colleges/index.html.

62. Raphael Fernandez, "Texas Colleges Prepare for the End of DEI," *Inside Higher Ed* (December 19, 2023), https://www.insidehighered.com/news/students/diversity/2023/12/19/texas-institutions-prepare-anti-dei-law-go-effect.

63. Quoted in Texas Public Policy Foundation, Post on X (May 17, 2024), https://twitter.com/TPPF/status/1791546188908425698.

64. Center for Media and Democracy, "Texas Public Policy Foundation" (2024), https://sfofexposed.org/texas-public-policy-foundation/.

65. Michael S. Schmidt and Michael C. Bender, "University of Virginia President Resigns Under Pressure from Trump Administration," *New York Times* (June 27, 2025), https://www.nytimes.com/2025/06/27/us/politics/uva-president-resigns-jim-ryan-trump.html; and Minyvonne Burke and Joe

Kottke, "Univ. of Virginia President Resigns amid Trump Administration Inquiry into Diversity Initiatives," NBC News (June 27, 2025), https://www.nbcnews.com/news/us-news/university-virginia-president-resigns-trump-admin-investigation-divers-rcna215597.

Chapter 6

1. "The Story Behind the Join or Die Snake Cartoon" (Philadelphia: National Constitutional Center, May 9, 2024), https://www.presidency.ucsb.edu/documents/letter-reply-horace-greeley-slavery-and-the-union-the-restoration-the-union-the-paramount.

2. Patrick Henry, Speech before the Virginia Convention of 1788 (June 5, 1788), https://www.redhill.org/speeches-writings/liberty-or-empire/#:~:text=This%20Constitution%20is%20said%20to,breast%20of%20every%20true%20American%3F.

3. Abraham Lincoln to Horace Greeley, on Slavery and the Union (August 22, 1862), University of California, Santa Barabara, American Presidency Project, https://www.presidency.ucsb.edu/documents/letter-reply-horace-greeley-slavery-and-the-union-the-restoration-the-union-the-paramount.

4. *New State Ice Co. v. Liebmann*, 285 U.S. 262 (1932), at 311, https://supreme.justia.com/cases/federal/us/285/262/.

5. Christopher A. Bracey, "Louis Brandeis and the Race Question," *Alabama Law Review* 52:3 (2001), 908.

6. In an earlier book, I developed the argument about how results depend on location. See Donald F. Kettl, *The Divided States of America: Why Federalism Doesn't Work* (Princeton: Princeton University Press, 2020).

7. David Siders, "Republican AGs Take Blowtorch to Biden Agenda," *Politico* (March 21, 2021), https://www.politico.com/news/2021/03/21/gop-attorneys-general-biden-477365.

8. *Biden v. Nebraska*, 600 US 477 (2023), https://www.oyez.org/cases/2022/22-506.

9. Heather Willard, "Attorney General Defends Filing Dozens of Cases Against Trump Administration," Fox31 News (April 8, 2025), https://kdvr.com/news/politics/colorado-politics-news/attorney-general-defends-filing-dozens-of-cases-against-trump-administration/.

10. Eliza Collins and John McCormick, "The Democrats Who Are Fighting—and Winning—Against Trump in Court," *Wall Street Journal* (March 30,

2025), https://www.wsj.com/politics/policy/trump-democrats-lawsuits-states-8b765117.

11. Raj Chetty, Will Dobbie, Benjamin Goldman, Sonya R. Porter, and Crystal S. Yang, "Changing Opportunity: Sociological Mechanisms Underlying Growing Class Gaps and Shrinking Race Gaps in Economic Mobility" (NBER Working Paper No. 32697, Opportunity Insights, July 2024), https://opportunityinsights.org/paper/changingopportunity/.

12. John P. Kaminski et al., eds., *The Documentary History of the Ratification of the Constitution*, vol. 10: *Virginia* [3] (Madison: Wisconsin Historical Society Press, 1993), 1609–12, https://csac.history.wisc.edu/wp-content/uploads/sites/281/2024/04/DC3-04-08-07_The-Impartial-Examiner-IV_11Jun88.pdf.

13. Kaminski et al., *Virginia*, 57–60, https://csac.history.wisc.edu/wp-content/uploads/sites/281/2024/04/DC3-04-08-02_Philadelphiensis-IX_6Feb88.pdf.

14. Quoted by Andrew Moesel, "Justice Scalia Speaks at Law School," *Chicago Maroon* (May 9, 2003), https://perma.cc/WQ3K-SZYP.

15. Antonin Scalia, "Originalism: The Lesser Evil," *University of Cincinnati Law Review* 57 (1989), 862.

16. "National Review," Ballotpedia, https://ballotpedia.org/National_Review.

17. Luke Savage, "The Quiet Death of National Review," *Jacobin* (October 1, 2024), https://jacobin.com/2024/10/the-quiet-death-of-national-review/.

18. "Read the Full Transcript of Donald Trump's '100 Days' Interview with TIME," *Time* (April 25, 2025), https://time.com/7280114/donald-trump-2025-interview-transcript/.

19. Sophia Shams, "Preserving Faithful Execution: An Examination into the Original Meaning of the Take Care Clause and the Measures to Preserve It," *Georgetown Journal of Law and Public Policy* 20:805 (2022), 805–824.

20. Jack Goldsmith and John F. Manning, "The Protean Take Care Clause," *University of Pennsylvania Law Review* 164:7 (2016), 1838.

21. *Marbury v. Madison* 5 U.S. 137 (1803), https://www.oyez.org/cases/1789-1850/5us137.

22. *Kendall v. United States ex Rel. Stokes*, 37 U.S. 524 (1838), https://supreme.justia.com/cases/federal/us/37/524/.

23. *Myers v. US*, 272 U.S. 52 (1926), 117.

24. *Youngstown Sheet & Tube Co. v. Sawyer*, 343 U.S. 579 (1952).

25. Dwight Waldo, *The Administrative State: A Study of the Political Theory of American Public Administration* (New York: Ronald Press, 1948).

26. Jed Handelsman Shugerman, "The Imaginary Unitary Executive," Lawfare (July 6, 2020), https://www.lawfaremedia.org/article/imaginary-unitary-executive.

27. Charles L. Heatherly, ed., *Mandate for Leadership: Policy Management in a Conservative Administration* (Washington, DC: Heritage Foundation, 1981).

28. Ronald Reagan, "Remarks at a Dinner Honoring Representative Jack F. Kemp of New York" (Reagan Presidential Library, December 1, 1988), https://www.reaganlibrary.gov/archives/speech/remarks-dinner-honoring-representative-jack-f-kemp-new-york.

29. Janet Hook, "Republicans Criticize Obama's Push to Use Executive Power," *Wall Street Journal* (January 28, 2014), https://www.wsj.com/articles/republicans-criticize-obama8217s-push-to-use-executive-power-1390949791.

30. Aaron Blake, "The GOP's Oversimplified Pushback on Biden's Executive Actions," *Washington Post* (January 21, 2021), https://www.washingtonpost.com/politics/2021/01/21/gops-oversimplified-pushback-bidens-executive-actions/.

31. *Biden v. Nebraska.*

32. Lauren Irwin, "74 Percent of Republicans Say It's Fine for Trump to Be Dictator for a Day," *The Hill* (February 7, 2024), https://thehill.com/homenews/campaign/4453457-74-percent-of-republicans-say-its-fine-for-trump-to-be-dictator-for-a-day/.

33. For a broader examination, see Stephen E. Hanson and Jeffrey S. Kopstein, *The Assault on the State: How the Global Attack on Modern Government Endangers Our Future* (Cambridge: Polity, 2024).

34. Saikrishna Bangalore Prakash, *The Living Presidency: An Originalist Argument against Its Ever-Expanding Powers* (Cambridge, MA: Harvard University Press, 2020), 4.

35. Donald J. Trump and Tony Schwartz, *Trump: The Art of the Deal* (New York: Ballantine Books, 1987); and Tony Schwartz, "Trump Is a Lost Cause. We Have to Change Ourselves," Medium (September 15, 2020), https://gen.medium.com/trump-is-a-lost-cause-we-have-to-change-ourselves-dd3d412e3aa8.

36. John D. Miller, "We Created a Monster: Trump Was a TV Fantasy Invented for 'The Apprentice,'" *US News* (October 16, 2024), https://www.usnews.com/opinion/articles/2024-10-16/we-created-a-tv-illusion-for-the-apprentice-but-the-real-trump-threatens-america.

37. "President Donald Trump," *Psychology Today* (undated), https://www.psychologytoday.com/us/basics/president-donald-trump; Bandy X. Lee, ed., *The Dangerous Case of Donald Trump: 27 Psychiatrists and Mental Health Experts Assess a President* (New York: St. Martin's Press, 2017).

38. Mary L. Trump, *Too Much and Never Enough: How My Family Created the World's Most Dangerous Man* (New York: Simeon and Schuster, 2020).

39. Francis Fukuyama, "100 Days of Ressentiment," Persuasion (April 30, 2025), https://www.persuasion.community/p/100-days-of-ressentiment?utm_source=post-email-title&publication_id=61579&post_id=162524320&utm_campaign=email-post-title&isFreemail=false&r=su09y&triedRedirect=true&utm_medium=email.

40. Doyle McManus, "Trump Is Creating an Imperial Presidency—And He's Doing It by Decree," *Los Angeles Times* (February 3, 2025), https://www.latimes.com/world-nation/story/2025-02-03/column-trump-is-creating-an-imperial-presidency-and-hes-doing-it-by-decree.

41. Arthur M. Schlesinger Jr., *The Imperial Presidency* (Boston: Houghton Mifflin Company, 1973), xxvii.

42. Molly Redden, Andy Kroll, and Nick Surgey, "'Put Them in Trauma': A Key MAGA Leader's Plans for Civil Servants, Troops, and More," Defense One (October 28, 2024), https://www.defenseone.com/policy/2024/10/put-them-trauma-inside-key-maga-leaders-plans-new-trump-agenda/400614/.

43. "Russ Vought: Donald Trump's Holy Warrior," *The Economist* (January 3, 2025), https://www.economist.com/united-states/2025/01/03/russ-vought-donald-trumps-holy-warrior.

44. Russell Vought, "Renewing American Purpose," The American Mind (September 29, 2022), https://americanmind.org/salvo/renewing-american-purpose/.

45. Thomas Paine, *The Rights of Man: Being an Answer to Mr. Burke's Attack on the French Revolution* (London: J.S. Jordan, 1791), https://oll.libertyfund.org/titles/paine-the-rights-of-man-part-i-1791-ed.

46. John Marini, "Abandoning the Constitution," *Claremont Review of Books* 12:2 (2012), https://claremontreviewofbooks.com/abandoning-the-constitution/.

47. John Marini, *Unmasking the Administrative State: The Crisis of American Politics in the Twenty-First Century* (New York: Encounter Books, 2019).

48. Paine, *The Rights of Man*.

49. Thomas E. Mann and Norman J. Ornstein, *The Broken Branch: How Congress Is Falling Apart and How to Get It Back on Track* (New York: Oxford University Press, 2006); *It's Even Worse Than It Looks: How the American Constitutional System Collided with the New Politics of Extremism* (New York: Basic Books, 2012); and Norman J. Ornstein, "The Republicans Broke Congress. Democrats Can Fix It," *New Republic* (November 9, 2018), https://newrepublic.com/article/152127/republicans-broke-congress-democrats-can-fix-it.

50. Donald Trump, Truth Social (March 19, 2024), https://truthsocial.com/@realDonaldTrump/posts/112121873535738974; Jason Lalljee, "'Deranged' Milwaukee Judge's Arrest a Warning to Others, Bondi Says," *Axios* (April 25, 2025), https://www.axios.com/2025/04/25/hannah-dugan-trump-bondi-fbi-arrest; Avery Lotz and Sareen Habeshian, "Leavitt Says Supreme Court 'Must Put an End' to Tariff Saga," *Axios* (May 29, 2025), https://www.axios.com/2025/05/29/leavitt-tariff-ruling-trump-trade-court; and Sareen Habeshian, "Trump Administration Escalates Attacks on Judges," *Axios* (May 29, 2025), https://www.axios.com/2025/05/29/trump-administration-courts-judges.

51. *Trump v. Casa*, 606 U.S. ___ (2025), https://www.supremecourt.gov/opinions/24pdf/24a884_8n59.pdf.

52. *Mahmoud v. Taylor*, 606 U.S. ___ (2025) https://www.supremecourt.gov/opinions/24pdf/24-297_4f14.pdf.

53. Moms for Liberty, "Liberty in Action Weekly" (June 29, 2025), email.

Chapter 7

1. Tim Miller, "Maybe You Can Get Tired of All the Winning?," *Bulwark: Morning Shots* (December 22, 2024), https://www.thebulwark.com/p/maybe-you-can-get-tired-of-all-the?utm_campaign=email-half-post&r=su09y&utm_source=substack&utm_medium=email.

2. "Javier Milei, Free-Market Revolutionary," *The Economist* (November 28, 2024), https://www.economist.com/the-americas/2024/11/28/javier-milei-free-market-revolutionary.

3. "A Fresh Wave of Hard-Right Populism Is Stalking Europe," *The Economist* (September 14, 2023), https://www.economist.com/leaders/2023/09/14/a-fresh-wave-of-hard-right-populism-is-stalking-europe.

4. Murray N. Rothbard, *Man, Economy, and State: A Treatise on Economic Principles, with Power and Market: Government and the Economy*, 2nd ed. (Auburn, AL: Ludwig von Mises Institute, 1970), esp. 85, https://mises.org/library/book/man-economy-and-state-power-and-market.

5. Vivek Ramaswamy, X (November 18, 2024), https://x.com/VivekGRamaswamy/status/1858559544202502250. More broadly, see Claire Donnelly and Meghna Chakrabarti, "Why Argentina's Javier Milei Has the Attention of Trump's Advisors," "On Point" (Boston: WBUR, December 19, 2024), https://www.wbur.org/onpoint/2024/12/19/shock-therapy-javier-milei-government-argentina.

6. E. J. Hobsbawm, *The Age of Revolution: 1789–1848* (New York: New American Library, 1962).

7. M. de Montesquieu, *De L'Espirit des Loix* [The Spirit of Laws] (London: T. Evans, 1777).

8. Max Fisher, "'Irony Lady': How a Moscow Propagandist Gave Margaret Thatcher Her Famous Nickname," *Washington Post* (April 8, 2013), https://www.washingtonpost.com/news/worldviews/wp/2013/04/08/irony-lady-how-a-moscow-propagandist-gave-margaret-thatcher-her-famous-nickname/.

9. Vivien Ann Schmidt and Mark Thatcher, eds., *Resilient Liberalism in Europe's Political Economy* (Cambridge: Cambridge University Press, 2013).

10. Schmidt and Thatcher, *Resilient Liberalism in Europe*.

11. Carlos Vacas Soriano, "A Picture of Income Inequality and Middle Classes Across the EU," Centre for Economic Policy Research (October 8, 2024), https://cepr.org/voxeu/columns/picture-income-inequality-and-middle-classes-across-eu#:~:text=Against%20the%20well%2Destablishe d%20public,countries%2C%20although%20to%20varying%20degrees.

12. World Population Review, "Happiest Countries in the World 2024," https://worldpopulationreview.com/country-rankings/happiest-countries-in-the-world.

13. Steven Hahn, *Illiberal America: A History* (New York: Norton, 2024).

14. Lucy Pawle, "Some British People Only Worried About Brown Migrants, Bishop Says," BBC (June 28, 2023), https://www.bbc.com/news/uk-england-kent-66044153.

15. Matthew Chance and Benjamin Brown, "Anti-Immigrant Anger Rises at Scene of German Market Attack," CNN (December 23, 2024), https://www.

cnn.com/2024/12/22/europe/anti-immigrant-anger-magdeburg-market-attack-intl/index.html.

16. Erika Solomon, "Germany Deems Youth Wing of Far-Right Party an Extremist Group," *New York Times* (April 26, 2023), https://www.nytimes.com/2023/04/26/world/europe/germany-afd-youth-wing-extremist.html.

17. Zselyke Csaky and Nate Schenkkan, "Confronting Illiberalism," Freedom House (2018), https://freedomhouse.org/report/nations-transit/2018/confronting-illiberalism.

18. Ruth Green, "The Year of Elections: The Rise of Europe's Far Right," International Bar Association (September 30, 2024), https://www.ibanet.org/The-year-of-elections-The-rise-of-Europes-far-right.

19. Cas Mudde, *The Far Right Today* (Cambridge: Polity, 2019), 1, 2.

20. Klaus von Beyme, "Right-Wing Extremism in Western Europe," *West European Politics* 11:2 (1988), 1–18.

21. Mudde, *The Far Right Today*, 10–23. See also Cas Mudde and Cristobal Rovira Kaltwasser, *Populism: A Very Short Introduction* (Oxford: Oxford University Press 2017).

22. Cas Mudde, "Democracy Is in a Doom Spiral—But It Isn't Dead Yet," *Prospect* (December 4, 2024), https://www.prospectmagazine.co.uk/politics/democracy/68694/democracy-doom-spiral-elections.

23. Alexander Smith and Carlo Angerer, "Why Europe's Far Right Is So Happy Trump Won," NBC News (November 8, 2024), https://www.nbcnews.com/news/world/trump-election-win-delights-orban-europes-far-right-rcna178938; see also Mike Allen, "Hard-Right Politics Grow Across the Globe," *Axios* (September 18. 2023), https://www.axios.com/2023/09/18/trump-global-right-2024-election?t.

24. Dalibor Rohac, "European Democracy Is Going Backwards," Persuasion (November 5, 2024), https://www.persuasion.community/p/european-democracy-is-going-backwards?utm_source=post-email-title&publication_id=61579&post_id=151219534&utm_campaign=email-post-title&isFreemail=false&r=su09y&triedRedirect=true.

25. The countries were France, Germany, Italy, the United Arab Emirates, Singapore, Ireland, India, South Africa, China, Kenya, Brazil, Japan, South Korea, Thailand, Sweden, Malaysia, Australia, Saudi Arabia, Mexico, and Nigeria. There were separate reports for the Asian-Pacific region, the Middle East and Africa, and Europe.

26. Edelman, "2012 Edelman Trust Barometer Executive Summary" (2012).

27. Edelman, "2024 Edelman Trust Barometer: Global Report" (2024), 7, 9. Data cited in the text from 2024 come from this source. https://www.edelman. com/trust/2024/trust-barometer.

28. Haifeng Huang, Chanita Intawan, and Stephen P. Nicholson, "In Government We Trust: Implicit Political Trust and Regime Support in China," *Perspectives on Politics* 21:4 (2023); 1357–1375. doi:10.1017/S1537592722001037.

29. There are differences here with the Edelman survey, with a different collection of countries—thirty for the OECD, versus twenty-eight for Edelman—and with a focus on the national government for the OECD, versus a generic government question for Edelman. Trust in subnational governments tends to be higher than for the national government. The United States was not included in this survey.

30. OECD, *OECD Survey on Drivers of Trust in Public Institutions—2024 Results: Building Trust in a Complex Policy Environment* (Paris: OECD Publishing, 2024), https://doi.org/10.1787/9a20554b-en.

31. OECD, *Trust in Government* (Paris: OECD, 2024), https://www.oecd. org/en/topics/sub-issues/trust-in-government.html.

32. Washington State Republican Convention, Resolution 20, "Resolution Supporting the Repeal of the 17th Amendment to the U.S. Constitution" (April 2024), https://www.documentcloud.org/documents/24602349-wa-gop-repeal-17th-resolution.

33. 2024 Washington State Republican Party Resolutions, "Resolution 1—Resolution Supporting our Republic vs. Democracy" (April 2024), https://www.documentcloud.org/documents/24602348-2024-gop-resolutions.

34. TheReallFrFamily, "Is America a Democracy or Constitutional Republic? What's the Difference? Share this with someone if you got value from it" (April 21, 2024), https://www.instagram.com/thereallfrfamily/reel/C6B4CzZLM4u/.

35. beforeitstoolate1 (January 2, 2024), https://www.instagram.com/beforeitstoolate1/reel/C1nqWDUxxbs/.

36. John Adams to John Taylor (December 17, 1814), https://founders. archives.gov/documents/Adams/99-02-02-6371.

37. Danny Westneat, "The WA GOP Put It in Writing That They're Not into Democracy," *Seattle Times* (April 24, 2024), https://www.seattletimes.com/seattle-news/politics/the-wa-gop-put-it-in-writing-that-theyre-not-into-democracy/.

38. "The Rachel Maddow Show," MSNBC (April 29, 2024), https://archive.org/details/MSNBCW_20240430_010000_The_Rachel_Maddow_Show.

39. Victor Davis Hanson, "The Mob Is Coming for You," Hoover Institution (September 30, 2015), https://www.hoover.org/research/mob-coming-you.

40. James Druckman, Samara Klar, Yanna Krupnikov, Matthew Levendusky, and John Barry Ryan, *Partisan Hostility and American Democracy: Explaining Political Divisions and When They Matter* (Chicago: University of Chicago Press, 2024).

41. David Andreatta, "Does It Matter How Much Democrats and Republicans Hate Each Other? Yes, It Does," University of Rochester News Center (June 13, 2024), https://www.rochester.edu/newscenter/partisan-hostility-and-american-democracy-polarization-610522/.

Chapter 8

1. David DiSalvo, "How the Left Got Lazy," *Forbes* (October 3, 2011), https://www.forbes.com/sites/daviddisalvo/2011/09/14/how-the-left-got-lazy/?sh=7fea25c01163.

2. E. J. Dionne Jr., *Why The Right Went Wrong: Conservatism—From Goldwater to Trump and Beyond* (New York: Simon and Schuster, 2016).

3. Elena Kagan, Dissent, *Dobbs v. Jackson Women's Health Organization*, 597 U.S. 215 (2022), https://supreme.justia.com/cases/federal/us/597/19-1392/#tab-opinion-4600822.

4. Adriana Gomez Licon, "Musk Waves a Chainsaw and Charms Conservatives Talking Up Trump's Cost-Cutting Efforts," AP (February 21, 2025), https://apnews.com/article/musk-chainsaw-trump-doge-6568e9e0cfc42ad6cdcfd58a409eb312.

5. Alana Newhouse, "Brokenism," *Tablet* (November 21, 2022), https://www.tabletmag.com/sections/news/articles/brokenism-alana-newhouse.

6. "Latest US Opinion Polls," Ipsos (November 18, 2024), https://www.ipsos.com/en-us/latest-us-opinion-polls.

7. David Dagan, "The Great Demolition," Persuasion (March 21, 2025), https://www.persuasion.community/p/the-great-demolition?utm_source=post-email-title&publication_id=61579&post_id=159499071&utm_campaign=email-post-title&isFreemail=false&r=su09y&triedRedirect=true&utm_medium=email.

8. Ben Smith, "The Group Chats That Changed America," Semafor (April 27, 2025), https://www.semafor.com/article/04/27/2025/the-group-chats-

that-changed-america. Quotations in the paragraphs that follow that are not otherwise attributed come from Smith's reporting.

9. Markokenya, "The Tech Bros Were Democrats, What Happened?," *Medium* (January 27, 2025), https://markokenya.medium.com/the-tech-bros-were-democrats-what-happened-5a8287526145.

10. Robby Soave, "The Tech Bros Love Trump Because the Democrats Pushed Them Away," *Reason* (January 20, 2025), https://reason.com/2025/01/20/the-tech-bros-love-trump-because-the-democrats-pushed-them-away/.

11. Noah Smith, X (April 26, 2025), https://x.com/Noahpinion/status/19161850967571460022.

12. Sriram Krishnan, "Group Chats Rule the World" (May 19, 2024), https://sriramk.com/group-chats-rule-the-world.

13. Quoted by Smith, "Group Chats."

14. Smith, "Group Chats."

15. Francis Fukuyama, *The End of History and the Last Man* (New York: Free Press, 1992).

16. Hailey Fuchs, "Two Anonymous $425 Million Donations Give Dark Money Conservative Group a Massive Haul," *Politico* (November 16, 2022), https://www.politico.com/news/2022/11/16/two-anonymous-425-million-donations-gives-dark-money-conservative-group-a-massive-haul-00067493.

17. Jaden Edison, "School Choice, Vouchers and the Future of Texas Education," *Texas Tribune* (January 23, 2025), https://www.texastribune.org/2025/01/23/texas-vouchers/.

18. Jeremy Schwartz, "Former Far-Right Hard-Liner Says Billionaires Are Using School Board Races to Sow Distrust in Public Education," *ProPublica* (May 15, 2024), https://www.propublica.org/article/texas-tim-dunn-wilks-brothers-vouchers-courtney-gore.

19. Eleanor Klibanoff, "How 'Wildly Successful' Anti-Trans Ads Fired Up Texas Voters for Republicans," *Texas Tribune* (November 8, 2024), https://www.texastribune.org/2024/11/08/transgender-ads-motivate-texas-republicans/.

20. Sandra González-Bailón, Valeria d'Andrea, Deen Freelon, and Manlio De Domenico, "The Advantage of the Right in Social Media News Sharing," *PNAS Nexus* 1:3 (2022), pgac137, https://doi.org/10.1093/pnasnexus/pgac137, and https://pmc.ncbi.nlm.nih.gov/articles/PMC9896954/.

21. Samantha Wooley, "Surging Violence and Far-Right Extremism: Unpacking Social Media's Role in the 2024 Election," *Georgetown Security Studies Review* (April 23, 2024), https://georgetownsecuritystudiesreview.org/2024/04/25/surging-violence-and-far-right-extremism-unpacking-social-medias-role-in-the-2024-election/; and Kateira Aryaeinejad and Thomas Leo Schere, " The Role of the Internet and Social Media on Radicalization: What Research Sponsored by the National Institute of Justice Tells Us" (Washington, DC: National Institute of Justice, April 2024), https://www.ojp.gov/ncjrs/virtual-library/abstracts/role-internet-and-social-media-radicalization-what-research.

22. Franklin Foer, "Trump Has Found His Class Enemy," *The Atlantic* (April 13, 2025), https://www.theatlantic.com/ideas/archive/2025/04/trump-waging-war-professional-class/682409/.

23. Henrik Temp, " Congress Less Popular Than Head Lice" (Washington, DC: American Enterprise Institute, January 8, 2013), https://www.aei.org/politics-and-public-opinion/polls/congress-less-popular-than-head-lice/.

24. Donald F. Kettl, *Can Governments Earn Our Trust?* (Cambridge: Polity, 2017).

25. Katie Colton, Ashka Dave, Erez Eizenman, Marcy Jacobs, Kunal Modi, and Sarah Tucker-Ray, "Great Expectations: How US Government Agencies Can Meet Public Demand for Better Service", McKinsey (December 5, 2023), https://www.mckinsey.com/industries/public-sector/our-insights/great-expectations-how-us-government-agencies-can-meet-public-demand-for-better-service.

26. Interview (June 7, 2023).

Chapter 9

1. Letter by Gil Carter to his wife, *The Ox-Bow Incident* (1941), https://www.imdb.com/title/tt0036244/characters/nm0000020.

2. Ambrose Bierce, *The Devil's Dictionary* (1911), https://www.thedevilsdictionary.com/c.html.

3. Katherine Stewart, *Money, Lies, and God: Inside the Movement to Destroy American Democracy* (New York: Bloomsbury Publishing, 2025).

4. Anne Applebaum, *Twilight of Democracy: The Seductive Lure of Authoritarianism* (New York: Anchor Books, 2020), 22.

5. However, there are other statements of conservative principles, including "The Sharon Statement," which a group of conservatives crafted in 1960

at William F. Buckley's Sharon, Connecticut, home. See New Guard Staff, "'We, as Young Conservatives, Believe': The Sharon Statement at 60" (September 12, 2200), https://yaf.org/news/we-as-young-conservatives-believe-the-sharon-statement-at-60/.

6. Kathryn Joyce, "'The Florida of Today Is the America of Tomorrow': Ron DeSantis's New College Takeover Is Just the Beginning of the Right's Higher Ed Crusade," *Vanity Fair* (February 10, 2023), https://www.vanityfair.com/news/2023/02/ron-desantis-new-college-florida; and Kathryn Joyce, "The New College Gambit," In These Times (December 9, 2024), https://inthesetimes.com/article/new-college-florida-republicans-higher-ed.

7. John Ismay, "Who's In and Who's Out at the Naval Academy's Library?," *New York Times* (April 11, 2025), https://www.nytimes.com/2025/04/11/us/politics/naval-academy-banned-books.html.

8. Alex Mitchell, "Long Island Town Begs Trump to help fight state's Native American Logo Ban: 'Where Does It End?,'" *New York Post* (April 7, 2025), https://nypost.com/2025/04/07/us-news/long-island-town-begs-trump-to-help-fight-states-native-american-logo-ban-where-does-it-end/; see also Tony Closson, "Trump Joins a Bitter Fight on Long Island Over a School Mascot," New York Times (April 22, 2025), https://www.nytimes.com/2025/04/22/nyregion/trump-massapequa-school-mascot.html.

9. Donald J. Trump, X (April 21, 2025), https://x.com/TrumpDailyPosts/status/1914413233424814264.

10. Hannah Schoenbaum and Mike Stobbe, "RFK Jr. Says He Plans to Tell CDC to Stop Recommending Fluoride in Drinking Water," AP (April 7, 2025), https://apnews.com/article/fluoride-cdc-epa-6f4dbc64b5dc511f712a82cd2d252d76.

11. Felicia Mason-Edwards, "The Child Welfare System: State and Faith," Focus on the Family (January 11, 2021), https://www.focusonthefamily.com/pro-life/the-child-welfare-system-state-and-faith/.

12. Focus on the Family, https://www.focusonthefamily.com/pro-life/.

13. Committee on Ways and Means, US House of Representatives, "Support for Pro-Family Policies Fast-Growing Among Conservatives" (February 13, 2024), https://waysandmeans.house.gov/2024/02/13/support-for-pro-family-policies-fast-growing-among-conservatives/.

14. Dana Mattioli, "The Tactics Elon Musk Uses to Manage His 'Legion' of Babies—and Their Mothers," *Wall Street Journal* (April 15, 2025), https://www.wsj.com/politics/elon-musk-children-mothers-ashley-st-clair-grimes-dc7ba05c.

15. Emma Green, "The Family Plan," *New Yorker* 100:38 (November 18, 2024).

16. The Heritage Foundation, "Marriage and Family," https://www.heritage.org/marriage-and-family.

17. "Fact Sheet: President Donald J. Trump Expands Access to In Vitro Fertilization (IVF)" (February 18, 2025), https://www.whitehouse.gov/fact-sheets/2025/02/fact-sheet-president-donald-j-trump-expands-access-to-in-vitro-fertilization-ivf/.

18. "Presidential Message on Super Bowl LIX" (February 9, 2025), https://www.whitehouse.gov/briefings-statements/2025/02/presidential-message-on-super-bowl-lix/.

19. Email, "Liberty in Action Weekly: White House, Supreme Court & More!" (April 26, 2025).

20. Dominick Mastrangelo, "Trump Knocks 'Kooky' Carlson over Iran Criticism," *The Hill* (June 16, 2025), https://thehill.com/homenews/media/5353896-trump-knocks-kooky-carlson-over-iran-criticism/.

21. "Does America Now Have a Woke Right?," *The Economist* (June 14, 2025).

22. Moms for Liberty, "'Moms for Liberty Day' at the White House" (June 16, 2025), email blog.

23. Survey undertaken for the National Academy of Public Administration by Frank Luntz, "The Language of Good Government." See National Academy of Public Administration, "Presentation from Terry Gerton on The Language of Good Government for EOM Standing Panel" (September 27, 2024), https://napawash.org/standing-panel-blog/presentation-from-terry-gerton-on-the-language-of-good-government-for-eom-standing-panel.

24. Winston S. Churchill, *The World Crisis*, vol. 3 (New York: Charles Scribner's Sons, 1927), 136.

25. James Madison, "Federalist 10" (November 23, 1787), https://avalon.law.yale.edu/18th_century/fed10.asp.

26. *Marbury v. Madison*, 5 U.S. 137 (1803).

27. Walter Berns, "Do We Have a Living Constitution?," *National Forum: Toward the Bicentennial of the Constitution*, Honor Society of Phi Kappa Phi (Fall 1984), 30.

28. John Adams, *Thoughts on Government* (Philadelphia: John Dunlap, 1776), https://oll.libertyfund.org/titles/adams-the-works-of-john-adams-vol-4.

29. Bruce P. Frohnen, "Burke's Defense of Natural Rights and the Limits of Political Power," Russell Kirk Center for Cultural Renewal (October 18, 2020), https://kirkcenter.org/essays/burkes-defense-of-natural-rights-and-the-limits-of-political-power/. See also Francis Fukuyama, "Boredom at the End of History," American Purpose (May 28, 2024), https://www.americanpurpose.com/articles/boredom-at-the-end-of-history-part-i/#scroll_to_steady_paywall.

30. Beth Reinhard, "Trump Loyalist Pushes 'Post-Constitutional' Vision for Second Term," Washington Post (June 8. 2024), https://www.washingtonpost.com/politics/2024/06/08/russ-vought-trump-second-term-radical-constitutional/.

31. Trump v. United States, 603 U.S. ___ (2024), https://www.supremecourt.gov/opinions/23pdf/23-939_e2pg.pdf.

32. Alexander Hamilton, "Federalist 77" (April 4, 1788), The Federalist Papers, https://avalon.law.yale.edu/18th_century/fed77.asp.

33. "The Supreme Court Protects the Presidency in Trump v. U.S.," Wall Street Journal (July 1, 2024), https://www.wsj.com/articles/trump-v-u-s-supreme-court-presidential-immunity-official-acts-john-roberts-january-6-c4d5eddc?mod=opinion_lead_pos1.

34. A Man for All Seasons (1966), https://www.imdb.com/title/tt0060665/quotes/?ref_=tt_trv_qu.

35. Thomas Jefferson to John Adams (August 1, 1816), https://founders.archives.gov/documents/Jefferson/03-10-02-0173; and John Adams to Thomas Jefferson (August 9, 1816), https://founders.archives.gov/documents/Jefferson/03-10-02-0191.

36. Vince Haley and Charles Ezell, "Merit Hiring Plan" (May 29, 2025), 18, https://www.chcoc.gov/content/merit-hiring-plan.

INDEX